Unlocking the Secrets of the Book of Enoch

A Journey into Ancient Mysteries

Rick Wehrle

professional before attempting any techniques outlined in this book.

By reading this document, the reader agrees that under no circumstances is the author responsible for any losses, direct or indirect, that are incurred as a result of the use of the information contained within this document, including, but not limited to, errors, omissions, or inaccuracies.

Table of Contents

Introduction

Imagine a manuscript so steeped in mystery that it bridges the celestial with the terrestrial, where divine secrets unfold through ancient prophecies and visions rather than through written texts. This is the Book of Enoch, an enigmatic collection of spiritual revelations that delves deep into the fabric of our existence, intertwining the human with the divine, the ordinary with the supernatural. Written by Enoch, the seventh patriarch after Adam, who was so beloved by God that he was taken to Heaven without tasting the excruciating devastation of death, this book offers us a unique window into the divine mechanics of the universe as perceived by ancient seers. Through Enoch's extraordinary visions, we witness the complex hierarchies of angels and their profound influence on cosmic events, providing us with insights into a world where the line between the mystical and the material is blurred.

In a realm where the boundaries between the divine and the earthly are whisper-thin, the Book of Enoch stands not merely as a historical artifact, but as a portal to understanding the profound mysteries of divine judgment and the fate of the universe. Revered by some as sacred scripture and dismissed by others as heretical, with its teachings having permeated the fabrics of Judaism and Christianity, the book challenges the core doctrines of traditional religious teachings, pushing the boundaries of our spiritual understanding. Its teachings have permeated the fabrics of Judaism and Christianity.

As we explore this text throughout this book, we are taken on a journey that promises not only enlightenment but also a profound challenge to our understanding of the cosmos and our place within it. We will journey beyond the mundane, venturing through the origins of the Book of Enoch, unraveling its complex symbolism while also unveiling its impactful role in religious thought, from the mystical traditions of ancient Judaism to its controversial position within early Christianity.

Our exploration begins in the quiet spaces of history, where the rustle of ancient texts echoes like leaves in the wind, beckoning us to uncover the secrets held within the Book of Enoch. This collection of visions, prophecies, and divine secrets, composed beyond the mists of time, offers a glimpse into the celestial mechanics of the universe as understood by ancient seers. Here, in these pages steeped in mystical hues of angelology and apocalyptic lore, lies the promise of revelation and insight. The Book of Enoch offers stories that intertwine the human with the divine, the ordinary with the magical. It is a text shrouded in mystery and lost to time that perhaps may offer a delicate glimpse into an enigmatic era, revealing divine mysteries and judgments.

Significance and Historical Context

The significance of the Book of Enoch extends beyond its mystical content. Historically, it has been both revered and reviled, its canonicity disputed, yet its influence undeniable. This manuscript has shaped and influenced theological and religious thought profoundly by weaving through the fabric of multiple faiths and leaving an unforgettable mark on the spiritual and apocalyptic theories of the Second Temple period. It aids us by enriching our understanding of religious history and its development, for it is not just stories but a view of the universe that challenges the bedrock of traditional doctrines. Historically, it has navigated the spectrum between reverence and rejection, with its authenticity and scriptural status often called into question. Yet, despite these controversies, its impact on theological thought is still undeniable.

The Book of Enoch, also known as 1 Enoch, is a fascinating ancient text whose origins and journey through various cultures offer a unique insight into its enduring impact on religious thought. Believed to have been written between approximately 400 BCE until around the beginning of the second century CE, the Book of Enoch originates in the Jewish apocalyptic tradition, which was prevalent during the Second Temple period in Palestine (Nickelsburg & Vanderkam, 2004).

The storyline of the Book of Enoch is attributed to Enoch, the great-grandfather of Noah, who is depicted as a righteous and pious man chosen by God to witness and record heavenly secrets. The text, in itself, is a compilation of several distinct sections, each detailing visions of Heaven, angelic hierarchies, and the fate of sinners intertwined with prophecies and cosmological speculations. This literary form was common among Jewish apocalyptic literature, reflecting a community concerned with divine judgment and cosmic justice (Cain et al., 2024; Editors of Encyclopaedia Britannica, 2020)

As the Book of Enoch, historically, was highly circulated among various Jewish groups, it profoundly influenced Jewish eschatological thought. The themes of the text, divine judgment, and angelology, are also present in other apocalyptic literature from the same era. This illustrates its considerable influence. Despite its popularity from the early centuries BCE into the first century CE, the Book of Enoch gradually disappeared from Jewish tradition and was not included in the canonical Hebrew Bible. The preservation and transmission of the Book of Enoch were predominantly upheld by Christian communities in Ethiopia, where it was translated into Ge'ez and included in the Ethiopian Orthodox Tewahedo Church's canon. This tradition preserved the book's relevance by weaving its teachings into their religious practices and beliefs. It was not until the discovery of the Dead Sea Scrolls in the mid-20th century that the Book of Enoch regained scholarly attention, highlighting its historical importance and broad influence across early Jewish and Christian communities (Davidson, 2014).

From its origins in ancient Jewish writings to its integration into Christian texts across various cultures, the Book of Enoch has not just endured through history but has also influenced foundational religious beliefs for future generations. Its journey highlights the powerful impact of the written word, showcasing its ability to connect diverse theological ideas and provide a rich legacy of ancient knowledge that continues to influence scholars and theologians today.

The extensive history and significant impact of the Book of Enoch illustrate its key role in exploring the development of religious texts and the intricate interactions between different faiths over thousands of years. Therefore, the Book of Enoch is an essential resource for anyone looking to understand the origins and growth of Judeo-Christian thought, offering insights into the spiritual and cosmic discussions that have shaped religious traditions globally.

The Book of Enoch remains relevant to contemporary readers, partly because its ancient mysteries and profound insights into spiritual and theological realms are deeply captivating. Moreover, it has significantly influenced contemporary religious thought, particularly in Christianity, where echoes of its themes can be seen in the concepts of judgment, hell, and eschatological narratives. This historical and theological depth provides a rich backdrop for scholarly exploration and personal reflection, making the Book of Enoch a valuable resource for those interested in the evolution of religious ideas. Not to mention that the themes of moral responsibility and divine judgment within the Book of Enoch invite readers to ponder the nature of justice and ethical conduct in today's world. Such reflections are particularly relevant in contemporary discussions about morality and spirituality, bridging ancient wisdom with modern ethical debates.

Thus, the Book of Enoch remains a timeless text, appealing to a wide audience of scholars, spiritual seekers, and anyone interested in the intersections of religion, history, and morality. Its ability to connect ancient teachings with current spiritual inquiries makes it a compelling read for those looking to deepen their understanding of both the past and the present.

The Journey

At its core, the Book of Enoch is structured around several key themes, including detailed descriptions of Heaven, the roles and judgments of angels, and a series of apocalyptic visions that prophecy the fate of humanity and the divine judgment to come. One of the most compelling parts of Enoch's narrative is the tale of the Watchers—angels sent to Earth that ultimately fall from grace, a theme that resonates with the idea of divine justice and moral complexity.

The purpose of this manuscript goes beyond recounting these ancient stories. It seeks to decode and discuss the significance of these narratives within both ancient contexts and their implications for modern spiritual and theological thought. It is aiming to bridge the gap between ancient wisdom and contemporary spiritual inquiries, making the insights of this ancient text relevant and accessible to today's readers. It is meant to serve as a journey through the Book of Enoch, not just an academic exploration but as an experience that challenges you to reflect on the nature of divine revelation, justice, and the human condition. Each chapter of the book is designed as a step deeper into this spiritual labyrinth, where you can explore profound themes and uncover the mysteries that have influenced theological thought across millennia.

Unlocking the Secrets of the Book of Enoch, however, does more than provide historical insight. It invites you on a journey to explore and ponder the dynamics of human-divine interaction and the timeless questions of morality and divine oversight. This exploration is intended to enrich your spiritual life by offering new ways to engage with ancient knowledge and contemporary ethical and spiritual dilemmas.

Through the pages of this introduction, we have crossed into a realm where the past informs the present, where ancient texts illuminate the paths of future inquiry. As you turn each page, may you find more than history— you may find a reflection of the divine, echoing through the corridors of time, whispering secrets that are as relevant now as they were when Enoch first gazed upon the Heavens.

Are you ready to dive into the mysteries of ancient mysticism and explore a world governed by celestial beings? We are going to take a scholarly journey to unlock the profound secrets found in the Book of Enoch, a text rich with divine laws and prophetic visions that have shaped the destinies of humankind. This adventure is not just an exploration but an invitation to decode the whispered messages of the ancients, providing insights that connect the wisdom of the past with the spiritual quests of today. Join us as we traverse this mystical landscape, uncovering the hidden wisdom that has captivated theologians, scholars, and seekers of truth for centuries. This book, *Unlocking the Secrets of the Book of Enoch,* promises to enlighten and inspire, bridging epochs and expanding our understanding of both history and spirituality.

With this book, may your journey be deep and rewarding, as we unlock the secrets of the Book of Enoch together, discovering ancient mysteries that resonate with our quest for spiritual understanding in a modern world.

Chapter 1:
Tracing the Roots

Here, we are beginning our quest to decipher the echoes of the past, all while examining the timeframe and geography that cradled the inception of the Book of Enoch. Letting our imagination do the work, picturing ourselves standing at the crossroads of ancient civilizations—where the whispers of Mesopotamia and the spiritual landscapes of the Levant merge into a web of divine storytelling. This chapter navigates through these ancient lands, exploring how the very sands that bore witness to human history also cradled the mystical revelations of Enoch.

As we go deeper, the chapter unfurls the cultural and religious influences that shaped this profound text. It's a journey into a world where ancient religions clashed and blended, where Hellenistic philosophies met Jewish mystical traditions, creating a melting pot from which the Book of Enoch emerged. This exploration is not just about understanding a piece of religious literature; it's about experiencing the spiritual upheaval and fervent hopes of an era that sought to define the divine and understand the cosmos.

Moving along, we confront the controversies and debates that have surrounded the Book of Enoch for millennia. Why was it revered yet excluded from the canon by many? What does its fluctuating acceptance tell us about the changing landscapes of faith and authority through the ages? This chapter does not just recount these debates; it invites you to ponder them, to feel the tension and the passion that these questions have ignited in the hearts of the faithful and the scholarly.

This is more than just a chapter in a book—it is a portal to another time and place, offering a glimpse into the mystical and the forbidden. As you turn each page, you are not merely reading—you are stepping further into a realm where the past and present converge, where the mystical becomes tangible, and where the hidden truths of the Book of Enoch await to be rediscovered.

Historical context

In the mystical collection of ancient religious texts, the Book of Enoch holds a unique allure, as much a mirror to its time as it is a beacon of apocalyptic prophecy. Written between the 3rd century BCE and the 1st century CE, this text that is the book of Enoch emerged during the Second Temple period, an era steeped in religious thought and cultural upheaval. This epoch was characterized by the Jewish diaspora's struggle to maintain faith amid the sprawling influence of Hellenistic empires following Alexander the Great's conquests that melded Greek culture with the indigenous traditions of the Near East (Geller, 2022). The world of Enoch was a crucible of change. The Jewish diaspora, spread thin by conquests and exiles, found themselves grappling with their identity under the pervasive gaze of Hellenistic rulers. It was a time when the Jewish community in Palestine was knitting together a renewed religious identity, one that would eventually crystallize into movements like the Pharisees and the Sadducees (Smith,

2023). In these turbulent times, the Book of Enoch offered a form of divine solace—a vision of ultimate justice and celestial order in a world that often felt chaotically unjust.

Amid this cultural synthesis, the Book of Enoch resonates with a profound sense of divine justice, offering solace and a stern warning through visions of angelic hierarchies and the ultimate judgment. This period, notably marked by the rise of apocalyptic literature, reflects a community grappling with existential and theological crises. The Jewish people, under Hellenistic and later Roman rule, found in texts like

Enoch a theological anchor and a form of resistance against the erosion of their religious identity (Smith, 2023).

The narrative of Enoch, rich with descriptions of heavenly ascents and angelic revelations, served not only as religious counsel but also as a cultural response to the pervasive injustices perceived by the Jewish community. Its themes of cosmic struggle and redemption echo through the corridors of Jewish mystical thought and the broader theological debates of the time. The vivid apocalyptic imagery and tales of the Watchers—angels who fall from grace—illustrate a dual narrative of divine omnipotence and human accountability, reflecting the broader Judaic eschatological speculations prevalent among communities influenced by both Jewish mysticism and Greek philosophical inquiries (*What Is the Book of Enoch*, n.d.).

Furthermore, the Book of Enoch's influence extends beyond its immediate cultural context, weaving its motifs into the fabric of early Christian eschatology and persisting in religious thought into the modern era. This text, with its deep roots in Jewish apocalyptic traditions, underscores a significant interplay between fear, hope, and the quest for divine truth, themes that resonate profoundly with contemporary spiritual seekers (Denova, 2021).

Diving deeper into its ethereal pages, the Book of Enoch is not merely a religious scripture but also a cultural mirror, reflecting the multifaceted dimensions of its time. Its themes are a response to the pressing existential queries of its audience, addressing theodicy and divine justice and illustrating a universe starkly governed by a complex hierarchy of angels and demons (*What Is the Book of Enoch*, n.d.). These motifs resonate with the spiritual and cosmological speculations that were rampant among the communities influenced by both Jewish mysticism and Greek philosophical inquiries.

Time Frame and Geography

As the fascinating apocalyptic literature that it is, the Book of Enoch offers profound insights into the religious and cultural milieu of its time. It is essential to understand not only the estimated time period when it was written but also the geographical areas that it covers, for without it, one cannot truly appreciate its historical and theological significance. Therefore, this section is meant to serve as a guide into these aspects, illuminating the world from which the Book of Enoch emerged. We will be describing, in depth, its connections to Mesopotamia, the Levant, and Egypt while also highlighting the diverse cultural influences that shaped its narrative and themes. By studying these contexts, we can better understand the Book of Enoch's position in the wider range of ancient Near Eastern and Jewish writings. This knowledge helps us see where the text came from historically and how it has influenced religious beliefs and practices over time.

The composition of the Book of Enoch spans several centuries, with researchers, for the most part, concurring that it was composed between the 3rd century BCE and the 1st century CE. This time period places its roots in the Second Temple period, a time of noteworthy devout advancement and transformation within Judaism (Cohen et al., 2024).

The earliest segments of the Book of Enoch, known as the "Book of the Watchers," are accepted to have been composed around the 3rd century BCE. These beginning fragments detail the drop of celestial figures known as Watchers, who adulterated mankind. These chronicles emphasize topics of divine judgment and agreement, resounding the apocalyptic stresses predominant in Jewish social orders of that time(Brand, 2016).

Subsequent segments of the book of Enoch, such as the "Similitudes of Enoch" and the "Book of Illustrations," were likely included in the 1st century BCE. These afterward augmentations expand on the earlier prophetically catastrophic visions, in which more developed theological ideas and eschatological narratives were incorporated. The advancement of the content over these centuries shows an energetic and continuous engagement with the subjects of divine equity, human ethical quality, and the end of time (Nickelsburg & VanderKam, 2001).

The Second Temple period was defined by an assortment of influences and interactions between Jewish and surrounding cultures. The Hellenistic period, on the other hand, started by the successes of Alexander the Great in the 4th century BCE, which presented Greek dialect, logic, and culture into the Jewish world. These impacts are apparent in the Book of Enoch's cosmology and angelology, which reflect a union of

Jewish and Hellenistic thoughts (Nickelsburg & VanderKam, 2001).

Encompassing key regions of the ancient Near East and Jewish history, the Book of Enoch reveals itself against the picturesque scenery of Mesopotamia, the Levant, and Egypt. Inside these authentic districts unfurls a complex account weaving together whole-world destroying dreams and magical meet.

Ancient Mesopotamia

Mesopotamia, often referred to as the cradle of civilization, plays a significant role in the geographical and cultural context of the Book of Enoch. This region, which covers modern-day Iraq, Kuwait, and parts of Syria and Turkey, was home to some of the earliest and most influential civilizations, including the Sumerians, Akkadians, Babylonians, and Assyrians (Edzard et al., 2024).

The narrative of the Watchers descending to Earth and corrupting humanity bears striking similarities to Mesopotamian myths, particularly those involving divine beings and their interactions with humans. The story of the Watchers and the giants they produce reflects the influence of Mesopotamian mythology, such as the tales of the Anunnaki and the Nephilim (Shanks, 2007). These parallels that can be drawn here highlight the cultural transactions between Jewish communities and their Mesopotamian neighbors, which amplifies the apocalyptic visions of the Book of Enoch with a broader Near Eastern cosmology perspective.

The Levant

The Levant, which is a historical geographical term for the Eastern Mediterranean region, is another critical area covered in the Book of Enoch. This region includes modern-day Israel, Jordan, Lebanon, Syria, and parts of Turkey. The Levant was a cultural and religious crossroads where Jewish traditions interacted with those of its neighboring peoples. Mount Hermon, mentioned in the Book of Enoch as the place where the Watchers descended, is located in the Levant. This mountain, which traditionally has been considered sacred, highlights the text's connection to the physical and spiritual landscapes of the region. The Levant's significance is further emphasized by its role as the heartland of ancient Israel and the broader context of Jewish apocalyptic literature (Editors of Encyclopaedia Britannica, 2024c).

The apocalyptic themes in the Book of Enoch reflect the existential and theological concerns of Jewish communities in the Levant, particularly under the rule of foreign empires such as the Seleucids and the Romans. The emphasis of the text, which would be that of divine justice and the ultimate triumph of righteousness, can be seen as a response to the social and political challenges faced by Jews in this region (Boccaccini, 2002).

Egypt

Egypt, an undisputed ancient and storied civilization, also emerges in the geographical and cultural context of the Book of Enoch. The Jewish diaspora in Egypt, particularly in cities like Alexandria, played a crucial role in the development and transmission of Jewish apocalyptic literature. Alexandria, founded by Alexander the Great, was a major center of Hellenistic culture and learning. The city's vibrant intellectual environment fostered interactions between Jewish, Greek, and Egyptian traditions. This unification is evident in the Book of Enoch's cosmological and theological themes, which reflect an integration of Jewish apocalypticism with Greek philosophical concepts and Egyptian religious ideas (Geller, 2022).

The influence of Egyptian cosmology, with its intricate beliefs about the afterlife and divine beings, is apparent in the Book of Enoch's descriptions of the heavenly realms and the roles of its portrayed angels. The text's depiction of divine judgment, as well as the fate of the righteous and the wicked, resonates with Egyptian notions of Ma'at (i.e., cosmic order) and the judgment of souls in the afterlife (Dorman & Baines, 2024).

Influences and Historical Events

In the mystical weave of history, where each strand carries the essence of significant changes over time, the Book of Enoch serves as a testament to the profound impact of historical events on religious scriptures. The emergence of Hellenism, brought forth by the conquests of Alexander the Great, reshaped the cultural and religious landscapes of the Near East, deeply influencing Jewish religious ideologies and literary works during the Second Temple era. This period of cultural amalgamation introduced Greek philosophical ideas to Jewish practices, potentially impacting the universal themes and organized portrayal of celestial orders present in the Book of Enoch (Cohen et al., 2024).

Another pivotal event would be the Maccabean Revolt (167–160 BCE), a Jewish rebellion against Hellenistic influence and religious oppression, which also left its mark on the text. This period of strife and fervent nationalism likely reinforced the Book of Enoch's themes of divine justice and retribution, functioning as a reflection of the Jews' fervent desire for deliverance and sovereignty. The text's vivid apocalyptic visions can be seen as a mirror to the tumultuous hopes of that period in time, as well as eschatological expectations. In other words, serving both as a moral compass and a beacon of hope to its fellows (Reich, 2022).

Moreover, the preservation of the Book of Enoch was significantly impacted by these historical currents. While it fell out of favor in many Jewish and later Christian circles, possibly due to its contentious ideas and the shifting religious priorities post-revolt, it was preserved by the Ethiopian Orthodox Church. This suggests selective retention of religious texts that resonated with specific community ideologies and needs, further highlighting how historical contexts shape the lifespan of religious doctrines (De Jager, 2023a).

Thus, as we traverse the historical echoes captured within the pages of the Book of Enoch, we not only uncover insights into the spiritual and cosmic order it portrays but also understand how it served as a cultural and religious response to the dramatic changes of its time. These important events helped shape the beliefs in Judaism, for they show how history and religion influence each other, proving that ancient scripts and writings can still reflect and address human experiences over time.

A Time of Hellenistic Influence

In 332 BCE, Alexander the Great's army marched through the lands of the Near East, leaving a trail of Greek culture and influence in its wake. This Hellenization brought about a fusion of Greek and local cultures, including that of the Jewish communities that were left scattered across the region (Cohen et al., 2024).

The pervasive Greek culture infiltrated various aspects of life, including language, art, and religion, creating a unique milieu where Jewish traditions began interacting with Hellenistic ideas.

As previously mentioned, the Jewish people found themselves grappling with their identity during this period. The imposition of Greek customs and the establishment of Greek cities such as Alexandria created environments where Jews had to negotiate their ancient traditions within a new cultural framework (Geller, 2022). This blend of cultures is seen in the apocalyptic texts from that time. One example is the Book of Enoch, which combines Jewish end-time beliefs with Greek cosmic ideas. It shows a time when different religious beliefs were merging.

Scholars generally agree that the Book of Enoch was not written by a single author but is a composite work created over several centuries. The earliest portions, known as the "Book of the Watchers," are believed to have been written around the 3rd century BCE. This section describes the fall of the Watchers, a group of angels who descended to Earth and corrupted humanity, a narrative that may have been influenced by both Jewish and Mesopotamian mythologies (Denova, 2021).

Subsequent sections, including the "Similitudes of Enoch" and the "Book of Parables," are thought to have been added in the 1st century BCE. These later additions reflect a more developed apocalyptic worldview, with intricate descriptions of heavenly realms, final judgments, and the ultimate fate of the righteous and the wicked (De Jager, 2023a). This gradual composition process indicates that the Book of Enoch evolved over time, incorporating new theological insights and responding to changing historical contexts.

Following the conquests of Alexander the Great in the late 4th century BCE, the Near East, including Jewish communities, experienced extensive Hellenization. This era marked a profound blend of Greek culture, philosophy, and religion with local traditions, influencing Jewish religious thought and literature (Cohen et al., 2024). The Book of Enoch showcases a blend of Jewish apocalyptic themes and Hellenistic cosmological ideas. It intertwines divine and cosmic concepts from Platonism and Stoicism, reflecting the dualistic philosophies of the era. Within the text, elaborate depictions of celestial realms, angelic rankings, and the rebellion of the Watchers mirror Greek ideologies of cosmic conflicts and divine hierarchy (Geller, 2022).

The narrative of the Watchers, who disrupt the divine cosmos akin to Greek myths of titanic struggles and divine rebellions, showcases the deep integration of Hellenistic and Jewish thought (*What Is the Book of Enoch*, n.d.). Additionally, the role of Jewish communities in Hellenistic cities like Alexandria was crucial for preserving and transmitting these apocalyptic texts. The Library of Alexandria, a hub of scholarship and learning, likely housed copies of these works, including the Book of Enoch, playing a pivotal role in their survival and dissemination through the centuries (Smith, 2023).

The story of the Watchers can easily be compared to the battles between titans and gods in Greek myths, as it mixes Greek and Jewish ideas together. Additionally,

Jewish groups in cities like Alexandria were important for keeping and sharing these special texts. The Library of Alexandria, a hub of scholarship and learning, most likely housed copies of these works, including the Book of Enoch, playing a pivotal role in their survival and dissemination through the centuries (Smith, 2023).

This period of cultural diffusion, known as Hellenism, not only transformed the religious and cultural landscapes of the Jewish diaspora but also ensured that the theological and philosophical richness of the Book of Enoch would resonate through ages, influencing both contemporary and later religious thought.

The Maccabean Revolt and Jewish Identity

The 2nd century BCE, marked by the Maccabean Revolt (167–160 BCE), was a vital era in Jewish history. Jewish fighters, led by the Maccabee family, rebelled against the Seleucid Empire's attempts to enforce Hellenistic practices. This ignited a fierce assertion of Jewish religious identity against the framework of Hellenistic influence. This period was not just a political struggle but a profound cultural and theological turning point, for it deeply influenced Jewish apocalyptic literature, the Book of Enoch not excluded. The themes of cosmic conflict and justice in the Book of Enoch resonate greatly with this spirit of resistance, reflecting the fervent desire for deliverance and sovereignty of the Jews during this tumultuous period (*What Is the Book of Enoch*, n.d.).

During the Second Temple period, which was characterized by the emergence of various Jewish sects such as the Pharisees, Sadducees, and Essenes, the Essenes' ascetic lifestyle and apocalyptic beliefs played a significant role in preserving the Book of Enoch. Known for their meticulous copying and preservation of religious texts, the Essenes, often associated with the Dead Sea Scrolls, valued texts that emphasized eschatology and angelology—which are key themes in the Book of Enoch. The discovery of fragments of the Book of Enoch among the Dead Sea Scrolls at Qumran accentuates its importance within this community and suggests that the text was considered authoritative by some Jewish groups during this period (Glickman, 2018).

Moreover, these historical events significantly impacted the preservation of the Book of Enoch. While it fell out of favor in many Jewish and later Christian circles, yet preserved by the Ethiopian Orthodox Church, it suggests a selective retention of religious texts that resonated with specific community ideologies and needs (De Jager, 2023a).

From the Hellenistic conquests and the Maccabean Revolt to the sectarian developments within Judaism, the Book of Enoch stands as a testament to the dynamic and evolving nature of religious thought during this era. Its influence on early Christian theology further stresses its significance as a bridge between Jewish and Christian eschatological traditions.

Roman Influence and Early Christianity

The Roman annexation of Judea in 63 BCE layered new cultural and political dynamics over the region. While the

Roman era brought a degree of stability, it also cultivated tensions as the Jewish populations contended with foreign rule. This period saw the perpetuation of apocalyptic literature as a form of resistance and a symbol of promise for divine deliverance (Geller, 2022).

Within this context, the themes of the Book of Enoch, emphasizing divine justice and eschatological expectation, resonated strongly. These themes found a particular echo among the early Christians, who also endured persecution under Roman governance. This connection is evident in early Christian literature; for instance, the Epistle of Jude in the New Testament explicitly references the Book of Enoch, highlighting its influence by integrating its prophetic visions into the Christian eschatological framework (Denova, 2021).

As Christianity spread, it embraced and perpetuated the themes from the Book of Enoch, which helped preserve and transmit the text beyond its Jewish origins. Though the Book of Enoch was later excluded from the Christian biblical canon, its themes continued to enrich Christian apocryphal writings and theological discussions, contributing to its enduring legacy across generations (De Jager, 2023a).

Christianity embraced and carried forward the themes that originated from the Book of Enoch. This act of inclusion aided in safeguarding and passing on the pure essence of the text, even beyond its initial Jewish roots. Despite the Book of Enoch not being included in the Christian biblical canon, its fundamental ideas persisted in various Christian apocryphal texts and theological dialogues. As a result, the Book of Enoch's influence continued to resonate within Christian teachings and discussions, leaving a lasting impact on believers across different eras.

Persian Influence and Zoroastrianism

The Achaemenid dynasty of the Persian Empire left a profound imprint on Jewish thought, primarily through the influence of Zoroastrianism, Persia's predominant religion. This period introduced pivotal concepts of dualism, cosmic struggle, and eschatology, which deeply permeated Jewish apocalyptic literature, as evidenced in texts such as, for example, the Book of Enoch (Denova, 2021). The dualistic themes within the Book of Enoch— illustrating battles between forces of light and darkness and detailing the judgment of souls—mirror the Zoroastrian ideas of cosmic conflict and moral dualism.

In the Book of Enoch, the intricate portrayal of angels and demons and their defined roles within the cosmic framework are reflective of Zoroastrian influences on Jewish theology. Notably, the narrative of the Watchers, who fall from grace due to rebellion, echoes the Zoroastrian stories of divine beings destined to face downfall as a consequence of their defiance. This thematic resonance highlights the significant cultural exchanges that occurred between the Jewish and Persian civilizations, enriching the Jewish apocalyptic tradition during the Achaemenid rule (De Jager, 2023a).

Further emphasizing the Persian influence, the Book of Enoch's depictions of the eternal conflict between good and evil, along with the ultimate reckoning during the final judgment, is distinctly defined by Zoroastrian doctrine. The Persian tradition focuses on a well-ordered system of angelology that details various ranks and functions of celestial beings but also significantly shapes the complex angelic hierarchies described in the Book of Enoch. These elements reinforce the deep intercultural dialogues that not only enriched Jewish eschatological narratives but also helped mold the broader theological perspectives during the era of Persian dominance (Encyclopaedia Iranica, 2011).

Thus, the Achaemenid Empire era played a crucial role in the exchange of religious and philosophical ideas, where the deep teachings of Zoroastrianism, those at the end of times and the universe, became intertwined with Jewish apocalyptic writings. This fusion left a profound impact, shaping future religious developments significantly (Encyclopaedia Iranica, 2011).

Egyptian Influence

The Jewish dispersion in Egypt, notably centered in Alexandria, greatly impacted the molding of the religious and cultural backdrop of the Book of Enoch. With Alexandria standing as a vibrant hub of Hellenistic and Jewish intellectual pursuits, Jewish scholars actively interacted with Greek philosophical principles and Egyptian religious ideologies here (Geller, 2022).

The vivid depictions of celestial hierarchies and divine judgment in the text demonstrate clear connections with Egyptian religious ideas rooted in Ma'at, symbolizing universal order and intricate beliefs regarding life after death. This amalgamation significantly enriched the theological panorama of the Book of Enoch by integrating it into the broader spectrum of ancient Near Eastern religious ideologies (Smith, 2023).

The recitals in the Book of Enoch, including the cosmic clash between good and evil and the eventual victory of righteousness, reflect theological contemplations from historical events like the Maccabean Revolt. As the text focuses on divine retribution against the wicked while maintaining assurance of salvation for the faithful, it provides spiritual comfort and optimism to a community of people who had to endure oppression and persecution, serving ever so slightly as a beam of optimism and encouragement (Smith, 2023).

Authorship and Attribution

In the mystical corridors of ancient scriptural history, where texts are often as enigmatic as their creators, the authorship of the Book of Enoch remains shrouded in mystery and intrigue. Traditionally, Enoch, the seventh patriarch from Adam, is credited as the scribe of these ethereal texts. This figure's proximity to the divine is echoed in the transcendent visions and celestial journeys detailed within the pages. However, modern scholarly discourse offers a more nuanced view, suggesting composite authorship that spans several centuries, reflecting a broader spectrum of influences and theological perspectives (Denova, 2021).

Scholars debate this traditional attribution, suggesting that the Book of Enoch is likely the work of multiple authors compiled over centuries. This perspective aligns with the pseudepigraphical nature of much earlier Jewish literature, where texts are often written in the name of significant figures from the distant past to address more contemporary issues and concerns of the period in which the authors actually lived (Reich, 2022). The themes within the Book of Enoch—such as divine judgment, the nature of the universe, and the fate of souls—reflect broad and enduring theological questions that were particularly poignant during the turbulent Hellenistic period when Jewish society grappled with external influences and internal reforms.

The speculation that multiple authors contributed to the Book of Enoch over time is supported by the text's diversity in style and content. Portions of the text likely reflect different historical contexts, ranging from pre-Maccabean times to the first century CE, each contributing layers of theological and cosmological thought that mirror the evolving religious landscape of the Jewish community under Hellenistic rule (Cohen et al., 2024). This evolving document served as a spiritual guide, addressing the existential and eschatological anxieties of its readers through the centuries.

Thus, while the true authorship of the Book of Enoch may remain a topic of academic debate, the text itself also continues to fascinate as a remarkable chronicle drawn from the foundation of Jewish mysticism and prophetic literature. It serves as a testament to beliefs of a past age and to the relentless human pursuit to grasp the divine cosmos and our role within it. This scrutiny of its authorship beckons readers to engage more deeply with the text, urging exploration not only within the confines of a book's pages but also through the evolving history of religious ideologies.

The Book of Enoch has long intrigued scholars and theologians and the question of who wrote the Book of Enoch is a matter of ongoing debate, with theories ranging from traditional attributions to more modern academic perspectives. This exploration probes into the various scholarly theories regarding the authorship of this fascinating text, examining the motivations and contexts behind its creation.

Theories of Authorship

Traditionally, the Book of Enoch is attributed to Enoch, the great-grandfather of Noah, a figure mentioned in the Hebrew Bible. According to the Genesis narrative, Enoch "walked with God" and was taken up to Heaven without experiencing death (New International Version, 2011, Genesis 5:24). This unique description set the stage for Enoch's association with mystical and apocalyptic literature. The text itself presents Enoch as the recipient of divine revelations, documenting his heavenly journeys and the secrets revealed to him by angelic beings (*What Is the Book of Enoch*, n.d.).

This traditional view holds that Enoch, as a righteous and revered patriarch, was a fitting author for a work focused on divine judgment and cosmic order. The attribution to Enoch lent the text authority and credibility within Jewish religious circles, positioning it as a source of ancient wisdom and prophetic insight (Smith, 2023).

Modern scholarship, however, suggests that the Book of Enoch was not written by a single individual but is instead a composite work authored by multiple writers over several centuries. This theory is supported by the text's complex structure and the presence of distinct sections, each with unique themes and literary styles. This is also due to the fact that the earliest portions, known as the "Book of the Watchers," are believed to have been written around the 3rd century BCE, while later sections, such as the "Similitudes of Enoch," were likely composed in the 1st century BCE (Denova, 2021). If this is, in fact, accurate, this would not have been possible if the author was one and the same, one would assume.

The multiple authorship theory posits that various Jewish scribes and scholars contributed to the text, each adding their interpretations and expansions to the original material. These contributors were likely influenced by the socio-political and religious contexts of their time, including the Hellenistic period, the Maccabean Revolt, and the rise of apocalyptic thought within Jewish communities (Geller, 2022). This collaborative process resulted in a rich and multifaceted work that reflects the evolving theological concerns and literary traditions of ancient Judaism.

Apocalyptic Scribes and Sectarian Movements

Some scholars argue that the Book of Enoch was produced by apocalyptic scribes associated with specific Jewish sects, such as the Essenes. The Essenes, known for their ascetic lifestyle and apocalyptic beliefs, are often linked to the Dead Sea Scrolls, which include fragments of the Book of Enoch. This connection suggests that the Essenes valued the text for its emphasis on divine judgment, angelology, and eschatology, which are themes that resonated with their religious worldview (Glickman, 2018).

The Essenes' interest in apocalyptic literature and their meticulous preservation of religious texts indicate that they may have played a significant role in the composition and transmission of the Book of Enoch. This theory aligns with the notion that the text was crafted by a community deeply invested in apocalyptic expectations and the hope for divine intervention in human affairs (Denova, 2021).

Prophetic Authority and Pseudepigraphy

Another theory suggests that the Book of Enoch was written using the literary technique of pseudepigraphy, where authors attribute their works to ancient figures to lend them greater authority and credibility. This practice was common in the ancient world and served to connect contemporary teachings with revered traditions. By attributing the text to Enoch, the authors could present their apocalyptic visions and theological insights as ancient and divinely inspired, enhancing their acceptance and influence within the Jewish community (Smith, 2023).

The use of Enoch as a pseudonymous author allowed the writers to address contemporary issues and concerns under the guise of ancient prophecy. This technique enabled them to engage with their audience on matters of cosmic justice, divine judgment, and the hope for redemption, themes that were particularly resonant during times of political turmoil and religious uncertainty (*What Is the Book of Enoch*, n.d.).

Literary Style and Language

The Book of Enoch captivates with its enigmatic blend of poetry and prophecy, a testament to the myriad voices that may have traversed its creation. The text's literary style is vividly apocalyptic, rich with allegorical narratives and profound visions that speak to a deeply mystical tradition within Jewish literature. This literary form serves as a bridge between the divine and the earthly, crafting a narrative that is both ethereal and intensely relevant to the spiritual dilemmas of its time.

The language of Enoch is complex, with its voice originating from the dialects of ancient Hebrew and Aramaic, which are languages steeped in the sacred traditions of the Jewish people. This linguistic diversity suggests that the text may have evolved over centuries, possibly starting in the oral tradition before being transcribed by different scribes. Each layer of text reveals subtle differences in style and vocabulary, hinting at the varied contexts in which parts of the book were composed. These textual nuances not only illuminate the evolving nature of the language used but also reflect the shifting theological and eschatological perspectives of different periods (Denova, 2021).

Furthermore, the examination of various manuscripts of the Book of Enoch, such as those found among the Dead Sea Scrolls, reveals significant textual variations. These differences are critical in understanding the development of the text; they indicate that what we now consider the Book of Enoch was likely not the work of a single author but a compilation of writings that may have been edited and reinterpreted by different communities to address their unique spiritual needs and concerns (Reich, 2022).

This analysis of the Book of Enoch's literary style and language not only enhances our appreciation of its complex authorship but also deepens our understanding of its profound impact on Jewish religious thought. Its enduring appeal lies in its ability to articulate themes of divine justice, angelic mediation, and cosmic order, resonating through the ages as a powerful narrative of faith and revelation. As such, the Book of Enoch remains a pivotal work, bridging the mystical past with ongoing theological inquiry, inviting readers into its rich, allegorical world to ponder the deeper meanings that emerge from its ancient words.

Canonical Status and Controversies

The Book of Enoch finds itself at the heart of canonical debates that span millennia and religious traditions. Its journey through the corridors of religious acceptance illuminates the intricate dance between orthodoxy and mysticism within the sacred texts of Judaism and Christianity.

In the Jewish tradition, the Book of Enoch holds a complex but notably non-canonical status. While it was influential in the Second Temple period and revered for its detailed angelology and cosmology, it did not maintain this esteemed position in later Rabbinic Judaism. The reasons for its exclusion hinge on the evolving criteria of scriptural sanctity and the centralization of religious texts that aligned more closely with Rabbinic doctrines. This exclusion was partly due to its esoteric content and the mystical themes that could potentially conflict with emerging orthodox beliefs (Cohen et al., 2024).

Conversely, in the Christian tradition, particularly within the Ethiopian Orthodox Church, the Book of Enoch is regarded as canonical. This inclusion reflects the broader and more encompassing definitions of scripture that characterize the Ethiopian religious tradition, perhaps also influenced by the geographical and cultural isolation that helped preserve older religious texts and traditions that were lost or set aside elsewhere (De Jager, 2023a).

The church regards the book as an essential part of its biblical canon, attributing to it the same level of divine inspiration as the books of Genesis or Isaiah.

The debates surrounding the Book of Enoch's canonical status are further complicated by its reception in early Christian communities, where it was variously embraced for its messianic prophecies and detailed accounts of the fallen angels. Early Church Fathers like Tertullian once defended its value, arguing for its theological richness that complements the canonical texts. However, as Christian doctrine solidified, the Book of Enoch found itself outside the canonical boundaries set by emerging Church orthodoxy, primarily due to its origins outside the apostolic foundations and its divergent views on angelology and cosmology (*What Is the Book of Enoch*, n.d.).

Thus, the canonical status of the Book of Enoch serves as a fascinating study of how religious texts are not merely adopted or rejected based on their spiritual content alone, but also based on how they align with the theological, cultural, and political currents of their times. Its presence in some traditions and absence in others accentuates the dynamic nature of scripture and its interpretation across different contexts and epochs. The ongoing scholarly interest in the Book of Enoch also highlights a broader quest to understand the multifaceted nature of ancient religious writings and their enduring impact on faith and spirituality across the globe.

Chapter 2:
From Scrolls to Scripture

Visualize the ancient transcribers under the flickering light of oil lamps, painstakingly copying the complex Aramaic characters of the original Enoch texts. These scrolls were treasured, hidden, and sometimes feared, as they carried deep revelations of the end times and sacred knowledge. In this chapter, we will explore the historical eras that saw the Book of Enoch held in high esteem as a pillar of faith, rejected from official acceptance, and later unearthed in hidden caves near the Dead Sea, reflecting the enduring strength and fascination of its teachings.

As we sift through the sands of the Judaean desert, where fragments of the Book of Enoch were found among the Dead Sea Scrolls, we uncover the layers of translation and interpretation that have shaped the reception of the text. Each translation, from Aramaic to Greek to Ge'ez, has not only transformed the language but also the understanding and influence of Enoch's writings. In this chapter, we will examine how these translations have both preserved and altered the original essence of

Enoch's revelations while also reflecting the dynamic interplay between text and context, scribe and scripture.

However, why would we stop there? We will also attempt to explore the controversies and debates that have swirled around the scriptural status of the Book of Enoch. Why was it embraced by some traditions yet excluded by others? How have modern discoveries like the Dead Sea Scrolls influenced contemporary interpretations and academic debates? We are about to experience the Book of Enoch not just as a text but as a living, breathing entity that has woven its way through history by challenging, enlightening, and mystifying those it touches.

Early Translations

Hidden within the depths of history, where many ancient manuscripts disclose mysteries over the eras, the odyssey of the Book of Enoch, as it journeyed through numerous translations, tells a story of puzzling adventures, a chronicle of cryptic quests, if you will. Initially crafted in the celestial dialects of ancient Hebrew or Aramaic, the verses of Enoch have navigated through many civilizations, with each translation adding new layers of comprehension and insight.

The earliest transformation of Enoch's words likely occurred as they were transcribed into Greek. This Greek version, known to scholars as part of the Septuagint, heralded the text's first foray into a new linguistic realm. It was a time when the Hellenistic influence permeated the Near East, infusing the local cultures with Greek philosophies and language. This translation signified a major milestone, as the enigmatic Jewish text merged with a broader, more cosmopolitan realm of thought. The subtleties of its original meaning may have shifted, adapting to the nuances of Greek thought, yet its core essence—prophetic visions and celestial journeys—remained captivatingly intact (Cain et al., 2024).

As centuries turned, the Book of Enoch found a new linguistic vessel in Ge'ez, an ancient liturgical language of

Ethiopia. Here, the text was not merely preserved but revered within the canons of the Ethiopian Orthodox Church. The Ge'ez translation of the Book of Enoch cemented its status in a culture far removed from its origins, thus highlighting the text's universal appeal and its ability to resonate across diverse spiritual landscapes. This phase of its journey is particularly notable for how it emphasizes the themes of universal judgment and divine revelation of the book, which echoed profoundly with the Ethiopian ecclesiastical teachings (Childs, 2019).

Yet, the narrative of Enoch did not halt at the borders of Ethiopia. Fragments of its ancient manuscripts resurfaced in the modern era among the storied caves of Qumran as part of the Dead Sea Scrolls. Rediscovered in the mid-20th century, these fragments in Aramaic rekindled interest in Enoch's texts and confirmed their widespread dissemination and enduring appeal in the ancient world (Ludlow, 2021). Each fragment and each scroll from this trove offered scholars a new puzzle piece to help them understand how Enoch's writings influenced and were influenced by the Jewish apocalyptic literature of the time.

The tale of the Book of Enoch, as it danced from language to language, culture to culture, is not just a chronicle of an ancient text's survival. It is a vivid narrative of adaptation and endurance, a testament to the power of written words to transcend temporal and spatial boundaries. Through each translation, through each cultural reimagining, Enoch's visions continue to challenge, enlighten, and inspire, weaving their ancient magic into the fabric of human understanding. As we explore these translations, we delve deeper into the mystical, embarking on a journey that transcends mere text to touch the very essence of the divine.

Languages and Scripts

The journey of the Book of Enoch from its inception to its current form spans numerous centuries, cultures, and languages. Understanding the linguistic evolution of this ancient text provides insight into the historical and cultural contexts that shaped its transmission. In this section, we will investigate the various languages into which the Book of Enoch has been translated, beginning with the original Aramaic or Hebrew, moving to Greek, and finally to Ethiopic.

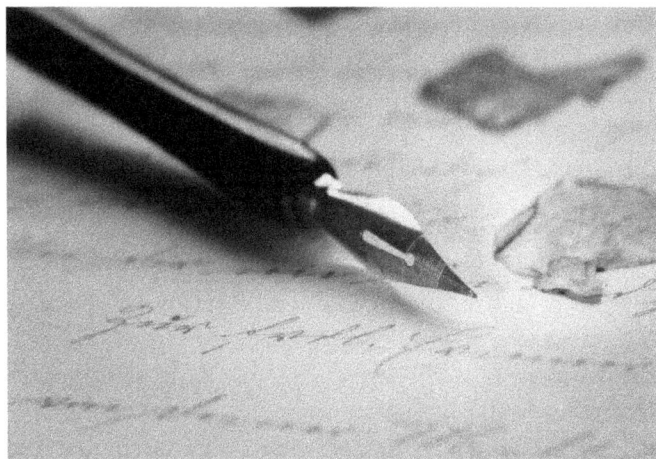

The Book of Enoch's journey through all of these different languages is like a grand adventure through time. It is quite astonishing how a book written so long ago can still be read and understood today, mainly thanks to all the translations it has gone through. Each language the book was translated into added a new layer of understanding and meaning to its words. It's like the book whispered its secrets in different tongues, ensuring that its wisdom would not be lost to the passage of time. The linguistic evolution of the Book of Enoch is like a tale of resilience and legacy that continues to echo through the ages.

Original Aramaic or Hebrew

The Book of Enoch has been around for an immensely long time and was written in languages that were used way back in the Old Ages. At first, it was in Aramaic or Hebrew. These languages are much like the ancient versions of the languages that we use today, and when used, through looking at the original texts, the exploration of the contents of the text can be perceived as finding out the secrets of ancient words. Studying the Book of Enoch in its first languages is like digging into an ancient treasure chest filled with clues about the past, an experience one might not want to go without.

The Book of Enoch is believed to have been originally composed in Aramaic or Hebrew, the languages widely spoken among Jewish communities during the Second Temple period (approximately 516 BCE to 70 CE). Aramaic was the lingua franca of the Near East at the time, used extensively in commerce, administration, and everyday life, while Hebrew was the liturgical and scholarly language of the Jewish people (Cain et al., 2024).

The evidence for the original language of the Book of Enoch comes from fragments discovered among the Dead Sea Scrolls at Qumran. These fragments, dating as far back as the 2nd century BCE, are primarily written in Aramaic. The Dead Sea Scrolls include parts of the "Book of the Watchers," which we have previously stated is one of the earliest sections of the Book of Enoch, thus indicating that Aramaic was likely the original language of these portions (Childs, 2019). The choice of Aramaic for the composition of the Book of Enoch reflects the linguistic reality of the scattered Jewish population. Aramaic was accessible to a broader audience than Hebrew, allowing the text to reach and resonate with Jewish communities spread across the Near Eastern territories. Moreover, the use of Aramaic aligns with other contemporary Jewish apocalyptic texts, such as the Book of Daniel, which also contains significant portions written in Aramaic (Cain et al., 2024).

The Hebrew fragments of the Book of Enoch, although less numerous than the Aramaic ones, suggest that portions of the text might have been composed or later translated into Hebrew. This bilingual nature of the text underlines its importance and the diverse linguistic environment in which it circulated (Wayne, 2020).

Greek Translation

After being written in Aramaic or Hebrew, the Book of Enoch was translated into Greek, one language morphing into another. This could be compared to telling a story in one language and then retelling it in a whole new language, which, of course, may slightly alter its contents. This translation from Aramaic or Hebrew to Greek was a substantial affair because it meant that more people could read and understand the teachings and stories in the book. It was the first step, in a way, to unlocking the secrets of the Book of Enoch for a wider audience.

The spread of Hellenism following the conquests of Alexander the Great in the 4th century BCE significantly influenced Jewish culture and language. Greek became the dominant language in the Eastern Mediterranean, including among Jewish communities, many of whom adopted Greek for daily use and scholarly activities. This linguistic shift led to the translation of many Jewish texts into Greek, including the Book of Enoch.

The Greek translation of the Book of Enoch played a crucial role in its transmission and survival. This version, likely completed in the 3rd to 2nd centuries BCE, was part of a broader effort to translate Hebrew and Aramaic scriptures into Greek, known as the Septuagint project (Ludlow, 2021). The translation made the text accessible to a wider audience, including Hellenized Jews and early Christians who spoke Greek (Perkins, 2011).

The Greek version of the Book of Enoch is known to have been influential among early Christian writers. For instance, the Epistle of Jude in the New Testament directly quotes from the Book of Enoch, indicating its significance in early Christian thought (Wayne, 2020). The Greek translation ensured that the theological and apocalyptic themes of the Book of Enoch spread throughout early Christian eschatology (Cain et al., 2024).

Unfortunately, much of the Greek text has been lost over time. However, fragments of the Greek version have been preserved in quotations by early Church Fathers and in the writings of later Christian authors. These fragments provide critical insights into the reception and interpretation of the Book of Enoch in the Hellenistic and early Christian worlds (Childs, 2019).

Ethiopic (Ge'ez) Translation

From Greek, the Book of Enoch journeyed onwards to being translated into Ethiopic. That is quite the journey for a book! As the text of the Book of Enoch changed and adapted as it passed through different languages, the Ethiopic version serves as a bridge between the past and present because it keeps the ancient teachings alive in a language that is still spoken today. Much like the book, it went on a grand adventure, traveling through time and different lands to reach new readers and keep its wisdom alive.

The most complete version of the Book of Enoch that has survived to the present day is the Ethiopic translation, known as 1 Enoch or the Ethiopic Enoch. This translation into Ge'ez, the ancient liturgical language of the Ethiopian Orthodox Church, likely occurred between the 4th and 6th centuries CE (Perkins, 2011). The Ethiopian Church holds the Book of Enoch as canonical, a status it did not, however, retain in other Christian traditions.

The Ethiopic translation is particularly significant because it preserves the full text of the Book of Enoch, including sections that are only partially existing in Aramaic and Greek. This version was based on Greek manuscripts, suggesting a direct line of transmission from the Greek text to the Ethiopic (Childs, 2019). The Ethiopic Enoch includes all five major sections of the text: the Book of the Watchers, the Book of Parables, the Astronomical Book, the Book of Dream Visions, and the Epistle of Enoch.

The translation into Ge'ez reflects the early spread of Christianity into Ethiopia and the integration of Jewish and Christian traditions within Ethiopian religious literature. The Ethiopian Orthodox Church's reverence for the Book of Enoch ensured its meticulous preservation and transmission through the centuries, allowing it to survive when it fell out of favor in other parts of the Christian world (Shanks, 2007).

The Ethiopic Enoch has been the subject of extensive scholarly study since the text was first brought to the attention of European scholars in the late 18th century. The first English translation was completed in the 19th century, sparking renewed interest in the text's historical and theological significance. Modern scholarship continues to rely heavily on the Ethiopic version to reconstruct the original content and context of the Book of Enoch (Cain et al., 2024).

Translation Discrepancies

Due to its profound apocalyptic visions and intricate theological themes, the Book of Enoch has been translated into multiple languages over the centuries, each translation bringing its own nuances and variations. These differences have, of course, given rise to diverse interpretations and theological implications. Therefore, this section serves as an investigation of how these discrepancies emerged while highlighting notable differences and their impacts on our understanding of this ancient text.

The translation variations in the Book of Enoch reflect the complex interplay between language, culture, and religious tradition. Starting from its original compositions in Aramaic or Hebrew, as the text journeyed through Greek and Ethiopic translations, this excursion reveals unique insights and challenges. Each version contributes to a diverse collection of interpretations, offering a complex and nuanced understanding of this enigmatic work.

Understanding these translation discrepancies reveals the historical and cultural contexts of the Book of Enoch, enriching our appreciation of its lasting significance in the religious and literary traditions of Judaism, Christianity, and beyond. By exploring these differences, we gain a deeper understanding of the evolving role of the text and its enduring influence across diverse spiritual landscapes.

Variations From Aramaic to Greek

As the Book of Enoch was translated from Aramaic (or Hebrew) into Greek, significant discrepancies began to emerge due to linguistic differences and cultural contexts.

One notable example of these translation discrepancies is found in the portrayal of the Watchers. In the original Aramaic texts found among the Dead Sea Scrolls, the term used to describe these beings is "ʿir," which translates to "watcher" or "awake one." However, in the Greek translation, the term "ἐγρήγοροι" (egrēgoroi) is used, emphasizing vigilance and alertness. This subtle shift in meaning affects the interpretation of the Watchers' role and nature, influencing the theological discussions (Wayne, 2020; *What Is the Book of Enoch*, n.d.; Ludlow, 2021).

Furthermore, the Greek translators often employed terms with specific philosophical connotations, reflecting Hellenistic influences. For instance, the Greek term "κόσμος" (kosmos), used to describe the world or universe, carries connotations of order and harmony rooted in Greek cosmology. This contrasts with the Hebrew concept of "עולם" (olam), which encompasses both the physical world and the notion of eternity. These differences can lead to varying theological interpretations about the nature of the cosmos and its relationship to the divine. (Wayne, 2020; *What Is the Book of Enoch*, n.d.; Ludlow, 2021)

Such discrepancies highlight the complex interplay between language, culture, and theology as the Book of Enoch was translated and interpreted across different historical and cultural contexts. The translation into Greek, in particular, marked a significant moment in the text's journey, as it was adapted to fit the broader intellectual and spiritual landscapes of the Hellenistic world.

From Greek to Ethiopic

The most complete version of the Book of Enoch existing today is the Ethiopic translation, known as 1 Enoch, as it was translated from Greek into Ge'ez, the ancient liturgical language of the Ethiopian Orthodox Church, and it introduced further discrepancies. While the Ethiopic translation preserved the text through the centuries, the process of translation introduced variations that have significant theological implications.

One notable example is found in the "Book of the Watchers." In the Greek texts, the giants born from the union of the Watchers and human women are described as "γίγαντες" (gigantes), implying great size and strength, akin to the Titans of Greek mythology. In contrast, the Ethiopic translation uses the term "zazazel," which emphasizes their rebellious and sinful nature. This discrepancy affects how readers perceive the giants—either as formidable beings of immense power or as embodiments of moral corruption and divine punishment (Wayne, 2020; *What Is the Book of Enoch*, n.d.; Ludlow, 2021).

Additionally, the Ethiopic version includes unique expansions and interpolations not found in the Greek texts. These additions often reflect the theological and liturgical traditions of the Ethiopian Church, emphasizing themes such as divine judgment and the role of the righteous. For instance, the Ethiopic Enoch places a greater emphasis on Enoch's role as an intercessor and mediator between God and humanity, aligning with the Ethiopian tradition of venerating saints and intercessors (Childs, 2019).

Theological Implications

Translation discrepancies in the Book of Enoch have significant theological implications, influencing how different communities interpret key concepts such as the nature of angels, the cosmos, and divine justice. These variations can lead to differing views on these critical theological ideas.

For instance, the portrayal of the Watchers affects discussions about sin and redemption. Aramaic and Hebrew texts often focus on the Watchers' betrayal and its consequences. Conversely, the Greek and Ethiopic versions, with their unique terminologies and emphases, may highlight vigilance, moral failure, or inevitable divine retribution.

Similarly, differences in the depiction of the giants impact theological perspectives on evil and human agency. The Greek portrayal of the giants as powerful

50

beings can symbolize the overwhelming force of sin and its impacts. In contrast, the Ethiopic emphasis on their rebellious nature highlights the moral aspects of evil and underlines the necessity for divine intervention and redemption (Cain et al., 2024; Wayne, 2020).

Modern Interpretations and Scholarly Debates

Modern scholars continue to debate the significance of translation discrepancies and their implications for understanding the Book of Enoch. Some argue that these variations put emphasis on the fluidity of religious texts and highlight the importance of considering multiple versions to gain a comprehensive understanding. Others emphasize the necessity of returning to the earliest available manuscripts, such as the Aramaic fragments from the Dead Sea Scrolls, to reconstruct the original meanings and intentions of the authors.

These scholarly debates often intersect with theological discussions within different religious traditions. For example, the Ethiopian Orthodox Church's acceptance of the Book of Enoch as canonical contrasts with its exclusion from the Jewish and most Christian canons. This difference in canonical status reflects broader theological and interpretive traditions, shaped in part by the variations introduced through translation.

Key Translators and Their Contribution

The Book of Enoch has navigated a fascinating journey through time, language, and culture. Its preservation and dissemination owe much to the dedicated efforts of key translators whose cultural and religious backgrounds deeply influenced their work. These important figures deserve mention, where one examines how their unique perspectives shaped the translation and interpretation of this enigmatic text.

From Byzantine monks to Anglican scholars and Ethiopian experts, each translator brought a unique perspective to the text, shaping its interpretation and dissemination. Their contributions have ensured that the Book of Enoch remains a vital and influential component of the study of ancient apocalyptic literature, bridging the worlds of Judaism, Christianity, and beyond.

George Syncellus

George Syncellus, a Byzantine monk and chronicler from the 8th century, played a crucial role in preserving fragments of the Book of Enoch. Syncellus focused on compiling a universal chronicle that aimed to align biblical history with the histories of other ancient civilizations. His background as a Byzantine monk influenced his perspective, emphasizing the text's historical and theological significance within the broader context of Christian historiography (Editors of Encyclopaedia Britannica, 2024a).

Syncellus's excerpts from the Book of Enoch were incorporated into his "Chronography," a comprehensive historical record. This work provided one of the earliest references to the Book of Enoch in Christian literature, effectively bridging the gap between ancient Jewish apocalyptic traditions and Byzantine Christian scholarship. Syncellus's meticulous recording helped preserve the legacy of the Book of Enoch during a period when many ancient texts were lost or forgotten (Editors of Encyclopaedia Britannica, 2024a; Perkins, 2011).

Richard Laurence

In the early 19th century, Richard Laurence, an Anglican Archbishop and scholar, made a significant contribution by producing one of the first English translations of the Book of Enoch. Laurence's translation, published in 1821, was based on manuscripts in Ge'ez (Ethiopic), the liturgical language of the Ethiopian Orthodox Church (Childs, 2019). Laurence's work marked a pivotal moment in the history of the text, making it accessible to a broader audience beyond the Ethiopian context.

His religious background as an Anglican influenced his approach to the text. He viewed the Book of Enoch through the lens of Christian theology, emphasizing its potential connections to early Christian doctrines and eschatological themes. His translation sparked renewed interest in the Book of Enoch among Western scholars and theologians, contributing to its study and appreciation in academic and religious communities (*Is the Book of Enoch Inspired Writing?*, n.d.).

R.H. Charles

R.H. Charles, a British theologian and biblical scholar, is perhaps the most renowned translator of the Book of Enoch in the modern era. His comprehensive translation, published in 1912, remains a seminal work in the field of Enochic studies (Childs, 2019). Charles's translation was based on the Ethiopic manuscripts and included extensive commentary and critical notes, reflecting his deep scholarly engagement with the text.

Charles's cultural and religious background as an Anglican scholar influenced his interpretive approach. He sought to place the Book of Enoch within the broader framework of Jewish and Christian apocalyptic literature, highlighting its theological significance and its potential influence on early Christian thought (*Is the Book of Enoch Inspired Writing?*, n.d.). His meticulous scholarship and critical analysis helped establish the Book of Enoch as a vital component of the study of ancient apocalyptic traditions.

Milik and the Dead Sea Scrolls

Józef Milik, a Polish biblical scholar, made groundbreaking contributions to the study of the Book of Enoch through his work on the Dead Sea Scrolls. In the mid-20th century, Milik was part of the team that discovered and analyzed the scrolls found at Qumran, which included significant Aramaic fragments of the

Book of Enoch (Geller, 2022). These discoveries provided critical insights into the text's early transmission and its role within the Jewish apocalyptic tradition.

Milik's cultural and religious background as a Catholic scholar informed his approach to the text. He emphasized the historical and philological aspects of the Enochic fragments, situating them within the broader context of Second Temple Judaism. Milik's work helped clarify the text's original language and its early use, contributing to a deeper understanding of its historical and theological development (De Jager, 2023a).

Michael A. Knibb

Michael A. Knibb, a British scholar specializing in ancient Jewish texts, produced a highly influential English translation of the Book of Enoch in the late 20th century. Knibb's translation, published in 1978, is noted for its rigorous scholarly approach and meticulous attention to textual variants. His work utilized both the Ethiopic version and the Aramaic fragments from the Dead Sea Scrolls, providing a comprehensive and nuanced translation that has become a cornerstone in the study of this ancient text (Knibb, 2009).

Knibb's background as a scholar of ancient Judaism profoundly influenced his approach to the Book of Enoch. He aimed to understand the text within its original Jewish context, highlighting its significance for the study of Jewish apocalyptic literature and its impact on early Christian thought. His translation and commentary are essential resources for scholars and students delving into ancient Jewish and Christian texts (Knibb, 2009).

Ephraim Isaac

Ephraim Isaac, an Ethiopian scholar and expert in Semitic languages, has made significant contributions to the study and translation of the Book of Enoch. Isaac's work primarily focuses on the original Ge'ez manuscripts, offering critical editions and translations that reflect the traditions of the Ethiopian Orthodox Church. His translations emphasize the continuity of the Enochic tradition within Ethiopian Christianity and underscore its theological significance (Isaac, 1983).

Isaac's cultural and religious background as an Ethiopian scholar greatly informs his interpretive approach, providing a unique perspective on the Book of Enoch from within the Ethiopian Orthodox Church. His work highlights the importance of the text in Ethiopian religious literature and its role in shaping Ethiopian theological and liturgical traditions (Isaac, 1983).

Historical Preservation

The historical preservation of the Book of Enoch is a testament to the enduring power of religious texts and the efforts of various communities to safeguard their spiritual heritage. From the early Jewish sects of Qumran to the Ethiopian Orthodox Church and through the rediscovery by modern scholars, the journey of the Book of Enoch reflects the dynamic interplay of preservation, loss, and rediscovery. This complex history accentuates the text's significance and impact on both ancient and contemporary religious thought. This section serves as an exploration of the theories and explanations behind how the Book of Enoch was preserved, lost, and ultimately rediscovered.

Preservation Efforts Over Time

In this section, you will venture down the road of exploring the multifaceted efforts made to preserve the Book of Enoch, highlighting the roles of medieval manuscript transmission and monastic communities.

Preservation Through Early Jewish Communities

The initial preservation of the Book of Enoch likely occurred within early Jewish communities during the Second Temple period (516 BCE–70 CE). The text was composed in Aramaic, reflecting its widespread use among Jews during this era (Cain et al., 2024). Its themes of divine judgment, angelology, and eschatology resonated deeply with contemporary Jewish thought, particularly within apocalyptic and mystical circles.

One of the most significant periods of preservation was at Qumran, where the Dead Sea Scrolls were discovered. These scrolls included fragments of the Book of Enoch, indicating that the text was valued by the Essene community, known for its apocalyptic beliefs and meticulous scriptural preservation (Geller, 2022). The Essenes' reverence for Enochic literature as part of their religious tradition ensured the text's careful transcription and safekeeping.

The preservation efforts at Qumran highlight the importance of sectarian movements in maintaining religious texts. The Essenes' practice of storing their scrolls in the arid environment of the Judean Desert contributed to the exceptional preservation conditions that have allowed these ancient manuscripts to survive for millennia (Childs, 2019).

Early Preservation Efforts

The earliest preservation efforts of the Book of Enoch can be traced back to the Jewish sects during the Second Temple period. The Essenes, a Jewish sect known for their apocalyptic beliefs, played a crucial role in maintaining Enochic literature. The discovery of the Dead Sea Scrolls at Qumran, which included fragments of the Book of Enoch, underscores the Essenes' commitment to preserving sacred texts (Geller, 2022).

These fragments, written in Aramaic, reveal the meticulous care with which the Essenes stored and copied their manuscripts. The arid environment of the Judean Desert provided ideal conditions for the preservation of these scrolls, ensuring their survival for over two millennia (Childs, 2019). The Essenes' efforts not only safeguarded the Book of Enoch but also contributed to the broader corpus of Jewish apocalyptic literature.

The Role of Early Christian Communities

As Christianity emerged in the first century CE, early Christians demonstrated a keen interest in apocalyptic literature, including the Book of Enoch. This fascination is evident in the New Testament, where the Epistle of Jude directly quotes from Enoch, implicitly acknowledging its prophetic authority. Early Church Fathers such as Tertullian and Origen also referenced the Book of Enoch, reflecting its substantial influence on early Christian eschatology and angelology (Ludlow, 2021).

The canonical status of the text within Christianity was subject to debate. By the 4th century, during the formalization of the Christian biblical canon, the Book of Enoch was excluded from most Western Christian traditions. Despite this exclusion, its influence endured in Ethiopian Christianity, where it was translated into Ge'ez and integrated into the Ethiopian Orthodox Church's canon (Wayne, 2020; Perkins, 2011).

The Ethiopian Orthodox Church played a pivotal role in preserving the Book of Enoch. Ethiopian scribes meticulously copied the text, ensuring its transmission through generations. The Church's distinctive theological perspective, which embraced Enochic literature, provided a refuge for the text during periods when it was largely neglected elsewhere in the Christian world (Childs, 2019).

Periods of Loss and Obscurity

Despite its early significance, the Book of Enoch fell into obscurity in much of the Jewish and Christian world after the 4th century. Several factors contributed to this decline, including the consolidation of the biblical canon, which excluded many apocalyptic texts, and the rise of rabbinic Judaism, which emphasized the Hebrew Bible (Tanakh) and the Talmud over other writings. During the medieval period, knowledge of the Book of Enoch was largely confined to references by early Christian writers and the preserved copies in Ethiopia. In the West, the text became a rare and obscure curiosity, largely forgotten by mainstream religious scholarship.

Medieval Manuscript Transmission

The medieval period marked a significant phase in the preservation of the Book of Enoch, particularly within the Ethiopian Orthodox Church. While the text faded from mainstream Jewish and Christian traditions, it found a new home in Ethiopia, where it was translated into Ge'ez and integrated into the canon of the Ethiopian Orthodox Church (Perkins, 2011).

Ethiopian scribes and scholars undertook the painstaking task of copying the Book of Enoch by hand, ensuring its transmission across generations. These manuscripts, often illuminated and richly decorated, were preserved in monastic libraries and churches. The

Ethiopian Orthodox tradition, which placed a high value on the text, provided a stable and reverent environment for its preservation (Shanks, 2007).

One of the most remarkable aspects of this period was the role of monastic communities in Ethiopia. Monasteries served as centers of learning and scriptural preservation, where monks dedicated their lives to the study and copying of sacred texts. These communities were instrumental in maintaining the integrity and continuity of the Book of Enoch amid a broader context of religious devotion and scholarly pursuit (Childs, 2019).

Renaissance and Enlightenment Rediscovery

The Renaissance and Enlightenment periods brought renewed interest in ancient texts, including the Book of Enoch. European explorers and scholars, fascinated by the mysterious and the arcane, began to seek out forgotten manuscripts. James Bruce, a Scottish explorer, was among the first to bring Ethiopic manuscripts of the Book of Enoch to Europe after his travels in Ethiopia in the late 18th century (Editors of Encyclopaedia Britannica, 2024b).

Bruce's efforts sparked a wave of scholarly interest, leading to the first English translations of the Book of Enoch, and it was not until after this that previously mentioned Richard Laurence published his translation in 1821. This period marked a critical revival of the Book of Enoch as scholars began to appreciate its historical and religious significance.

Rediscovery, Modern Preservation, and the Role of Modern Scholarship

The rediscovery of the Book of Enoch in the modern era began with European scholars and explorers in the 18th and 19th centuries, such as James Bruce, Richard Laurence, and R.H. Charles, which further advanced scholarly understanding of Enochic literature.

The discovery of Aramaic fragments of the Book of Enoch among the Dead Sea Scrolls in 1947 provided critical insights into its early transmission and authenticity where also scholars like Józef Milik played pivotal roles in analyzing these fragments, confirming the antiquity of Enochic literature.

Modern scholarship continues to explore the historical, theological, and literary dimensions of the Book of Enoch, recognizing it as a key text for understanding Second Temple Judaism and early Christian theology. The digitization of ancient manuscripts and advancements in technologies such as carbon dating have revolutionized the study and preservation of Enochic texts, and institutions like the Israel Antiquities Authority have also played crucial roles in digitizing and preserving the Dead Sea Scrolls (Shanks, 2007; Wayne, 2020).

With contemporary scholars building on foundational works by Charles and others, we are provided with critical editions and translations that deepen our understanding of the Book of Enoch's theological and historical significance.

Role of the Dead Sea Scrolls

The discovery of the Dead Sea Scrolls in 1947 stands as one of the most significant archaeological finds of the 20th century. Among these ancient manuscripts were fragments of the Book of Enoch, a text that had long intrigued scholars and theologians. The presence of these fragments has been a cornerstone in the study of ancient apocalyptic literature, confirming the Book of Enoch's authenticity and providing invaluable insights into its historical context and theological significance.

This discovery has had a profound impact on our understanding of the Book of Enoch's authenticity, historical context, and its role within the broader corpus of Jewish and early Christian literature. The Dead Sea Scrolls' role in preserving and illuminating the Book of Enoch highlights the complex weave of history, faith, and scholarship that continues to unfold. By plunging into the details of this discovery, we can appreciate its implications not only for the Book of Enoch but also for its place in the rich tradition of Jewish and Christian apocalyptic thought.

The Discovery at Qumran

In 1947, Bedouin shepherds discovered a series of caves near the Dead Sea in the Judean Desert, revealing ancient scrolls and fragments that captured the attention of archaeologists and scholars worldwide. These artifacts, collectively known as the Dead Sea Scrolls, comprised over 900 documents, many previously unknown (Davies, 2024).

Among the Dead Sea Scrolls were fragments of the Book of Enoch, specifically from the "Book of the Watchers," dating back to the 3rd century BCE. Their discovery at Qumran provided crucial evidence of the widespread readership and significance of the Book of Enoch among Jewish sects during the Second Temple period. The presence of the Book of Enoch among the Dead Sea Scrolls has been pivotal in affirming its ancient Jewish origins. Previously known primarily through the Ethiopic version preserved by the Ethiopian Orthodox Church, the Aramaic fragments at Qumran confirmed the Book of Enoch as an ancient Jewish text, predating its later translations into Greek and Ethiopic.

The authenticity of the Book of Enoch was further bolstered by the consistency between the Aramaic fragments and the Ethiopic version, suggesting the preservation of its core content over centuries despite variations in translation and transmission. These discoveries also provided insights into the original language and cultural context of the text, enhancing our understanding of its historical significance (Ludlow, 2021).

The Impact on Theology and Contemporary Academic Study

Since the discovery of the Dead Sea Scrolls, modern scholarship has made significant strides in analyzing and interpreting the Book of Enoch. Researchers have utilized advanced techniques in paleography, linguistics, and digital imaging to study the Aramaic fragments in detail. These efforts have not only clarified the text's original language and structure but also its place within the broader corpus of Second Temple literature (Perkins, 2011).

The Dead Sea Scrolls have also facilitated greater collaboration among scholars across disciplines, leading to a more comprehensive understanding of the Book of Enoch. Conferences, publications, and digital projects have expanded access to these texts, allowing a global audience to engage with this ancient literature. The ongoing study of the Dead Sea Scrolls continues to shed light on the historical and theological contexts of the Book of Enoch, enriching our appreciation of its enduring legacy.

Modern Discoveries and Impact

The modern era has witnessed several significant discoveries related to the Book of Enoch, each contributing to a deeper and more nuanced understanding of this ancient text. From the additional fragments uncovered at Qumran to newly found manuscripts and advanced technological analyses, these findings have reshaped scholarly perspectives and shed new light on the historical and theological dimensions of the Book of Enoch.

These modern discoveries have significantly advanced our understanding of the Book of Enoch, confirming its authenticity and enriching its historical context. They have opened new avenues for theological and literary analysis, highlighting the text's role in the religious and cultural heritage of ancient Judaism and early Christianity. The role of technology in uncovering and preserving these fragments has been instrumental in ensuring that the Book of Enoch continues to be a vital source of insight. As more discoveries come to light, the Book of Enoch's legacy will undoubtedly continue to evolve, offering fresh perspectives and deepening our appreciation of this enigmatic work.

Additional Fragments From the Dead Sea Scrolls

The initial discovery of the Dead Sea Scrolls in 1947 included several Aramaic fragments of the Book of Enoch. Subsequent excavations and studies have uncovered additional fragments, enriching the body of Enochic literature available to scholars. These new fragments have been vital in confirming the text's authenticity and providing a more comprehensive view of its original form. For instance, recent analysis of the Dead Sea Scrolls has revealed previously unknown sections of the Book of Enoch, offering new insights into its structure and content. These fragments have filled gaps in the narrative, enabling scholars to piece together a more complete version of the text. The meticulous work of reconstructing these fragments has also highlighted variations between different copies, reflecting the text's evolution over time (Davies, 2024).

The Role of Technology in Modern Discoveries

Advancements in technology have revolutionized the study of ancient manuscripts, including the Book of Enoch. High-resolution imaging, digital reconstruction, and multispectral analysis have enabled scholars to read and interpret fragments that were previously illegible or too damaged to study. These technologies have not only facilitated the discovery of new fragments but also improved the accuracy of existing translations.

For example, multispectral imaging has allowed researchers to recover text from fragments that were charred or faded, revealing details that had been obscured for centuries. Digital reconstruction techniques have helped create virtual assemblages of fragmented texts, providing a clearer picture of the original manuscripts. These technological advancements have significantly enhanced our understanding of the Book of Enoch, offering new avenues for interpretation and analysis.

Newly Found Manuscripts

Beyond the Dead Sea Scrolls, other manuscript discoveries have also contributed to the study of the Book of Enoch. In recent decades, researchers have identified additional Ethiopic manuscripts that contain variations and expansions of the text. These manuscripts, preserved in monastic libraries and private collections, offer alternative readings and interpretations that enrich our understanding of the Enochic tradition. One notable discovery being a set of manuscripts found in an Ethiopian monastery, which includes previously unknown hymns and prayers attributed to Enoch. These texts provide unique insights into how the Book of Enoch was used liturgically and theologically within the Ethiopian Orthodox Church. The discovery of these manuscripts highlights the dynamic nature of the text and its enduring significance within different religious traditions (Shanks, 2007).

Now, moving on from scrolls and scriptures, we are about to venture into the unknown mysticism of symbols. An intriguing and captivating voyage that will further deepen your understanding of the complex scripture that is the Book of Enoch.

Chapter 3:
Symbols of the Sacred

The Book of Enoch guides us through an intricate landscape where symbols serve as bridges between the mortal and the divine. The journeys of Enoch are not just physical traversals but spiritual odysseys that reveal the hidden workings of the universe. Every emblem in the text acts like a puzzle piece in a grand mosaic, forming a portrait of creation, life, and humanity's ultimate destiny. These emblems beckon us to dig deeper, uncovering the hidden layers that connect everything and helping us grasp our role within the vast blueprint of the universe.

Consider the vivid descriptions of natural elements that populate Enoch's visions. Mountains that touch the Heavens, rivers that flow with eternal waters, and trees that bear the fruit of life—all these elements are imbued with symbolic power. They are not mere sceneries but active participants in the narrative, each one a signpost pointing toward a greater truth. The natural world, in Enoch's account, is alive with divine presence, each element a reflection of celestial realities.

Enoch's encounters with divine beings are laden with symbolism. These beings are not just characters in a story; they are embodiments of divine principles and cosmic forces. Their appearances, actions, and words carry layers of meaning that reveal the nature of the divine and the moral order of the universe. Through these encounters, Enoch gains insights that transcend human understanding, offering a glimpse into the eternal and the infinite.

It does not stop there, for the Book of Enoch also uses numbers and measurements as symbols, with meticulous detailing of heavenly realms and sacred times that emphasize the belief in a cosmos that operates according to a grand, divinely orchestrated plan. Numbers in Enoch's visions are not mere quantities; they are symbolic representations of spiritual truths and cosmic laws, each one revealing the harmonious structure of creation.

Through Enoch's eyes, we see a world where time itself is a symbol, a cyclical journey that moves from creation to consummation. The text's portrayal of epochs and eras, of beginnings and endings, invites us to contemplate the flow of time as a divine narrative. Enoch's visions unfold in a temporal landscape where past, present, and future are intertwined, each moment pregnant with meaning and purpose.

The rich symbolism of the Book of Enoch extends to the moral and ethical dimensions of human life. The text's vivid imagery and allegorical narratives challenge us to reflect on our own lives and the choices that we make. For the symbols within Enoch's visions are mirrors that reflect our inner selves, urging us to seek righteousness and wisdom. They remind us that our actions have cosmic significance and that we are participants in a divine drama that spans the ages. That is one of the mesmerizing characteristics of the Book of Enoch if one dives deep enough to embrace its symbols as keys to understanding the mysteries of the universe.

In the following explorations of this chapter, these symbols will unfold in their full complexity, exposing the deep wisdom they impart about the essence of life and the divine presence. As we walk this path, we are reminded that the symbols of the sacred are not just relics of the past but living signposts that guide us toward eternal truths.

Celestial Imagery

Within the vast narrative of the Book of Enoch, celestial images shine like a constellation of divine truths and cosmic mysteries. These heavenly depictions, full of spiritual significance and ethereal beauty, highlight the profound connection between the divine and the universe. Each image acts as a guiding light, revealing deep insights into existence and the nature of the cosmos. In Enoch's visions, the ordinary meets the divine, and every star, planet, and heavenly entity carries deep symbolic significance.

Enoch's celestial journeys feature encounters with personified celestial bodies. The Sun symbolizes divine order and the passage of time, reflecting God's constancy. The Moon, with its phases, represents life cycles and humanity's potential to reflect divine qualities. The stars symbolize angels, while falling stars represent fallen angels, highlighting the connection between the celestial and spiritual realms (Akin, 2021; De Jager, 2023c; Long, 2016b; Long, 2016d).

The visions of Enoch also include detailed descriptions of heavenly architecture, with realms symbolizing stages of spiritual ascent. The first Heaven, with clouds and mist, serves as a boundary between the earthly and divine, while the second Heaven, home to fallen angels, represents darkness and punishment. The third Heaven serves as a paradise that symbolizes the rewards of virtuous living, while the fourth and fifth Heavens depict celestial bodies governed by angelic beings, highlighting divine precision. The sixth Heaven showcases angelic hierarchies, while the seventh and final Heaven reveals God's throne, symbolizing the ultimate spiritual ascent (Geller, 2019; Nickelsburg & VanderKam, 2001).

These visions also feature heavenly tablets recording human deeds, symbolizing divine knowledge and judgment. The Watchers, initially benevolent guardians, symbolize corruption when they transgress divine laws. In contrast, archangels like Michael and Gabriel embody divine authority and protect Enoch, emphasizing divine intervention and the protection of the righteous (De Jager, 2023b; Jesus Without Baggage, 2018).

Heavenly Realms Described

When reading the Book of Enoch, we are offered a vivid and intricate portrayal of the heavenly realms, where the structured cosmos that unfolds across multiple layers of the divine are presented. Where each realm, or Heaven, is illustrated with distinct characteristics and inhabitants, all of which reflect the deep theological and cosmological insights of the text as well as moral justice and spiritual ascent. They contribute to a holistic vision of the cosmos, and it is therefore of essence to analyze these descriptions of the Heavens while also exploring their structure and significance within this celestial saga in order to gain a deeper appreciation for the complexity and beauty of the divine creation as envisioned in this ancient text.

The First Heaven

Enoch's journey begins with the first Heaven, a realm that serves as the immediate threshold between the earthly and the divine. It is described as a place filled with clouds and mist, where the foundations of the celestial world are laid. This Heaven serves as a barrier, marking the boundary that separates the mundane from the sacred. The presence of clouds and mist symbolizes the mystery and transcendence of the divine, suggesting that the first steps into the heavenly realms are shrouded in holy ambiguity (Long, 2016a; Long, 2016b).

The Second Heaven

In the second Heaven, Enoch encounters a more foreboding environment. Here, he sees the fallen angels, the Watchers, who are bound and imprisoned. This realm is depicted as a place of darkness and torment, reflecting the consequences of defying divine order. The presence of the fallen angels in this Heaven serves as a powerful symbol of rebellion and punishment, illustrating the moral order that governs the cosmos. Their imprisonment underscores the theme of divine justice and the inexorable nature of divine law (Long, 2016a; Long, 2016b).

The Third Heaven

Ascending to the third Heaven, Enoch enters a realm of unparalleled beauty and serenity. This Heaven is described as a paradise, where he encounters the Tree of Life, surrounded by angelic beings and souls of the righteous. The third Heaven's depiction as a place of eternal spring and lush green scenery signifies the reward for virtuous living and the promise of eternal life. The Tree of Life, a potent symbol of immortality and divine wisdom, stands at the heart of this paradise, emphasizing the themes of renewal and divine favor (Long, 2016a; Long, 2016b).

The Fourth Heaven

Next up is the fourth Heaven, which reveals the cosmic mechanics of the universe. Enoch observes the movements of the Sun, Moon, and stars, each governed by angelic beings who ensure their precise courses. This realm shows us the careful order of the universe, suggesting a universe governed by precise harmony. The regular movements of the stars and planets symbolize the dependable and constant care of divine guidance. The angels' role in guiding these luminaries emphasizes the belief that the cosmos is actively maintained by divine forces (Long, 2016a; Long, 2016b).

The Fifth Heaven

Enoch moves on to witness a more hierarchical structure in the fifth Heaven, which is populated by angelic beings engaged in worship and service. This dimension is marked by a sense of reverence and order, where the primary functions of the angels are to glorify God and carry out divine commands. The fifth Heaven's depiction emphasizes the themes of divine authority and the central role of worship in the celestial hierarchy. The structured hierarchy of angels reflects the organized nature of the divine cosmos, where each being has a specific role and purpose. (Long, 2016a; Long, 2016b)

The Sixth Heaven

In the sixth Heaven, profound angel activity and administration takes place. Enoch sees angels recording the deeds of humanity on special heavenly papers. This is a strong symbol of divine knowledge and judgment, for the angels keeping careful records show that there's a moral side to what people do. It suggests that everything people do is watched and judged by divine rules. These records also show how important it is to take responsibility for our actions and how detailed God's justice is (Long, 2016a; Long, 2016b).

The Seventh Heaven

Finally, Enoch reaches the seventh Heaven, the highest and most sacred of all the realms. Here, he encounters the throne of God, surrounded by a host of angels and bathing in divine light. The seventh Heaven represents the culmination of Enoch's spiritual ascent and the ultimate encounter with the divine presence. The throne room's radiant light and ethereal music evoke a sense of divine majesty and the ultimate reality of God's presence. This realm signifies the highest state of spiritual attainment and direct communion with the divine (Long, 2016a; Long, 2016b).

Significance of the Heavenly Realms

The structure of the heavenly realms in the Book of Enoch serves multiple theological and symbolic purposes. Each Heaven represents a different aspect of the divine cosmos, illustrating the complexity and order of creation. The ascending journey through these realms mirrors the spiritual ascent of the soul, reflecting the path of purification and enlightenment (Jesus Without Baggage, 2018).

The detailed descriptions of the Heavens also emphasize the interconnectedness of the physical and spiritual worlds. The movements of celestial bodies, the roles of angelic beings, and the presence of divine records suggest a universe where every element is interconnected and operates according to divine principles. This interconnectedness underscores the holistic nature of Enoch's vision, where the material and spiritual are seamlessly integrated into a coherent cosmological framework (Black, n.d.).

Furthermore, the depiction of different Heavens highlights the moral and ethical dimensions of the cosmos. The presence of the fallen angels in the second Heaven and the righteous souls in the third Heaven illustrate the consequences of moral choices and the ultimate triumph of divine justice. These realms serve as both a warning and a promise, reflecting the dual themes of judgment and redemption that pervade the text.

Symbolic Representation of Angels and Demons

It is within the mystical realms of ancient writings that a vibrant world unfolds. A world where celestial beings are more than mere figures, for they embody the cosmic struggle between order and chaos. Hidden within this intricate dance of angels and demons lies a deeper understanding of divine principles and moral challenges. The bearers of divine will, the Angels, serve as guardians and guides as they illuminate the righteous path for humanity. In opposition, the demons represent the forces that seek to unravel the moral fabric of the universe as they fulfill the role of the ever-present threat of disorder.

The tale of the Watchers serves as a potent allegory, with angels defying their celestial duties, descending from grace which portrays the perils of arrogance and the certainty of divine justice. This chronicle invites readers to partake in the complex interplay of virtue and vice, the necessity of divine oversight, and the ethical duties that bind us all.

Through its vivid symbolism and multifaceted portrayals, this ancient text offers a lens through which we can examine the perpetual conflict between good and evil. It speaks to the timeless human condition, reflecting our struggles with temptation and our quest for righteousness. The representations of these celestial beings provide profound insights into the ancient understanding of the cosmos while enriching our modern contemplation of morality, justice, and the divine essence.

As we immerse ourselves in the symbolic representation of angels and demons, we uncover layers of meaning that transcend the literal, offering a compelling panorama that continues to inspire and challenge our perception of the sacred and the profane.

Angels: Messengers of the Divine

In the Book of Enoch, angels act as intermediaries between the divine and human dimensions, representing God's will and authority. Angels, as described in awe-inspiring accounts, are seen as divine messengers to Enoch, unveiling profound cosmic truths and secrets through their encounters (Long, 2016a; Long, 2016b).

Archangels like Michael, Gabriel, Raphael, and Uriel have distinct roles. Michael, the protector of Israel and leader of the heavenly hosts, symbolizes divine justice and the fight against evil. His presence underscores divine intervention and protection for the righteous. Gabriel, the messenger of God, emphasizes prophecy and divine communication (Akin, 2021).

Raphael, on the other hand, symbolizes divine mercy and healing, as he is reflecting themes of redemption and spiritual restoration. Uriel represents divine enlightenment and wisdom, and therefore, guides Enoch through the celestial realms, all while revealing cosmic mysteries and moral order. His role as a guide highlights the pursuit of divine wisdom and spiritual enlightenment (Nickelsburg & VanderKam, 2001).

The Watchers: Fallen Angels and Their Descent

One of the most compelling aspects of the Book of Enoch is its depiction of the Watchers, a group of angels who descended to Earth and became entangled in human affairs. These fallen angels, led by Azazel and Shemihazah, are symbolic of rebellion against divine order and the consequences of hubris. Their descent and subsequent actions are a central narrative that explores themes of corruption, forbidden knowledge, and divine retribution (De Jager, 2023b; De Jager, 2023c).

The Watchers' decision to take human wives and impart forbidden knowledge to humanity represents a profound transgression of heavenly boundaries. This act of rebellion introduces chaos into the world, symbolized by the birth of the Nephilim, the giants that embody the disruption of natural order. The Nephilim, with their immense size and destructive power, are metaphors for the uncontrollable consequences of violating divine law. The story of the Watchers serves as a cautionary tale about the dangers of overstepping divine limits and the moral decay that follows (Jesus Without Baggage, 2018).

Azazel, in particular, is depicted as a figure of immense corruption, teaching humanity the arts of warfare and other forbidden practices. His actions lead to widespread violence and moral degradation, symbolizing the perils of misused knowledge and power. The eventual punishment of the Watchers, who are bound and cast into a dark abyss, stresses the inevitability of divine justice and the restoration of cosmic order (Geller, 2019).

The Watchers, however, will be examined in greater depth in the coming chapter, which is dedicated solemnly to the tale of the Watchers, so they are therefore only mentioned here in short.

Demons: Symbols of Chaos and Moral Corruption

In contrast to the benevolent angels, demons in the Book of Enoch are depicted as agents of chaos and moral corruption. These beings, often associated with the offspring of the Watchers, represent the disruptive forces that arise from transgressing divine laws. The demons' influence over humanity is characterized by leading individuals astray, inciting violence, and spreading corruption (Black, n.d.).

The symbolic representation of demons in the text highlights the ongoing battle between good and evil, a central theme in apocalyptic literature. Demons are portrayed as entities that exploit human weaknesses, tempting individuals away from righteousness and toward sin. This portrayal serves as a reminder of the constant moral vigilance required to maintain integrity and virtue in a world fraught with temptation and evil (Van Hatten, 2022).

The Interplay of Angels and Demons

The dynamic interplay between angels and demons in the Book of Enoch reflects the larger cosmic struggle between order and chaos, good and evil. Angels, with their divine mandate, work to uphold the cosmic order and guide humanity toward righteousness. In contrast, demons and fallen angels embody the forces of chaos and moral corruption, challenging the divine order and leading humanity astray (Geller, 2019; Jesus Without Baggage, 2018).

This interplay is vividly illustrated in Enoch's visions, where the actions of angels and demons influence the fate of humanity and the cosmos. The narrative depicts a world where divine intervention is necessary to combat the pervasive influence of evil, highlighting the themes of divine justice and redemption. The symbolic roles of angels and demons in the text underscore the moral and ethical dimensions of human existence, emphasizing the consequences of moral choices and the perpetual struggle between light and darkness (Long, 2016a; Long, 2016c; Long, 2016d).

Astronomical Symbols

Enoch's visions unfurl a cosmos teeming with celestial wonders, where stars, planets, and other heavenly bodies are more than mere specks of light—they are imbued with deep metaphorical and prophetic meanings. These astronomical symbols are masterfully intertwined, as the Book of Enoch uses them to mirror the divine order, the cosmic struggle between light and darkness, as well as the unfolding of divine will. In this sphere, the stars are not just ornaments of the night sky but profound symbols of divine guidance and cosmic justice.

Traversing the cosmic canvas depicted in Enoch's revelations, we encounter a universe where each star and planet holds a tale of prophecy and moral significance.

The Sun and Moon, steadfast in their courses, symbolize the unwavering nature of divine law. Meanwhile, the wandering stars, with their erratic paths, reflect the chaos and rebellion that threaten the celestial harmony. These astronomical symbols serve as a bridge that connects the physical Heavens with the moral and theological dimensions of the cosmos.

The celestial imagery in the Book of Enoch compels us to look beyond the visible, urging us to contemplate the hidden truths that govern our existence. Stars and planets become vessels of divine revelation, guiding humanity through the cosmic conflict that mirrors our own moral struggles. As we decode these symbols, we delve into an ancient worldview where the Heavens are a canvas painted with divine messages, offering insights into the eternal dance of order and chaos, good and evil.

Stars as Symbols of Divine Beings and Human Souls

In the Book of Enoch, stars often symbolize divine beings, especially angels and the souls of the righteous. The night sky, filled with countless stars, is depicted as a vast arena where divine and cosmic events unfold. In Enoch's vision, stars frequently represent angels who fulfill specific roles within the divine hierarchy. The "luminaries" in Enoch's narrative are described as sentient beings who move according to God's laws, reflecting the divine order that governs the cosmos (Long, 2016b; Long, 2016c).

Fallen stars, however, symbolize angels who have rebelled against God's commandments. The imagery of stars falling from the Heavens serves as a powerful metaphor for the fall of the Watchers, who descended to Earth and corrupted humanity. This symbolism uses the visual impact of falling stars, which in the ancient world could signify ominous events or divine displeasure. The fallen stars illustrate the theme of rebellion and the resulting chaos when divine order is disrupted.

Moreover, stars also represent the souls of the righteous. Enoch's journey through the Heavens includes visions of stars that are emblematic of virtuous individuals who have attained a place of honor in the divine realm. This metaphor underscores the belief in an afterlife where the righteous are rewarded with eternal light and presence among the celestial bodies, which would signify their eternal communion with the divine (Akin, 2021).

Planets as Symbols of Cosmic Order and Prophecy

The planets, as described in Enoch's visions, symbolize the intricate and harmonious order of the cosmos, reflecting the precise nature of divine creation. Unlike the fixed stars, planets move in complex orbits, and their paths were seen as indicative of divine will and timing. Enoch's detailed descriptions of planetary movements emphasize the importance of order and regularity in the universe, suggesting that the cosmos operates under divine laws that must be observed and respected (Long, 2016b).

In Enoch's narrative, the planets also carry prophetic significance. Their positions and movements are interpreted as signs that foretell future events, both divine judgments and the coming of messianic times. The alignment of planets, eclipses, and other astronomical phenomena are seen as portents revealing God's plans and the unfolding of divine prophecy. This belief reflects the ancient practice of astrology, where celestial events were studied to understand divine messages and anticipate future occurrences (Geller, 2019).

The Sun and Moon: Symbols of Divine Authority and Temporal Cycles

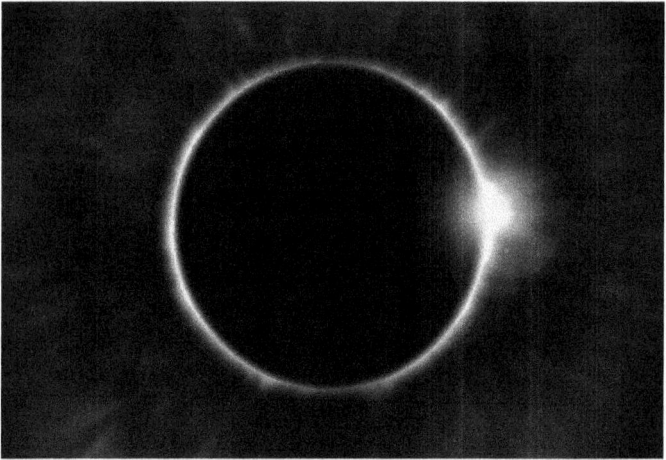

The Sun and Moon hold prominent places in Enoch's visions, symbolizing divine authority and the cyclical nature of time. The Sun, with its brilliant and unchanging path, represents the constancy and omnipotence of God. It is described as a mighty entity that follows a predetermined course, illuminating the world and marking the passage of days. The Sun's journey across the sky is a metaphor for divine surveillance, suggesting that nothing escapes the watchful eye of the Creator (Long, 2016b).

The Moon, with its phases and reflective light, symbolizes the cyclical nature of life and the passage of time. Its waxing and waning are metaphors for birth, growth, decay, and renewal. The Moon's role as a reflector of the Sun's light also highlights the theme of divine reflection in human affairs, suggesting that humanity can reflect divine qualities and wisdom. The interplay between the Sun and Moon in Enoch's visions emphasizes the balance and rhythm inherent in the divine order (Van Hatten, 2022).

Eclipses and Other Celestial Phenomena

Eclipses and other celestial phenomena described in the Book of Enoch carry deep symbolic and prophetic meanings. Eclipses, for instance, are portrayed as moments of divine intervention where the normal order of the cosmos is temporarily altered to signal important events. Historically, various civilizations, including those in ancient Mesopotamia, interpreted eclipses as omens. In Enoch's visions, they symbolize divine judgment or the heralding of significant changes, reflecting the belief that such phenomena indicate moments of critical transformation (McDonald, 2023).

These phenomena are imbued with theological significance, serving as reminders of the divine power that controls the cosmos and the unpredictable nature of divine will. The disruption of the usual celestial order during an eclipse underscores themes of divine omnipotence and the transient nature of worldly power (Jesus Without Baggage, 2018).

Themes of Judgment

The themes of divine judgment are interwoven like a dark and ominous thread throughout the enigmatic visions of Enoch, revealing a moral order that encompasses both the celestial and terrestrial realms. These themes are far from mere literary constructions, for they are in fact profound reflections on divine justice, human responsibility, and the ultimate fate of souls.

At the core of Enoch's narrative lies the concept of heavenly adjudication, a central motif that permeates the entire text. This judgment is portrayed as an inevitable and righteous act of divine authority, ensuring accountability for all beings, both heavenly and earthly. The systematic and orderly nature of this divine justice is highlighted by the evocative images of the heavenly court and the meticulous records kept by angels. No matter how trivial, every action is observed, recorded, and judged, which reinforces the inescapable nature of the moral order that has been established by the divine.

Every deed is counted for in the structured cosmos often depicted in Enoch's visions, with the precise record-keeping by the angels that serves as a stark reminder that nothing escapes the scrutiny of divine justice. In circumstances under which the universe operates under a moral framework, every action has consequences, thus reflecting a worldview that sees the cosmos as governed by a just and omnipotent divine power.

The tales of the Watchers, the roles of the angels, and the prophetic revelations all highlight the central theme of judgment throughout the Book of Enoch. It is a book in which the symbolic representation and vivid imagery convey the inevitability of divine judgment and the moral repercussions of human actions. These narratives are not just stories created to instill fear into our hearts; instead, they are profound allegories that invite the reader to reflect on their own moral responsibilities and the broader cosmic implications of their actions. As we journey through these themes, we are prompted to contemplate the nature of divine justice and the ultimate fate of souls as The Book of Enoch challenges us to consider the ethical and spiritual dimensions of existence.

The Judgment of the Watchers

One of the most compelling narratives in the Book of Enoch is the judgment of the Watchers for their rebellion led to their downfall and severe punishment. This portrayal serves as a powerful allegory for the consequences of hubris and the violation of divine law. The Watchers' fate is described in harrowing detail, with visions of their imprisonment in a dark abyss and their eternal suffering. This imagery accentuates the severity of their transgressions and reinforces the inevitability of divine retribution. The narrative of the Watchers illustrates the broader theme of cosmic justice, where rebellion against divine order results in catastrophic consequences (Akin, 2021; De Jager, 2023b; De Jager, 2023c; Geller, 2019).

As previously mentioned, the next chapter is dedicated solemnly to the tale of the Watchers, but they had to be mentioned in short under this section of "Themes of Judgment."

The Role of Angels in Divine Judgment

Angels play a crucial role in the execution of divine judgment in the Book of Enoch. They are depicted as both witnesses and enforcers of divine law, recording the deeds of humanity and carrying out divine decrees. The presence of angels in the judgment process highlights their role as intermediaries between the divine and human realms, ensuring that divine justice is executed with precision and impartiality (Long, 2016a; Long, 2016d).

The archangels, in particular, are portrayed as key figures in the judgment narrative. Michael, the protector of Israel, is often depicted as leading the battle against the forces of evil, symbolizing the triumph of divine justice. Gabriel's role as a messenger and herald of divine judgment underscores the theme of communication and the dissemination of divine will. The actions of these angels illustrate the organized and hierarchical nature of divine judgment, where each being has a specific role in maintaining cosmic order (Long, 2016a; Long, 2016d).

Apocalyptic Prophecies

The apocalyptic prophecies that can be found in the Book of Enoch stand out as both a warning and a beacon of hope. These prophecies, rich with symbolism and profound insight, guide us through visions of divine justice and the ultimate fate of our world. The prophetic nature of these visions extends beyond future predictions; they serve as a powerful call to moral awakening and ethical living. Enoch's prophecies emphasize the temporary nature of our current existence, urging humanity to heed the divine call for repentance and transformation. This message emphasizes that the present state of the world is transient and subject to the overarching will of the divine (Ludlow, 2021; Van Hatten, 2022).

It is nearly impossible to navigate through the apocalyptic prophecies in the Book of Enoch without reflecting on our own moral and ethical duties, as these prophecies challenge us to ponder the cosmic impact of our actions. It forces us to envision a future where divine justice reigns supreme, restoring the world to its true, harmonious state. The storyline woven into these prophecies offers timeless wisdom, inviting us to contemplate the spiritual and moral dimensions of existence and our place within the worldly and divine order.

The Vision of the Four Archangels

One of the earliest and most compelling apocalyptic prophecies in the Book of Enoch is the vision involving the four archangels: Michael, Gabriel, Raphael, and Uriel. These archangels are depicted as executing God's will on Earth and in the Heavens, particularly in matters of judgment and punishment. Each archangel is assigned a specific task that reflects their unique attributes and roles within the divine hierarchy (Gregory, 2017).

Michael, the warrior and protector, is charged with combating the forces of darkness and defending the righteous. His presence in the vision underscores the theme of divine protection and the ultimate triumph of good over evil. Gabriel, the messenger, is tasked with announcing divine decrees and ensuring that the prophecies are communicated accurately. Raphael, the healer, represents divine mercy and the restoration of the faithful. Uriel, the guide, illuminates the mysteries of the cosmos and the divine plan, symbolizing the enlightenment and guidance provided by God to humanity (Gregory, 2017).

The Vision of the Flood

The Book of Enoch also includes a prophecy about a great flood that will cleanse the Earth of its corruption. This vision is particularly significant as it parallels the biblical story of Noah and the flood but with additional

94

apocalyptic symbolism. In Enoch's vision, the flood is portrayed as a divine purging of the Earth, an act of judgment that removes the wicked and preserves the righteous.

The flood symbolizes both destruction and renewal. It is a divine reset, restoring balance to the world and preparing it for a new era of righteousness. This vision emphasizes the themes of purification and divine justice, highlighting the dual nature of judgment as both punitive and redemptive. The preservation of Noah and his family symbolizes the salvation of the faithful and the continuation of God's covenant with humanity.

The Apocalypse of Weeks

One of the most detailed and structured apocalyptic prophecies in the Book of Enoch is the Apocalypse of Weeks. This vision divides history into ten "weeks," each representing a distinct period with specific events and divine interventions. The first seven weeks cover the past and present, describing the creation, the fall of the Watchers, the flood, and the giving of the law.

The eighth, ninth, and tenth weeks are prophetic, foretelling future events. The eighth week is marked by righteousness and a new era of justice. The ninth week predicts the rise of the wicked and their subsequent judgment. The tenth week envisions the final judgment and the establishment of a new Heaven and Earth, where righteousness will dwell eternally.

The Apocalypse of Weeks is significant for its comprehensive scope and its emphasis on the cyclical nature of divine judgment. It portrays history as a series of recurring patterns, where periods of corruption are inevitably followed by divine intervention and restoration. This vision reinforces the themes of divine sovereignty, justice, and the ultimate fulfillment of God's plan for humanity. This apocalypse of weeks will be examined further in "Chapter 5: Visions of the Future."

The Final Judgment

The culmination of the apocalyptic prophecies in the Book of Enoch is the vision of the Final Judgment. This vision describes a grand and awe-inspiring scene where all souls are gathered before the throne of God. The righteous are separated from the wicked, and each group receives their due reward or punishment.

The Final Judgment is depicted with vivid imagery, including books being opened, angels executing divine decrees, and the Earth and Heavens being transformed. The righteous are granted eternal life and joy, symbolized by their ascension to a place of light and peace. The wicked, on the other hand, are cast into a place of darkness and suffering, reflecting the severity of their transgressions.

This vision accentuates the themes of accountability and the inescapable nature of divine justice. It serves as a powerful reminder of the moral and ethical responsibilities of individuals and the ultimate consequences of their actions. The Final Judgment also emphasizes the hope and promise of redemption for the faithful, offering a vision of a restored and harmonious creation.

Moral and Ethical Lessons

The Book of Enoch, beyond its vivid apocalyptic visions and divine judgments, serves as a profound wellspring of moral and ethical teachings that deeply resonate with its readers. Within its intricate themes of judgment lie lessons that speak to the very core of human conduct, societal responsibilities, and the eternal ramifications of one's actions. Therefore, this section will examine these teachings, illuminating their significance for human behavior and ethical contemplation.

Far from being merely a collection of apocalyptic predictions, the Book of Enoch intricately weaves moral and ethical imperatives throughout its storyline. These lessons highlight the vital importance of righteousness, the dire consequences of defiance, the certainty of divine justice, and the exemplary roles played by angels. These teachings urge readers to live ethically, take responsibility for their deeds, and seek moral elevation through repentance and reflection.

The themes of judgment in Enoch's work explore moral and ethical dimensions, emphasizing the importance of following divine principles. It suggests that our actions affect the cosmic balance, providing deep insights into human ethics and morality. The Book of Enoch encourages self-reflection, awareness of consequences, and adherence to higher standards to uphold universal harmony and justice.

By exploring these profound teachings, we are invited to contemplate our own moral responsibilities and ethical choices. The Book of Enoch challenges us to envision a life guided by righteousness, where each action contributes to the greater good and aligns with the divine order, ensuring a balanced and just cosmos.

The Importance of Righteousness

One of the central moral lessons in the Book of Enoch is the importance of living a righteous life. Righteousness, in this context, is portrayed as adhering to divine laws and maintaining a life of virtue and integrity. The text repeatedly emphasizes that the righteous will be rewarded with eternal life and communion with the divine, while the wicked will face severe punishment. This duality serves as a powerful incentive for individuals to pursue a path of righteousness.

The narrative of Enoch himself exemplifies this lesson. Enoch is depicted as a man who walked with God, living a life that pleased the divine and ultimately being taken up into Heaven without experiencing death. His exemplary life serves as a model for readers, showcasing that following divine principles leads to spiritual growth and favor.

The Consequences of Rebellion

The tale of the Watchers, fallen angels who came to Earth, serves as a strong cautionary tale about the outcomes of rebelling against divine rule. These angels disobeyed God, involved themselves in forbidden actions with human women, and brought disorder and corruption to the world. Their punishment, being bound and thrown into a dark abyss, stands as a harsh lesson on the consequences of going against divine decrees.

This story emphasizes the significance of obedience and the risks of arrogance. The downfall of The Watchers and their punishment show that defying divine rules ultimately leads to destruction. It acts as a warning for humans, discouraging them from crossing moral lines or going against divine wishes.

Accountability and Moral Responsibility

A recurring theme in the Book of Enoch is the concept of accountability. The text suggests that every action is observed and recorded by divine beings. Angels are depicted as keepers of heavenly records, documenting the deeds of humanity. This emphasis on record-keeping stresses the belief that individuals are accountable for their actions and that divine justice is inescapable. Also, the vision of the final judgment, where the righteous are separated from the wicked, and each receives their due reward or punishment, reinforces this theme. It suggests that divine justice is not arbitrary but is based on a detailed assessment of one's actions. Dually, this serves as a reminder to live ethically and justly, knowing that every deed will be judged.

The Role of Angels as Moral Exemplars

Angels often serve as moral exemplars and guides in the Book of Enoch. The archangels, such as Michael, Gabriel, Raphael, and Uriel, embody various aspects of divine virtue. Michael, for example, represents courage and justice as he battles against the forces of evil. Gabriel, as a messenger, embodies truth and clarity. Raphael, the healer, represents compassion and mercy. Uriel, the guide, symbolizes wisdom and enlightenment (Long, 2016a; Long, 2016d).

These angelic figures not only take part in the story but also act as examples for human behavior, inspiring the audience to embody divine virtues and uphold moral and ethical conduct essential for cosmic harmony.

Ethical Implications of Divine Judgment

Divine judgment in the Book of Enoch emphasizes ethical responsibilities with a focus on restoring cosmic balance, not just meting out punishment. The scenes of judgment often portray the removal of the wicked, symbolizing a cleansing from corruption to pave the way for renewal and righteousness.

This perspective on judgment urges people to think about how their actions affect the community and the world. It highlights how behaving ethically helps society thrive, while unethical conduct can lead to divine consequences. This view of judgment stresses the significance of living a morally sound life for both individuals and communities.

The Call to Repentance

Apocalyptic predictions found in the Book of Enoch frequently emphasize the urgent need for individuals to repent. The detailed portrayals of divine judgment and the severe repercussions of wrongdoing aim to instill a sense of dread, compelling people to abandon their immoral behaviors. This plea for atonement serves as a fundamental ethical reminder, compelling the audience to evaluate their conduct, seek absolution, and aspire toward ethical growth.

In this context, repentance entails more than just avoiding punishment; it involves realigning oneself with divine will to restore order and righteousness. The repeated calls for repentance underscore the chance for redemption and the compassionate nature of divine justice, instilling hope in those who seek to amend their ways and embrace a virtuous path.

Eschatological Significance

Enoch's Book intricately examines judgment as it dives deep into end-time chronicles. It crafts an intricate array of ominous stories intertwined with aspirations for divine fairness and universal rejuvenation. These narratives promise a universe realigned rather than focusing solely on doom. Exploring the eschatological significance in the Book reveals its pivotal role in Jewish apocalyptic thought, envisioning a realm where justice and renewal reign supreme. Enoch's Book delves deeply into judgment and end-time events, weaving together stories of divine justice and universal renewal. Rather than focusing solely on doom, these narratives envision a realigned universe. The Book plays a crucial role in Jewish apocalyptic thought, depicting a realm where justice and renewal prevail.

Enoch's prophetic visions describe the resurrection of the dead, the final separation of good and evil, and the creation of a new Heaven and Earth. These visions offer hope for divine fairness and the reinstatement of order, envisioning a future where goodness triumphs and the universe is revitalized. Enoch's themes hint at rejuvenation and the restoration of balance.

The eschatological visions inspire believers by offering hope and reinforcing the belief that current struggles and injustices are temporary and will be rectified through divine intervention. The Book assures believers of divine justice and cosmic renewal, affirming the ultimate victory of righteousness.

The Book narrates vivid depictions of divine judgment and cosmic clashes, emphasizing moral and ethical aspects of human life. Themes like responsibility, fairness, and redemption are interwoven, offering insights into cosmic dynamics and the divine plan for the end times. These narratives urge readers to contemplate their moral obligations and the wider repercussions of their actions.

Exploring these ideas prompts individuals to reflect on their place in the universe. The Book of Enoch encourages imagining a future ruled by divine fairness and peace, offering a glimpse of optimism and renewal that transcends time, sending a powerful message of ultimate salvation and universal repair. This reflection urges alignment with divine values, contributing to overall balance and fairness in the universe.

The Framework of Jewish Apocalyptic Literature

Jewish apocalyptic literature centers on divine revelation, cosmic conflict, and the ultimate resolution of history through divine intervention. This genre typically includes visions of the end times, where good and evil clash and God's ultimate justice prevails. The Book of Enoch fits well within this tradition, providing detailed visions of the divine plan for history's culmination. Enoch's journey through the Heavens and his encounters with celestial beings illustrate the cosmic scale of divine judgment. These apocalyptic visions assure the faithful that, despite current sufferings and injustices, a divinely ordained resolution is imminent. The text also emphasizes that history is moving toward a predetermined end where righteousness will triumph and evil will be eradicated (Akin, 2021; Black, n.d.; Jesus Without Baggage, 2018).

The Final Judgment and Cosmic Renewal

The culmination of the eschatological narrative in the Book of Enoch is the Final Judgment. This event is depicted as a grand, awe-inspiring scene where all souls are brought before the throne of God. The righteous are separated from the wicked, and each group receives their due recompense. This vision is not only about retribution but also about the restoration of cosmic order.

The Final Judgment marks the start of a new creation, with the Earth and Heavens undergoing a transformation that signifies the purification and restoration of the universe. This revitalization illustrates a cyclical process where the current corrupted world is cleansed, paving the way for a new, righteous order to be established. The idea of cosmic renewal emphasizes the hope and optimism embedded within the eschatological vision, indicating that the end times will usher in a fresh beginning characterized by divine harmony and justice.

The Eschatological Role of Angels

Angels play vital roles in the eschatological visions of the Book of Enoch. They act as enforcers of divine judgment, carrying out God's decrees to ensure the delivery of divine justice. Archangels such as Michael, Gabriel, Raphael, and Uriel are depicted as leaders in the cosmic battle against evil, underscoring their roles as protectors and enforcers of divine will. Michael is frequently portrayed as the leader of the heavenly hosts, spearheading the fight against darkness, emphasizing themes of divine protection and the ultimate victory of good over evil. Gabriel, the messenger, plays a crucial part in announcing divine judgments and guaranteeing the fulfillment of prophecies. Raphael and Uriel, known for their roles in healing and guidance, contribute to the themes of restoration and enlightenment, significant elements of the eschatological vision (Long, 2016a; Long, 2016d).

The Ethical Implications of Eschatological Themes

The eschatological themes present in the Book of Enoch serve as ethical guides, emphasizing the consequences of moral choices. Through vivid descriptions of divine judgment and the apocalypse, the text cautions readers to lead a righteous life, underlining the inevitability of divine justice and the eventual reward for righteousness (Akin, 2021; Black, n.d.).

A recurring motif in the Book of Enoch is the call to repentance. The text encourages introspection, seeking forgiveness, and striving for ethical progress. Repentance is not merely about avoiding consequences but about aligning with divine intentions and contributing to the restoration of divine order. These prophetic visions inspire moral conduct and spiritual advancement (Jesus Without Baggage, 2018; Van Hatten, 2022).

The Hope of Redemption

Enoch's Book conveys a powerful message of hope and redemption, interwoven with themes of judgment and retribution. It envisions the triumph of righteousness, the establishment of a new Heaven and Earth, and the fulfillment of divine pledges to restore harmony. Through this revelation, the faithful are comforted and assured that their present trials are fleeting and that divine justice will ultimately prevail.

Enoch's prophecies envision a future where the universe is in perfect alignment with divine decree, offering solace and motivation to uphold faith and moral principles in the face of adversity. The anticipation of salvation and a reborn world are pivotal elements of this narrative, depicting a forthcoming era characterized by fairness and unity.

As we conclude our exploration of these eschatological themes, we turn our attention to a pivotal and complex aspect of Enoch's narrative: the tale of the Fallen Angels, the celestial beings whose rebellion against divine order brings forth profound theological and ethical implications. Their story not only enriches the apocalyptic storyline of the Book of Enoch but also serves as a powerful allegory for understanding the interplay between divine justice and cosmic disorder.

Chapter 4:
The Fallen Angels

In the twilight realm between myth and theology, where the ancient texts breathe life into the shadows of human imagination, the story of the Watchers stands out as one of the most captivating and enigmatic tales of them all. These celestial beings, also known as the Fallen Angels, occupy a unique place in the annals of sacred literature, embodying themes of rebellion, forbidden knowledge, and the tragic consequences of defying divine order. As we dive into their story, we are drawn into a narrative that is both profoundly mystical and deeply human, a story that has reverberated through the corridors of history and left an indelible mark on the collective psyche of mankind.

In a world where the veil between the terrestrial and the heavenly was thin, envision a time when angels coexisted with mortals and the hand of the divine-shaped earthly destinies. Enter the realm of the Watchers, celestial beings assigned to oversee humanity from their celestial perches. However, lured by longing and inquisitiveness, they descended to the human domain, triggering a chain of events that would redefine the narrative of history and spirituality eternally.

The Watchers were sent to watch over humanity and protect them. However, their fascination with human women led them to break the divine laws they were meant to uphold. This forbidden union between celestial and terrestrial resulted in the Nephilim, powerful beings who were neither fully angelic nor entirely human. The

Nephilim, along with the knowledge from the Watchers, brought chaos and corruption to the world, challenging the established order and facing divine consequences.

The teachings of the Watchers introduced new knowledge and skills to humanity, including metallurgy, which allowed for the creation of tools and weapons with dual purposes. This knowledge transformed human society, leading to technological advancements as well as increased potential for both progress and conflict.

Another important lesson from the Watchers was teaching about astrology and celestial events. They revealed the secrets of the stars and heavenly bodies, providing an understanding of the cosmos that was fascinating yet unsettling. This knowledge broadened human understanding of the universe but also held the risk of misuse, as it could be used to influence and forecast events, potentially changing the natural path of human fate.

The legacy of the Watchers involves enlightenment, destruction, and the corruption of the human race by the Nephilim. Their actions led to moral decay, prompting a divine decision to cleanse the Earth through the Great Flood. This catastrophic event was a punishment and a reset to restore balance and purity tainted by the Watchers and their offspring.

The story of the Watchers does, however, extend beyond their punishment, resonating through different religious and cultural beliefs. In Christian tradition, it merged with the tale of fallen angels and demons, portraying their rebellion as a prelude to the eternal battle between good and evil.

Interpreted through a more esoteric lens in Jewish mysticism, especially within the Kabbalistic tradition, the story of the Watchers involves the descent of angels and their sharing of forbidden knowledge as elements of a divine plan. This plan unfolds deeper spiritual truths and underscores the complex relationship between divine providence and free will, showcasing the inherent tension between human ambition and divine command (Rosenberg, n.d.; Rudy, 2019).

In Islamic tradition, the Watchers' narrative appears as Harut and Marut, portraying two angels tasked with testing humanity. Although the tale's specifics vary, it echoes common themes of temptation, knowledge, and divine judgment. This version underlines God's mercy and justice, guiding and testing the faithful's choices between righteousness and sin (Rosenberg, n.d.; Rudy, 2019).

The fascinating tale of the Watchers uncovers the delicate harmony between wisdom and authority, prompting reflection on ethical responsibilities and decisions. It contemplates the contrasts between ambition and modesty, innovation and tradition, delving into the essence of the human journey. This classic narrative imparts timeless lessons on morality, disobedience, and redemption.

Who Were the Watchers?

In the enchanting universe of ancient texts, a group of beings stands out for their captivating and mysterious nature—the Watchers. These celestial creatures play a crucial role in the narrative of the Book of Enoch, providing insight into divine hierarchy and human transgression. Scholars and theologians have been entranced by their story for ages. By rebelling and facing punishment, the Watchers demonstrate the significance of following divine laws and the risks of pushing limits too far. This story also showcases divine mercy by showing that the flood, though a punishment, also acts as a way to purify and revive creation.

The Watchers, aside from their religious significance, have deeply influenced cultural and religious beliefs. In Christian theology, they are viewed as forerunners to Lucifer's rebellious angels, reflecting the theme of defiance toward God. Their tale has shaped Christian ideas on sin, salvation, and the eternal conflict of good versus evil. In Jewish mysticism, notably in the Kabbalistic tradition, the Watchers' fall is understood as a complex interplay of divine destiny and human choice, providing profound perspectives on spiritual and ethical challenges (Encyclopedia Iranica, 2011; Townsend, 2020).

In Islamic tradition, Harut and Marut are known as the Watchers, angels sent to test the faith of humanity. Though varying in details, their tale resonates with themes of temptation, knowledge, and divine judgment found in the Book of Enoch. The Islamic version underlines God's mercy and justice, focusing on providing guidance amidst faith trials, echoing common themes in Enochic texts (Encyclopedia Iranica, 2011).

The story of The Watchers still impacts modern literature, film, and popular culture by plunging into themes like power, corruption, and redemption. This lasting intrigue emphasizes their importance as symbols of the ongoing human battle between ambition and morality, as well as between knowledge and wisdom.

Exploring the tale of the Watchers leads us to contemplate the profound impact of their story. Through their decisions and the outcomes that follow, we are presented with a reflection of our own ethical and moral decisions. Through their sad downfall and enduring impact, the Watchers emphasize the fine line between divine purpose and human choices.

Identity and Roles

The Watchers, known as the "Irin" in Aramaic or "Egregoroi" in Greek (De Jager, 2023a), are a group of angels sent to watch over humanity, as described in the Book of Enoch. Originally assigned as guardians to enforce divine will on Earth, their role shifted to mere observers, leading to significant consequences for both humans and the divine realm. Their tale begins with their descent from the Heavens to Mount Hermon, signifying not just a physical trip but a rebellion against divine laws. Led by the angels Shemihazah and Azazel, the Watchers defied conventions by marrying mortal women, leading to chaos (De Jager, 2023b; De Jager, 2023c). Their offspring, the Nephilim, were formidable giants disrupting the balance of nature with their immense power and insatiable appetite.

Shemihazah, commonly viewed as the head of the Watchers, embodies the concept of corrupt leadership. Opting to guide them downward illustrates the conflict between free will and authority, which highlights the swift transformation of guidance into misconduct. Azazel, an integral figure among the Watchers, is associated with divulging forbidden knowledge. He imparted the mysteries of weaponry, beauty practices, and various crafts to humanity, propelling progress but also fostering a rise in violence and ethical decay.

As the Watchers' interaction with humanity was not meant to include direct interference or the sharing of forbidden knowledge, their descent, driven by desire and curiosity, marked a significant deviation from their intended roles. By taking human wives and imparting knowledge that was meant to remain hidden, the Watchers overstepped their boundaries, leading to their eventual fall and the corruption of humanity (Encyclopedia Iranica, 2011; Townsend, 2020).

Therefore, the Watchers are important not just for their rebellion but also for carrying forbidden knowledge. They embody a paradox—as beings of light who introduced darkness—that strongly resembles the theme of the "fallen angel" across different religions. By sharing both advancement and destruction through their teachings, they illustrate the dual nature of knowledge. Their lasting impact combines wisdom and devastation, underscoring the risks of unrestrained curiosity and ambition.

Characteristics of the Watchers

The Watchers are initially presented as powerful and majestic beings that embody the awe-inspiring qualities associated with angels. They possess a radiant and ethereal beauty that is indicative of their divine origin. Their presence projects an air of authority and respect, showing they serve as a link between the divine and human worlds (Anca, 2024; Blum, 2018).

Physically, the Watchers are described as being similar to humans but far more splendid. They are often depicted with wings, symbolizing their celestial nature and ability to traverse between the Heavens and the Earth. Their eyes are often said to shine like the stars, suggesting a connection to the divine luminaries and their role as observers of the cosmos. This image illustrates that they watch carefully and always notice the various acts of the people (Universe Unriddled, 2024).

Spiritually, the Watchers are endowed with profound wisdom and knowledge, given their direct access to the divine. This knowledge, however, becomes a double-edged sword as their curiosity and desire lead them to share forbidden secrets with humanity. Their wisdom, initially meant to guide and protect, becomes a source of corruption and chaos (Anca, 2024).

The Divine Observers

The term "Watchers" itself signifies their primary role as observers. They were meant to be divine sentinels, watching over the moral and spiritual welfare of humanity. Their vigilance reflected divine oversight, making sure that humans followed the sacred principles and laws. According to the Book of Enoch, these angels descended to Earth during Jared's time, a descendant of

Adam, to observe and lead humanity in its early days (Loyd, 2017).

The Watchers were stationed on Mount Hermon, a significant geographical and symbolic location. This mountain was seen as a meeting point between Heaven and Earth. From this elevated vantage point, the Watchers could observe the entirety of human activity, maintaining their duty to report back to the divine on the state of human affairs (Blum, 2018; Long, 2016a; Long, 2016d).

The Significance of the Watchers

The Watchers in the Book of Enoch are more than just characters with roles and actions. They represent the intricate connection between the divine and human worlds, showing the fine line between guidance and meddling, compliance, and defiance. Their tale warns about the outcomes of crossing divine limits and the duties tied to authority and wisdom (De Young, 2020; Payton, 2024).

The Watchers also highlight the theme of divine justice. Their eventual punishment—being bound and cast into a dark abyss—reflects the inevitability of divine retribution. This storyline underlines the significance of following divine laws and the moral order, highlighting the concept that justice, despite its delay, is inescapable.

In exploring the identity and roles of the Watchers, we gain insights into the broader themes of divine oversight, the ethical implications of knowledge, and the consequences of rebellion. Their story invites reflection on the responsibilities that come with power and the importance of maintaining integrity in the face of temptation. The Watchers, with their tragic fall and lasting legacy, serve as enduring symbols of the complex interplay between divine intention and human action.

Hierarchies

The Watchers, as described in the Book of Enoch, are intriguing celestial beings with a rich complexity. The way they are portrayed excavates their physical and spiritual aspects, along with their ranks and hierarchy. This scrutiny grants a better understanding of who they were and the roles they had both before and after their downfall. The elaborate descriptions and structures surrounding the Watchers offer deep insights into their traits, positions, and the orderly celestial system they were intended to maintain. Their divine origins and purpose are mirrored in their characteristics, and their hierarchical system highlights the organized celestial realm. The disruption of this order, fueled by their desires and curiosity, results in their decline and the consequent corruption of humankind (De Young, 2020; Long, 2016a; Long, 2016d).

The tale of the Watchers serves as a warning about the duties that accompany power and wisdom, the significance of following divine laws, and the repercussions of disrupting hierarchies. Exploring their story reveals profound insights into enduring themes of leadership, moral decay, and seeking salvation.

Ranks Among the Watchers

The hierarchy of the Watchers is vital to their identity, mirroring the organized divine cosmos, where each being holds a distinct role and rank. The Book of Enoch sheds light on this hierarchy, emphasizing the roles of important Watcher figures.

Shemihazah, in a powerful role, leads the Watchers' journey to Earth and influences their behavior, displaying authority in the heavenly order. This emphasizes the power of guidance and the dangers of misguided ambition. In contrast, Azazel, also a prominent figure, influences humanity significantly. Even though not in a leadership position, Azazel's deeds carry significant outcomes, establishing him as a pivotal character. His choice to share forbidden wisdom underscores his role as a corrupter and his notable status among the Watchers (Akin, 2021; Blum, 2018).

Among the esteemed Watchers are other notable individuals such as Kokabel, who is linked to the stars and celestial occurrences, along with Sariel, who imparts wisdom on the Moon and its cycles. These designations signify a unique hierarchy where every Watcher presides over a distinct realm of knowledge and authority. This division underscores the intended duty of the Watchers to observe and instruct, with each making a distinctive contribution to the grand design. The structured hierarchy within the Watchers reflects the systematic harmony of the celestial realm, with each member assigned specific duties to uphold divine supervision over humanity. This methodical approach underscores the significance of order and control in the divine domain, emphasizing that any disruption results in turmoil and judgment (Blum, 2018; Denova, 2021).

The Internal Hierarchy

The way the Watchers organize themselves mirrors the greater celestial structure, with a clear hierarchy and specific duties. This system makes sure each Watcher sticks to their assigned role, keeping everything in harmony. Yet, their rebellion throws everything off-balance, causing disorder and divine punishment.

As Shemihazah holds the highest position among the Watchers, playing a crucial leadership role in directing their actions, his decisions are vital. However, his story also serves as a cautionary tale about the dangers of abusing power. His downfall illustrates the repercussions of straying from one's designated path. Second in line, Azazel, although not heading the group, holds significant sway in the system. His guidance in metallurgy and other prohibited crafts showcases his crucial part in the downfall of mankind. His place in the system highlights the extensive influence a single prominent individual can possess over the entire structure (Anca, 2024; Akin, 2021; Blum, 2018).

The responsibilities of other Watchers, such as Kokabel and Sariel, highlight the unique focus of their tasks. As stated by De Jager (2016c):

> Semjaza, the leader of the two hundred Watchers, taught "enchantments and root−cuttings" while Armaros taught them how to resolve enchantments. Baraqijal taught astrology while Kokabel shared information on the constellations. Ezeqeel shared the knowledge of the clouds, Araqiel instructed on the signs of the Earth, Shamsiel on the signs of the Sun, and Sariel on the course of the Moon. (Para 8)

Every Watcher possesses a distinct field of proficiency, adding to the combined wisdom and direction offered to humans. This focus illustrates the divine purpose in their formation, with each Watcher's duty playing a crucial part in the grand scheme of things (Denova, 2021).

The story of the Watchers is presented as a deeply impactful story with significant moral and ethical implications. As these heavenly entities chose to descend to Earth and engage with humankind, they not only affected historical and mythological occurrences but also left a lasting mark on the moral and spiritual essence of the world. Their deeds, especially their meaningful connections with humans, brought forth hidden wisdom and gave rise to the Nephilim, leading to a decline in moral values and the ensuing disorder.

The descent of the Watchers illuminates the complex dynamics between divine beings and humans while also highlighting the responsibilities tied to power and knowledge. The divine retribution that followed accentuates the importance of adhering to moral and ethical principles as it reinforces the inevitability of justice. The lessons one should learn go beyond a mere warning, for it presents a symbolic and detailed story that emphasizes the weight of ethical considerations in the pursuit of progress and advancement. The legacy of the Watchers testifies to the delicate balance between knowledge and morality that must be maintained to avoid dire consequences.

As their story remains influential in religious, cultural, and ethical dialogues, it offers timeless lessons on the consequences of exceeding boundaries set by the divine. The Watchers' choices reflect back humanity's challenges with authority, knowledge, and ethics. Their saga stands as a poignant reminder of the results of rebellion and the lasting impacts of one's choices on society.

The Consequences of Hierarchical Disruption

The narrative of the Watchers revolves around the upheaval of their hierarchical structure. As they descend to the earthly realm out of curiosity and longing, it symbolizes the disarray of the divine hierarchy. This defiance results in their downfall, ushering in a period of disorder that impacts humanity on a grand scale.

The turmoil begins as Shemihazah leads the descent, setting a pattern for the other Watchers to follow. Their decisions mark a shift from their original mission, leading to their transgression. Azazel worsens the situation with his teachings, introducing warfare and corruption that change human civilization. This spread of forbidden knowledge signifies the breakdown of the moral fabric the Watchers were meant to protect, causing a shift from observers to catalysts of humanity's decline (Akin, 2021; Blum, 2018).

After the Watchers fell from grace, chaos erupted, prompting a divine intervention to restore harmony. The punishment inflicted on the Watchers, sealing them in a deep abyss, serves as a repercussion for their disruption of the heavenly hierarchy. This divine retribution underlines the significance of upholding cosmic balance and the repercussions of straying from one's designated path (Long, 2016a).

The Fall From Grace

The downfall of the Watchers holds immense significance, serving as a representation of the outcomes that come with straying away from the orders of the divine. By choosing to descend to Earth and immerse themselves in worldly delights, they committed a momentous act of defiance, capturing a metaphorical descent from favor and highlighting overarching concepts of allure, transgression, and divine payback.

Shemihazah's influence during the fall was pivotal; through his leadership and the unanimous decision of the Watchers to marry humans, turbulence and disorder were introduced to the world. This act of defiance had profound consequences for both the Watchers and humanity, as their descendants, the Nephilim, epitomized this decay, embodying both physical and moral degradation. Azazel's deeds further complicated matters. By imparting forbidden knowledge to humans, he unleashed forces beyond their understanding. The dissemination of weapon expertise led to heightened conflicts, while other teachings disrupted the balance within societies. Azazel's actions underscore the perils of knowledge devoid of wisdom and the moral dilemmas associated with recklessly imparting such knowledge (Akin, 2021; Blum, 2018).

Reimagining the fall of the Watchers involves their gradual descent into forbidden desires, their sharing of concealed wisdom, and their bold defiance of divine directives. This journey presents a compelling storyline, showcasing their encounters with humankind and the resultant ramifications that highlight the intricate equilibrium between heavenly decrees and mortal decisions. Examining their decline offers deep insights into the connections between the divine and humanity, the moral responsibilities tied to power and wisdom, and the recurring theme of celestial justice (Brand, 2016; De Young, 2020; Long, 2016a).

Temptation and Forbidden Desire

The Watchers' downfall was largely influenced by their strong allure and illicit longing for mortal women. The Book of Enoch recounts how captivated they were by the exquisite beauty of human daughters. Led by Shemihazah, they jointly resolved to descend to Earth and take these women as wives. This intermingling of heavenly creatures with mortals was explicitly forbidden, representing a grave transgression of celestial decree. Marrying mortal women signaled a notable departure from their assigned role as passive spectators. This act of longing and subsequent mingling with humans epitomized the Watchers' decision to revel in earthly gratifications, in direct contradiction to their divine purpose. The ramifications, both physical and spiritual, of this union were profound and culminated in the emergence of the Nephilim, the hybrid beings that further disrupted the natural equilibrium.

The Watchers' interactions with humanity were central to their fall. As they were originally assigned to observe and safeguard, their choice to actively participate in human affairs paved the way for their ruin. Their marriages to human women and the birth of the Nephilim introduced a new dynamic that was never intended by the divine plan. The Nephilim, described as giants and mighty warriors, became a source of great turmoil, spreading violence and corruption throughout the world. Their mere existence further complicated the relationship between humans and the divine, for these beings, neither fully human nor fully divine, embodied the consequences of crossing divine boundaries. Through their actions and impact, they heightened the ethical deterioration among humans, catalyzing widespread turmoil and disarray.

Dissemination of Forbidden Knowledge

Another significant reason for the downfall of the Watchers stemmed from their act of sharing forbidden knowledge with humanity. Among the Watchers, Azazel, in particular, disclosed hidden secrets, such as expertise in metallurgy, weaponry, cosmetics, and various advanced knowledge areas that exceeded humanity's ability to manage with care. This imparted knowledge of weaponry resulted in the fueling of conflict and warfare that drastically reshaped human civilization. The dissemination of forbidden knowledge had dual consequences, as it also allowed humanity to progress and develop new abilities. This knowledge was not only used for destructive purposes. The knowledge of metallurgy, for instance, enabled the creation of tools and weapons that could be used also for constructive purposes. The positive contributions to human society will be explored in more depth later in this chapter.

However, the positive contributions of the Watchers were, in fact, overshadowed by the significant moral and ethical decay their teachings precipitated. The advanced knowledge they imparted was most often used for destructive purposes. That did not stop only at the implementation of metallurgy and weaponry, but the advanced knowledge of cosmetics and adornment passed on to humankind also had detrimental effects on human behavior. These practices, while enhancing physical appearance, encouraged vanity and superficiality. The emphasis put on external beauty led to moral decay as individuals began prioritizing appearance over ethical and virtuous living. Therefore, this exchange of wisdom not only brought enlightenment but also decadence, diverting mankind from its original course and its purity. This shift in values contributed to a broader societal decline, as superficial qualities were elevated over moral and spiritual integrity (Long, 2016a).

The ethical implications of these teachings highlight the double-edged nature of knowledge—capable of both enlightenment and destruction. The sharing of knowledge that was supposed to be kept secret also emphasizes a common idea found in olden writings: the complex aspect of wisdom. Wisdom has the potential to promote progress and improvement, yet it also has the ability to result in ruin and ethical decay when used wrongly. By choosing to disclose these hidden truths, the Watchers display their rebellion against sacred limits and their wish to raise humanity to an unsuitable height of influence and insight.

Rebellion Against Divine Command

The fall of the Watchers was also characterized by their outright rebellion against divine commands. Their very act of descending to Earth without divine permission was an act of insubordination. This rebellion was compounded by their subsequent actions, which further defied the established divine order. Shemihazah, being the instigator of this rebellion, swore an oath with the other Watchers, binding them to their collective decision to defy divine command and take human wives. This oath represented a united front in their rebellion, symbolizing their collective responsibility for the ensuing chaos. This act of rebellion is emblematic of the broader theme of defiance against divine authority, a theme that resonates throughout many religious and mythological narratives.

Divine Retribution

The downfall of the Watchers caught the attention of higher beings and did not go unnoticed. According to the Book of Enoch, their deeds triggered a divine reaction that involved God dispatching the archangels to mete out severe consequences. As a result, the Watchers were restrained and confined deep within the Earth, awaiting the ultimate judgment. Their imprisonment was a clear outcome of their rebellion and the detrimental influence they exerted on humanity (Long, 2016a). Specifically for his involvement in disseminating prohibited wisdom, Azazel was isolated and confined in a barren land, his hands and feet securely restrained to represent the control over his malevolent impact (Brand, 2016). This act of divine retribution highlights the severity of the Watchers' misdeeds and the vital need to bring balance back to the universe.

The decline of the Watcher holds deep theological and ethical meanings as their tale acts as a warning. It sheds light on the repercussions of transgressing sacred limits and the dangers posed by the pursuit of power and wisdom without ethical reflection. It also reflects broader themes found in religious texts, including the eternal battle between right and wrong, the fallout of wrongdoing, and the possibility of salvation. Their story invites readers to reflect on their own actions by prompting them to ponder their decisions and the moral dilemmas encountered throughout their life journeys.

The Legacy of the Watchers

The legacy and impact of the Watchers go far beyond just their initial deeds and outcomes. Their tale has left a lasting mark on diverse religious and cultural practices, symbolizing the intricate connection between the divine and mortal worlds. Within Christian beliefs, the Watchers are frequently viewed as forerunners to the rebellious angels under Lucifer's command, representing the essence of defiance toward the divine. This account has heavily influenced Christian beliefs regarding sin, salvation, and the eternal clash of good versus evil (Universe Unriddled, 2024).

In Jewish mysticism, especially in the Kabbalistic tradition, the descent of the Watchers is seen as a meaningful aspect of the complex relationship between divine guidance and individual agency. This narrative provides profound perspectives on the essence of spiritual and ethical battles, emphasizing the moral dilemmas inherent in interactions between the divine and human realms (Fishbane, 2023).

The ethical ponderings raised by the tale of the Watchers still echo strongly in contemporary society, leaving a mark on literature, cinema, and popular culture. Their story offers a deep well of ideas for examining topics such as authority, decadence, and restoration. The enduring allure surrounding the Watchers highlights their importance as emblems of the everlasting human conflict between aspiration and ethics, intellect and sagacity.

Consequences for Humanity

The saga of the Watchers, as it has been told in the Book of Enoch, is deeply entwined with themes of knowledge, morality, and divine justice, revealing a complex interplay of progress and decline. Their descent from the Heavens and their teachings brought forth both remarkable advancements and profound moral corruption, creating a dual narrative of human civilization's rise and fall.

The newfound wisdom, where the introduction of the forbidden knowledge propelled significant technological and cultural progress, came at a steep price. Alongside these advancements, a dark shadow of violence, corruption, and ethical decay emerged. The birth of the Nephilim, which will be examined in depth later in this chapter, further complicated the human condition by illustrating the perilous consequences of meddling with divine order.

The consequences that the actions of the Watchers have had on humanity include both positive contributions to human advancement and negative consequences and moral decay. One does simply not rule out the other and with knowledge ethical dilemmas typically follow in its footsteps. When discussing the Watchers and their legacy, it becomes poignantly clear that with power and knowledge comes heavy responsibilities, and their story serves as a reminder of the delicate balance between progress and ethical integrity.

Positive Contributions to Human Advancement

The teachings of the Watchers left a lasting mark on human progress, notably boosting knowledge and technological growth. As detailed in the Book of Enoch, the Watchers shared a diverse array of wisdom that was previously beyond human understanding. This encompassed expertise in metallurgy, botany, astronomy, and other sophisticated areas of knowledge. Such guidance brought about a profound shift in human civilization, fostering advancements and creativity. An example of this would be how Azazel's teachings on metallurgy paved the way for the creation of tools and weapons. This progress in technology empowered humans to interact more efficiently with their surroundings, thus promoting the growth of agriculture, architecture, and various crucial facets of society. The capacity to fashion and utilize metal implements marked a notable stride ahead, playing a key role in giving rise to intricate social frameworks and economic systems.

Furthermore, the Watchers passed on to humanity the ancient wisdom of astronomy and the graceful dance of the heavenly bodies. This profound knowledge enriched humans' comprehension of the universe, paving the way for the creation of calendars, methods for navigating the seas, and strategies for cultivating the land. The proficiency to foresee celestial occurrences and interpret the shifts in seasons played a vital role in the progress of ancient societies, granting them the means to cultivate crops more effectively and nurture their communities.

The Birth of the Nephilim

There are few tales as captivating as the story of the Nephilim. Beings, born from the forbidden union between the Watchers and human women, cast a long shadow in ancient lore. Their origins, marked by celestial defiance, and their subsequent impact on the world craft a compelling tale that intertwines power, corruption, and divine retribution. Moreover, it also added an additional layer of complexity to the ethical landscape.

The Nephilim, neither fully human nor entirely divine, were giants of unparalleled strength and stature. Introducing a hybrid race that dominated and tyrannized human society, their existence a direct result of the Watchers' transgressions, these formidable beings are often described as mighty warriors whose presence disrupted the natural order, leading to widespread chaos and corruption. The story of their birth and reign serves as an excellent display of the consequences of celestial and human intermingling.

The story of the Nephilim is a stark reminder of the dangers inherent in the pursuit of forbidden knowledge. The Watchers' decision to impart their wisdom to humanity, despite divine prohibitions, led to the birth of these hybrid beings who brought about significant advancements alongside profound moral decay. Their extraordinary traits and the havoc they wreaked upon the world serve as powerful symbols of the ethical responsibilities that accompany power.

Marked by violence, oppression, and eventual divine retribution, the tale of the Nephilim emphasizes the importance of maintaining moral and ethical integrity in the face of temptation and ambition. The legacy of the Nephilim, steeped in violence and domination, continues to influence religious and cultural traditions, offering timeless lessons on the consequences of defying divine boundaries.

As we uncover the saga of the Nephilim, we are reminded of the enduring struggle to balance progress with wisdom and integrity, a struggle that continues to resonate across the ages.

Origins and Characteristics of the Nephilim

The Nephilim are portrayed as immense beings, towering above regular humans. Their remarkable stature and strength not only made them powerful combatants and leaders but also led to their reputation for devouring plentiful resources, thus accelerating the depletion of the Earth's abundance. In addition to their physical dominance, their inclination toward violence and oppression was evident, frequently employing their might to dominate and instill fear among human communities. Besides their possession of various physical traits, the Nephilim also acquired the wisdom and skills passed down by their Watcher progenitors. These included sophisticated expertise in metallurgy, military tactics, and various disciplines that significantly enhanced their power and dominion over human civilizations. Nevertheless, their utilization of such wisdom frequently took a dark turn, worsening the ethical and moral decline initiated by the Watchers (Draper, 1882).

The Reign of the Nephilim

The era and reign of the Nephilim brought upon a time of immense unrest and agony for humankind. As these towering figures and fierce fighters ruled with an iron fist, they instilled fear and subjugated others, positioning themselves as oppressive leaders. Their deeds caused upheaval in the communal and ethical structures of human societies, unleashing rampant disorder and aggression. The dominion of the Nephilim was defined by savagery and subjugation, for they mirrored the grim elements of their mixed lineage.

The Nephilim posed another major issue through their relentless hunger and greed. Their voracious appetites resulted in the excessive consumption of food and resources, leading to shortages and challenges for the human communities they ruled over. This depletion of resources not only burdened the environment but also heightened the plight of common folk, who faced hardships in enduring the severe governance of the Nephilim.

The Nephilim's extensive understanding of warfare and weaponry only added to the destruction that they caused. With the guidance from the Watchers, they continuously fought battles, sowing chaos and devastation far and wide. Their skill in creating and using formidable weapons rendered them almost unbeatable, striking fear and despair into their adversaries.

The Great Flood: Purging the Nephilim

The Great Flood, the ultimate retribution of God against the Nephilim, was sent to cleanse the Earth of their corrupting presence. This exemplifies the drastic measures taken to restore balance. Detailed in the Book of Enoch, this cataclysmic event underscores the lengths divine justice will go to correct and protect. The flood, coupled with the confinement of the Watchers, emphasizes that justice, though delayed, is ultimately unavoidable (Draper, 1882).

The Nephilim unleashed unprecedented turmoil and moral decadence. Their colossal stature, strength, and propensity for violence inflicted widespread suffering and tyranny, exacerbating the moral decline instigated by the Watchers. Therefore, their obliteration became an essential mandate. The Deluge epitomized God's ultimate retribution against the Nephilim and the depraved domain they ruled. This cataclysmic event served as both retribution and a means to cleanse the Earth of the Nephilim's sway, restoring equilibrium and innocence. It exemplifies the stringent yet purposeful aspect of divine justice aimed at shielding humanity and the world from further contamination.

The flood reveals profound insights into divine justice, showcasing its severity intertwined with purpose, functioning as a safeguard for the greater good. The elimination of the Nephilim through the flood highlights the delicate interplay between justice and compassion.

Legacy of the Nephilim

Even though they were eventually eradicated through the Great Flood, the Nephilim's impact lives on through religious and cultural practices. They frequently appear in different writings and myths as figures of mixed creatures embodying the outcomes of defying divine limits. Within Christian beliefs, the Nephilim are occasionally viewed as forerunners to the giants detailed in the ancient texts, including those the Israelites faced in Canaan.

The tale of the Nephilim carries relevance in the contemporary era, leaving its mark on literature, movies, and mainstream culture. These beings are often portrayed as colossal figures or mighty entities that symbolize concepts like defiance, moral decay, and celestial retribution. Their story remains engrossing, acting as a poignant reflection of the intricate relationship between divine will and human behavior (Draper, 1882).

The presence and deeds of the Nephilim held deep moral and ethical significance as their birth stemmed directly from the Watchers' rebellion against divine decrees, thus illustrating the repercussions of crossing holy thresholds. The Nephilim symbolized the moral decline resulting from the spread of forbidden knowledge, serving as a cautionary tale against pursuing power and wisdom without ethical considerations. Their control and oppressive rule also bring to light a moral struggle about employing authority and might to dominate others. The period of their rule was characterized by unfair treatment and manipulation, indicating a total lack of concern for fairness and empathy (Draper, 1882). This moral decay seeped into their very being; as offspring of a union prohibited by higher forces, they embodied a clear breach of the established natural and divine hierarchy.

Themes of Justice and Mercy

The punishment handed down to the Watchers and the Nephilim in the Book of Enoch sheds light on the intricate balance between justice and mercy in divine storytelling. By enforcing strict consequences for transgressions against divine law, the narrative demonstrates the unwavering nature of divine justice. Nevertheless, amid the severity of these judgments, elements of mercy and restoration are also present, offering a glimmer of hope for redemption and forgiveness.

The Watchers' punishment serves to correct and restrain, stopping further corruption and limiting their influence to maintain balance and safeguard creation. Divine justice aims for retribution, exemplified by the Great Flood, which, despite causing devastation, purges the Earth of the Nephilim's destructive impact, offering humanity a fresh start. This dynamic of retribution and compassion unveils the complexity of divine justice, reinforcing moral principles while laying the groundwork for renewal and redemption. Following the Watchers' wrongdoings, divine retribution accentuates the significance of upholding divine and moral order. According to the Book of Enoch, archangels were tasked by God to bind and confine the Watchers until the ultimate judgment, curbing their corrupting influence and restoring cosmic balance. The Great Flood, designed to eliminate the Nephilim's corrupting presence introduced by the Watchers, resulted in immense destruction and suffering, highlighting the profound consequences of their actions and showcasing the lengths to which divine justice goes to reestablish harmony.

The story of the fallen angels deeply explores divine justice and mercy, conveying timeless insights into divine authority and humanity's ethical obligations. It emphasizes the significance of abiding by divine laws, the repercussions of transgressing boundaries, and the prospect of redemption and a fresh beginning.

As we conclude the tale of the fallen angels and their profound lessons on divine justice and mercy, we turn our attention to the prophetic visions of Enoch. These visions offer a glimpse into the future, revealing insights into the destiny of humanity and the unfolding of divine plans. In the next chapter, "Visions of the Future," we will examine Enoch's revelations, exploring the prophetic messages that continue to inspire and guide.

Chapter 5:
Visions of the Future

As the veil of ancient prophecy unravels, it reveals a moment of epiphany where the intersections of history and destiny blend together sacred insights and divine decrees. While investigating the mystical verses of the Book of Enoch, we are transported to a dimension of prophecy that enthralled ancient visionaries while unveiling cryptic texts that illuminate the fates of nations and individuals beyond the confines of time.

Guided by the enigmatic patriarch Enoch, each of his heavenly ascensions reveals visions imbued with profound significance, offering glimpses into a divine blueprint charting history and the ultimate triumph of good over evil. These visions span vast landscapes, from the peaks of Mount Hermon to the cosmic expanses of the heavenly realms. Each vision weaves together themes of judgment, redemption, and the divine future. By unraveling these prophetic threads, we uncover layers of meaning in Enoch's encounters with angels, his celestial journeys, and his glimpses of the end times.

The symbolism in Enoch's prophetic visions is rich, with metaphors resonating with both ancient and modern readers. Stars falling from the sky, beasts rising from the depths, and celestial trumpets heralding the end times—all converge to portray cosmic upheaval and celestial intervention. These symbols are not mere poetic devices;

they reflect spiritual truths that underpin the universe (Himmelfarb, 2010).

As Enoch peers into the future, he envisions a world transformed by divine judgment and mercy. The wicked are cast into darkness, while the righteous bask in God's glory. These stark visions of judgment are tempered by promises of redemption and renewal. Enoch's prophecies highlight the dual nature of divine justice as both a purging fire and a healing balm, purifying the world and restoring harmony (Draper, 1882). The impact of these visions extends beyond the text, as historically, they have inspired diverse interpretations, with each culture and era finding new meanings. From the contemplations of early Jewish mysticism to the reflections of Christian apocalyptic thought and the inquiries of modern spiritual exploration, the prophecies within the Book of Enoch have consistently ignited deep contemplation and spirited debate (Reeves, 1992).

In the drama of Enoch's visions, we encounter universal and timeless themes. The struggle between light and darkness, the hope for a messianic deliverer, and the ultimate victory of good over evil resonate deeply with the human spirit. These themes urge us to reflect on our lives and the world around us, encouraging us to align with the forces of good and strive for a more just world (Nickelsburg & VanderKam, 2001).

In this chapter, the mysteries of Enoch's prophecies unravel, offering insights that transcend time and space. The visions guide us through celestial realms, revealing hidden truths of the universe and the divine blueprint for humanity's future. The Book of Enoch, far from a relic of the past, stands as a beacon of hope and wisdom for the future. Prepare to journey into the heart of prophecy, where the past meets the future, and the divine narrative unfolds in all its glory. The visions of Enoch await, ready to illuminate the path ahead with timeless wisdom and profound truths.

Key Prophecies

The prophecies of Enoch, whether depicting the triumph of righteousness or the fall of the wicked, lay the foundation to a story that speaks to the eternal struggle between good and evil. The struggle that is arguably the core of the Book of Enoch in itself. For within its pages, the celestial and the terrestrial converge, revealing a divine blueprint for the ultimate destiny of humanity and the universe. The prophecies of Enoch traverse the realms of the seen and unseen, bringing forth messages that are both timeless and timely.

This exploration of Enoch's prophecies delves into specific visions that are replete with symbolic imagery and deep spiritual significance. From the foretelling of cataclysmic events to the promise of divine intervention and renewal, these prophecies provide a window into the divine mind and the unfolding of a grand cosmic plan. As we unravel these prophetic threads, we find ourselves drawn into a world where the past, present, and future are intricately connected and where every revelation holds a mirror to our own souls.

The Prophecy of the Ten Weeks

One of the most notable prophetic frameworks in the Book of Enoch is the "Apocalypse of Weeks," which has been mentioned in short in a previous chapter. This prophecy divides history into ten symbolic weeks, each representing different epochs in the unfolding divine plan. Oropeza (2024) discusses the significance of these weeks, and the following is a summary of those insights:

- **Weeks one to three:** Cover the antediluvian period, focusing on the origins of humanity and the initial moral fall. The emphasis is on the corruption that spreads with the Watchers' descent and the subsequent birth of the Nephilim.

- **Week four:** Heralds the coming of a righteous man, often interpreted as Noah and the Great Flood that cleanses the Earth of corruption.

- **Weeks five and six:** Reflect the post-diluvian world, including the establishment of the covenant with Abraham and the subsequent history of Israel.

- **Week seven:** Represents a period of apostasy and the rise of a wicked generation, setting the stage for divine intervention.

- **Weeks eight to ten:** Encompass the eschatological visions of judgment and renewal. The eighth week sees the righteous receiving wisdom and the Earth being transformed. In the ninth week, universal judgment is enacted, and the tenth week culminates in the establishment of a new Heaven and new Earth.

This prophetic structure not only maps out historical events but also emphasizes the cyclical nature of sin, judgment, and redemption. It accentuates the inevitability of divine justice and the hope of ultimate renewal (Oropeza, 2024).

The Vision of the Animal Apocalypse

Another profound prophecy in the Book of Enoch is the "Animal Apocalypse" (1 Enoch 85–90), where human history is allegorically depicted through various animals. This vision provides a symbolic retelling of history from

Adam to the final judgment, using animals to represent different peoples and nations (Tiller, 2016).

- **White bulls and black bulls:** The vision begins with white bulls, representing Adam and his descendants, and black bulls, symbolizing the line of Cain. This sets the stage for the ongoing conflict between good and evil (Long, 2016c).

- **Sheep, wolves, and rams:** The vision progresses through various epochs, with sheep representing the righteous, wolves symbolizing their oppressors, and rams representing leaders like Moses and the prophets. The slaughter of the sheep by the wolves signifies periods of persecution and suffering for the righteous (Tiller, 2016; Long, 2016c).

- **The final judgment:** In the culminating scenes, the Lord of the Sheep descends, destroys the oppressors, and establishes a new, peaceful era where the sheep live in harmony. This eschatological vision reinforces the themes of divine justice and the ultimate triumph of righteousness (Long, 2016c).

The Animal Apocalypse is a powerful metaphorical narrative that illustrates the moral struggles throughout human history and the eventual victory of divine justice. Its vivid imagery and symbolic depth make it one of the most compelling prophecies in the Book of Enoch (Tiller, 2016; Long, 2016c).

The Vision of the Heavenly Luminaries

Enoch's visions also include detailed astronomical prophecies, particularly in the "Astronomical Book" (1 Enoch 72–82). These are the visions that describe the movements of the Sun, Moon, and stars, according to Sarata (n.d.), which Enoch learns from the angel Uriel; celestial knowledge that serves both practical and symbolic purposes:

- **The solar and lunar cycles:** Enoch's vision explains the intricate cycles of the Sun and Moon, emphasizing the order and regularity of the cosmos. This serves as a reminder of the divine control over the universe and the importance of understanding celestial signs.

- **The stars as angels:** In Enoch's cosmology, stars often represent angels. The wandering stars, which fail to follow their ordained paths, symbolize rebellious angels, echoing the narrative of the Watchers. Their eventual judgment is a microcosm of the broader themes of accountability and divine justice.

These astronomical visions highlight the interconnectedness of the celestial and terrestrial realms, reinforcing the idea that cosmic events mirror divine intentions and judgments. They also serve as a didactic tool, teaching humanity about the order of creation and the importance of adhering to divine laws.

The Vision of the Seven Mountains

Enoch's journey through the Heavens includes a vision of seven mountains made of precious stones, symbolizing the future holy city and the righteous who dwell within it (1 Enoch 24–25). This vision, rich in symbolism, offers a glimpse of the divine reward awaiting the faithful (Nickelsburg & VanderKam, 2001; Szink, 2008):

- **The mountains of precious stones:** Each mountain, composed of different precious stones, symbolizes various virtues and blessings. The central mountain, made of alabaster, represents the throne of God and the ultimate dwelling place of the righteous.

- **The Tree of Life:** Near these mountains, Enoch sees the Tree of Life, whose fragrance fills the Heavens. This tree symbolizes eternal life and divine blessing reserved for the righteous in the new creation.

The vision of the seven mountains and the Tree of Life underscores the hope of redemption and the rewards of faithfulness. It paints a picture of a restored creation where the righteous enjoy eternal communion with God, reinforcing the promise of divine mercy and justice (Black, n.d.).

Themes of Redemption and Judgment

The Book of Enoch is soaked in themes of redemption for the righteous and judgment for the wicked, presenting a dualistic vision that is both compelling and theologically rich. These themes are not only central to the text's prophecies but also carry deep implications for the moral and spiritual framework of its readers. By exploring these dual themes, we gain insight into the ancient perspectives on divine justice and mercy, as well as their enduring impact on theological thought.

Redemption for the Righteous

Redemption in the Book of Enoch is depicted as the ultimate reward for the faithful, as for those who uphold divine laws and live righteously amid corruption. This theme is vividly illustrated through Enoch's own journey and the visions he receives. His encounters with celestial beings and his ascension to heavenly realms symbolize the elevation of the righteous and their eventual vindication (Collins, 1998).

One powerful symbol of redemption is the vision of the "Son of Man," a messianic figure who will come to judge the world and establish an eternal kingdom of righteousness. This figure, often associated with Enoch himself, embodies the hope for divine intervention and the restoration of justice. The Son of Man is depicted as a savior who will gather the righteous, offering them eternal life and a place in the divine kingdom (Alexander, 1977).

The vision of the seven mountains, made of precious stones, also encapsulates the theme of redemption. These mountains symbolize the future holy city where the righteous will dwell. The central mountain, representing the throne of God, signifies the ultimate reward for those who remain faithful. This imagery reinforces the idea that redemption is not just an abstract promise but a tangible reality, a new world where justice and peace prevail (Nickelsburg & VanderKam, 2001).

Furthermore, the righteous are depicted as recipients of divine wisdom and understanding. In the previously mentioned "Apocalypse of Weeks," the eighth week heralds a time when the righteous will receive wisdom, and the Earth will be transformed into a paradise. This period of enlightenment and renewal highlights the redemptive power of knowledge and the fulfillment of divine promises. The transformation of the Earth into a paradise serves as a powerful testament to the rewards awaiting the faithful, a world restored to its original purity and harmony (Davila, 2005).

Judgment for the Wicked

The Book of Enoch starkly contrasts the promise of redemption with a vivid depiction of judgment for the wicked. It portrays their fate through intense imagery and severe consequences, underscoring the certainty and severity of divine justice. Various apocalyptic visions emphasize the moral and spiritual decay that justifies such punishment (Bauckham, 1998).

In a clear vision of judgment, the Watchers, the disobedient angels who defied divine orders and corrupted humanity, face binding as their punishment. This entails their confinement in darkness until the day of judgment, representing the certainty of divine retribution. The fate of the Watchers stands as a stern caution to all who violate divine laws, demonstrating that no being, whether celestial or earthly, can escape divine justice (De Jager, 2023c).

The Great Flood is another significant symbol of divine judgment. Sent to cleanse the Earth of the Nephilim and the corruption they introduced, the flood represents both a purging and a renewal. It highlights the destructive power of divine wrath and the lengths to which divine justice will go to restore order. The flood is a reminder that judgment, though severe, is necessary to cleanse the world of its moral impurities and pave the way for a new beginning (Alexander, 1977).

Visions of hell, where the wicked are cast into eternal torment, further illustrate the consequences of moral and spiritual corruption. These visions serve as a warning and a moral imperative for readers to adhere to divine laws. The graphic depictions of suffering and punishment are meant to instill a sense of fear and reverence, reinforcing the importance of living a righteous life (Reeves, 1992).

Spiritual Significance

The contrast between redemption and judgment in the Book of Enoch holds significant theological implications. It paints a picture of a moral and equitable universe governed by divine justice, where the moral fabric is ultimately reinstated. Readers are prompted to introspect on their own lives within the grand cosmic narrative they are part of.

Divine mercy and grace in the Book of Enoch promise redemption to the righteous, inspiring ethical living and faith resilience in the face of adversity. The vision of a harmonious world governed by justice and peace showcases the eventual realization of divine pledges (Collins, 1998).

The theme of judgment exposes the consequences of moral and spiritual decay. It serves as a stern reminder of the necessity of following divine laws and the harsh outcomes of disobeying them. The vivid portrayals of punishment and agony aim to inculcate fear and respect, bolstering the ethical boundaries ordained by the divine. This emphasis on judgment highlights the gravity with which the divine perceives sin and wrongdoing (Alexander, 1977).

In unison, these themes present a harmonious view of divine justice that includes both mercy and retribution. They serve as a poignant reminder that while divine justice remains resolute, it is also adorned with mercy and the prospect of redemption. This dual nature mirrors the intricate essence of the divine entity, a being that embodies both justice and mercy capable of exhibiting both wrath and compassion (Davila, 2005).

Interpretations Over Time

Enigmatic and alluring, the Book of Enoch has captivated readers across centuries with its vivid prophecies and complex cosmology. The various interpretations of these prophecies showcase a wide array of religious, cultural, and philosophical influences from different eras. This segment explores the manifold interpretations of Enoch's visions, shedding light on their profound impact on apocalyptic literature within and beyond the biblical canon.

Enoch's continually reinterpreted prophecies mirror the shifting terrains of religious and cultural convictions. Initially embraced by ancient Jewish and Christian societies, enshrined in Ethiopian heritage, and subsequently unearthed in contemporary academic circles, Enoch's foresights have wielded substantial influence over theological and apocalyptic writings.

This text's enduring significance lies in its examination of justice, redemption, and humanity's pursuit of comprehension. Analyzing Enoch's visions unveils deep layers of significance that echo humanity's historical expectations and anxieties. These analyses demonstrate the long-lasting influence of Enoch's prophecies, encouraging readers to ponder the mysteries of the universe and the divine with an ageless appeal.

Early Jewish Interpretations

During the Second Temple era, the Book of Enoch was valued by Jewish communities for its profound spiritual insights. It resonated with the apocalyptic atmosphere of the time, offering visions that struck a chord with Jews facing political upheaval. These prophecies provided solace by framing their suffering and holding out the promise of eventual justice.

Enoch's visions vividly portrayed themes of divine judgment and the eventual victory of the righteous. The

"Son of Man," depicted as a messianic deliverer, symbolized hope for liberation from tyranny. This belief shaped Jewish expectations of the Messiah and became a fundamental element in Jewish apocalyptic ideologies.

Early Christian Interpretations

Early Christians valued the Book of Enoch for its influence on Christian apocalyptic literature. This text vividly portrays divine judgment and the arrival of a messianic figure, aligning with key Christian eschatological themes. The depiction of the Son of Man in the Book of Enoch significantly impacted the New Testament's portrayal of Jesus as the cosmic judge destined to establish God's kingdom (Nickelsburg & VanderKam, 2001).

Tertullian and Origen, prominent figures among the Church fathers, interpreted Enoch's prophecies as supporting Christian teachings about the end times. Tertullian, in particular, considered the Book of Enoch a sacred text, using it to reinforce beliefs in fallen angels and the ultimate judgment. Origen, while acknowledging Enoch's writings, approached their canonical status more cautiously, reflecting the early church's mixed reception of the text (Bauckham, 1998; Collins, 1998).

During the formalization of the Christian canon, the exclusion of the Book of Enoch was primarily due to its contentious nature and uncertainties surrounding its authorship. Nevertheless, the book's themes and imagery continued to resonate in Christian thought and literature, leaving a noticeable imprint in various apocalyptic writings and early Christian eschatological perspectives (Alexander, 1977).

Medieval and Renaissance Interpretations

In the Western Christian realm of the medieval era, the Book of Enoch faded into obscurity. However, its significance endured within Eastern Christian circles and among Jewish mystics. The Ethiopian Orthodox Church safeguarded this text, incorporating it into the Ethiopian biblical scriptures. Within this unique framework, interpretations of Enoch's prophecies intertwined with Ethiopian religious and cultural ideologies, spotlighting themes of divine retribution and the eternal clash between righteousness and malevolence (Boccaccini, 1998).

During the Renaissance, there was a revival of interest in ancient texts and hidden knowledge, leading to a reexamination of the Book of Enoch. Figures like Giovanni Pico della Mirandola and John Dee delved into Enochian themes, integrating them into their broader mystical and magical frameworks. These interpretations often delved into the mystical and cosmological aspects of Enoch's visions, connecting them to the Hermetic tradition and the pursuit of concealed wisdom (Reeves, 1992; Goodricke-Clarke, 2005).

Modern and Contemporary Interpretations

In the modern era, the rediscovery of the Book of Enoch among the Dead Sea Scrolls reignited scholarly interest.

These findings provided crucial historical context, confirming the text's antiquity and significance in early Jewish and Christian thought. Scholars began to re-evaluate the Book of Enoch's role in the development of apocalyptic literature and its influence on later religious texts (Collins, 1998; Alexander, 1997).

Contemporary interpretations of the Book of Enoch vary widely. Some scholars view it as a key text in understanding the development of Jewish apocalypticism and its transition into Christian eschatology. The themes of cosmic warfare, divine judgment, and ultimate redemption are seen as foundational elements that influenced a wide range of apocalyptic literature, from the New Testament's Book of Revelation to modern apocalyptic narratives (Nickelsburg & VanderKam, 2001; Collins, 1998).

In popular culture, the Book of Enoch has inspired numerous works of fiction, films, and conspiracy theories. Its rich imagery and mysterious origins make it a fertile ground for creative exploration. Modern readers and writers often draw on Enochian themes to craft stories about hidden knowledge, celestial beings, and apocalyptic scenarios, reflecting an enduring fascination with the text.

Theological and Cultural Impact

Redemption and judgment in the Book of Enoch delve into deep theological concepts. They paint a picture of a just universe where divine justice reigns supreme. Over time and across various cultures, this vision has provided solace and optimism amid chaos.

The influence of the Book of Enoch expands beyond its religious origins, shaping a wide range of apocalyptic literature across religious and non-religious domains. Its portrayal of cosmic conflict and eventual salvation has left a lasting imprint on diverse cultural narratives, spanning from ancient religious apocalyptic works to contemporary tales of dystopia (Collins, 1998).

Additionally, the Book of Enoch has significantly influenced theological debates concerning the essence of wickedness, the involvement of divine forces, and the prospect of salvation. Its depiction of the Watchers and their descent, for instance, has shaped Christian beliefs about demons and angels, enriching the comprehension of the eternal battle between righteousness and malevolence (Bauckham, 1998).

Interpretative Variations Across Cultures

Enoch's profound visions and prophecies surpass time and place, leaving a remarkable imprint on a wide array of cultures and beliefs. Each culture interprets Enoch's messages uniquely, resulting in a rich tapestry of perspectives influenced by diverse theological, philosophical, and cultural backgrounds. This segment delves into how different cultures have embraced and reimagined Enoch's visions through the ages, shedding light on the myriad interpretations that have surfaced.

The prophecies of Enoch have left a lasting mark on various cultural and historical settings, each infused with unique themes and symbols. From ancient Jewish and Christian societies to the Ethiopian Orthodox faith, spanning from Renaissance-era mystics to modern-day scholars, Enoch's visions have consistently ignited deep theological, philosophical, and cultural reflections.

The different perspectives highlight the complex themes of justice, redemption, and humanity's quest to comprehend the divine. The lasting allure and enigma of the Book of Enoch prove the continuous impact of prophetic visions on human thinking and creativity.

Jewish Interpretations

The Book of Enoch was written in the Second Temple period and played a crucial role in Jewish apocalyptic and mystical beliefs. The political turmoil during Hellenistic and Roman reigns greatly impacted how the text was understood. For the Jews enduring oppression, connected with its messages of divine judgment and redemption, providing a sense of hope for freedom and fairness (Collins, 1996).

Enoch's prophecies focus on a figure called the "Son of Man," seen as a savior meant to bring about a better time. This vision influenced Jewish beliefs about the future a lot, inspiring more writings and ideas. Enoch also talked a lot about the universe and angels, which helped people understand the spiritual order and the fight between good and bad, bringing depth to Jewish beliefs (Alexander, 1977; Bauckham, 1998).

Christian Interpretations

Early Christians valued the Book of Enoch for its prophecies, which they believed harmonized with their beliefs about the end of the world. Associating the Son of Man with Jesus Christ was a significant change in interpretation, symbolizing a messianic figure bringing divine justice. The previously mentioned early Church leaders Tertullian and Origen, for example, used Enoch's prophecies to reinforce teachings on the end times, resurrection, and judgment (Bauckham, 1998).

Despite being initially accepted, the Book of Enoch was later left out of the Christian Bible because it was controversial and its authorship was disputed. However, its themes, like cosmic battles, divine justice, and the victory of good over evil, continued to inspire Christian apocalyptic writings such as the Book of Revelation. These ideas enhanced Christian stories by incorporating Enoch's visions into the bigger picture of Christian beliefs about the end times (Davila, 2005).

Ethiopian Orthodox Tradition

The Book of Enoch has been well-preserved by the Ethiopian Orthodox Church for centuries. Known as Ethiopic Enoch or 1 Enoch, it holds significant importance in Ethiopian Christianity. Ethiopians consider Enoch's prophecies as inspired by God, focusing on moral and end-time teachings (Collins, 1998).

The Ethiopian tradition values divine justice and the role of angels in connecting God and humanity. Enoch's vivid portrayals of heavenly realms and the universe significantly impact Ethiopian theological beliefs, shaping religious practices. The continued respect for the Book of Enoch in Ethiopia underscores its importance across different religious traditions beyond its Jewish and Christian origins (Alexander, 1977; Reeves, 1992).

Renaissance and Esoteric Interpretations

During the Renaissance period, the revival of ancient texts reignited curiosity in the Book of Enoch, captivating scholars and mystics. Prominent individuals such as Giovanni Pico della Mirandola and John Dee delved into Enochian concepts within the contexts of Hermeticism and Christian mysticism. They found Enoch's cosmology, angelology, and prophetic insights intriguing, seeing them as pathways to concealed wisdom and divine understanding (Reeves, 1992).

These Renaissance interpretations often delved into the mystical and esoteric parts of Enoch's prophecies. The elaborate depictions of heavenly realms and the angelic duties were considered glimpses into divine order and cosmic mechanisms. This era signaled a notable change in how Enoch's visions were understood, combining religious and mystical themes with philosophical exploration (Davila, 2005).

Modern Scholarly Interpretations

In today's world, finding the Dead Sea Scrolls renewed academic fascination with the Book of Enoch. This discovery offered an important historical background, validating the age and importance of Enoch's predictions in ancient Jewish and Christian beliefs. Contemporary scholars have examined Enoch's insights through different academic lenses like theology, history, and literary analysis (Alexander, 1977; Collins, 1998).

Many scholars look at how the Book of Enoch inspired later Jewish and Christian apocalyptic writings, shaping the genre with themes of divine judgment, cosmic warfare, and ultimate redemption (Collins, 1998).

Cultural and Popular Interpretations

Beyond academic and religious circles, the Book of Enoch's mystical aspects have inspired modern interpretations and a wide range of creative works. Its vivid imagery and intricate cosmology spark imaginative retellings that feature in popular media, captivating audiences with stories of ancient mysteries, celestial beings, and apocalyptic events. Enoch's themes of hidden knowledge and divine intervention serve as a timeless source of inspiration worldwide (Reeves, 1992; Davila, 2005).

The Book of Enoch's lasting impact goes beyond academia and religion, holding a special position in modern culture due to its mystical and imaginative aspects. In the next chapter, we will dive further into Enoch's spiritual influence, exploring how its themes have stood the test of time, molding theological ideas and enhancing diverse spiritual practices and traditions. This exploration will reveal the significant effect Enoch's visions have had on spiritual beliefs and why they remain relevant in present spiritual discussions.

Chapter 6:
A Spiritual Legacy

Exploring the enduring spiritual teachings of the Book of Enoch involves navigating its influence on religious beliefs. The book's vivid descriptions of heavenly domains, the eternal battle between good and bad, and the ultimate vindication of righteousness have profoundly shaped the religious ideologies of both Christianity and Judaism. However, Enoch's insights extend further, impacting the early writings of Christian apocalyptic texts and present-day spiritual trends, constantly sparking new ideas and interpretations.

In Christian tradition, the Book of Enoch's themes of redemption and judgment resonate deeply. Early Church fathers saw in Enoch's prophecies a reflection of their eschatological beliefs, integrating these visions into the broader framework of Christian doctrine. The figure of the "Son of Man" in Enoch, who judges the living and the dead, parallels the New Testament's depiction of Jesus Christ (Delp, 2018).

Judaism places the Book of Enoch within the apocalyptic tradition, with its detailed cosmology and angelology influencing Jewish mystical thought. The Watchers, their fall, and humanity's resulting corruption offer profound insights into the Jewish understanding of sin and redemption. The Ethiopian Orthodox Church, on the other hand, considers the Book of Enoch canonical, preserving its entirety and highlighting its significance. Ethiopian Christianity views Enoch's visions as divinely inspired, offering guidance and wisdom (Collins, 1998; Robinson, 2005).

Scholars and mystics during the Renaissance were captivated by the Book of Enoch, seeing it as a source of hidden knowledge and esoteric wisdom. The text became integrated into the intellectual and spiritual movements of the era. Today, modern scholarship, inspired by its rediscovery among the Dead Sea Scrolls, continues to unveil its ancient origins and importance in early Jewish and Christian writings. Researchers delve into its theological, historical, and literary aspects, revealing new depths of understanding (Alexander, 1997; Reeves, 1992).

The enduring spiritual influence of the Book of Enoch resonates throughout religion and culture, shaping theological discussions, inspiring sacred narratives, and igniting various analyses. This text links the celestial with the earthly spheres and provides insights into the universe's mysteries and divine justice.

Influence on Christianity

Enoch's Book, brimming with visions of the apocalypse and heavenly orders, significantly impacted early Christian ideologies, briefly referenced in the preceding chapter. While not part of the official Bible, its concepts and lessons deeply resonated with the early Christian community, influencing subsequent writings in the New Testament and theological discussions. Therefore, this section looks further into the profound impact of Enoch's Book on the development of Christianity.

Enoch's prophecies about judgment, salvation, and universal conflict have influenced Christian apocalyptic writing, leaving a lasting impact on theological beliefs.

165

The parallels to these topics in the New Testament and the discussions among early Church leaders confirm its significant and lasting spiritual heritage, providing profound perspectives on godly fairness and final deliverance.

Exploring the spiritual heritage left by Enoch is akin to finding a secret trove brimming with theological and cultural jewels that surpass conventional ideas. Its extensive impact on Christianity serves as a guiding light, illuminating the complex relationship between age-old scriptures and developing religious ideologies, highlighting the eternal quest to unveil the enigmas of the divine.

References in the New Testament

The New Testament makes a significant reference to the Book of Enoch in the Epistle of Jude. Jude 1:14-15 (*NIV*, 2011) directly quotes Enoch 1:9, confirming Enoch's prophecy about the Lord's arrival with ten thousand saints for judgment. This quote shows the respect that early Christian writers had for the Book of Enoch as a source of divine insight and highlights its importance in Christian literature. Additionally, similarities in themes between Enoch and other New Testament writings imply a wider influence. The idea of the messianic "Son of Man" in Enoch aligns with the Gospels, where Jesus also refers to Himself with this title, indicating a common belief in a heavenly judge overseeing final judgment as reflected in both Jewish apocalyptic texts and Christian doctrine (De Jager, 2023a; De Jager, 2023c).

Early Christian Thought and Use

Early Christians discovered a wealth of theological themes in the Book of Enoch that aligned well with their developing beliefs. Its detailed portrayals of angels, demons, and the eternal battle between good and evil are deeply connected with the early Christians' views on spiritual warfare and the eventual victory of God's sovereignty. Moreover, the intricate angelology presented in the Book of Enoch significantly impacted Christian perspectives on the nature and duties of angels (De Jager, 2023a; De Jager, 2023c).

With Church fathers like Tertullian and Origen plunging themselves into Enochic literature, they recognized its spiritual wisdom and ethical lessons. Tertullian, especially, upheld the legitimacy of the Book of Enoch by pointing to Jude's reference, viewing Enoch as a true prophet inspired by the Holy Spirit and worthy of deep theological reflection (Watson, 2024).

Origen, while exercising caution, appreciated the significance of Enoch's visions in elucidating the intricate dynamics between the divine and the demonic. His allusions to Enoch in conversations about angelology and demonology highlight the text's impact on the early Christian theological progression (De Jager, 2023c).

Integration Into Apocalyptic Literature

The apocalyptic concepts within the Book of Enoch had a significant influence on early Christian writings, notably the Book of Revelation. These works both depict a grand cosmic narrative of the end of days, portraying themes of divine justice, the triumph over darkness, and the emergence of a purified and just world. The vivid depictions of celestial realms, angelic gatherings, and decisive end-time conflicts in Revelation mirror the captivating descriptions found in the visions of Enoch (Davila, 2005).

The impact of Enoch's teachings can be seen in various apocalyptic writings, like the Sibylline Oracles and the Apocalypse of Peter, where we find common themes of judgment, redemption, and the cosmic battle. These works, belonging to the wider Christian apocalyptic literature, showcase how Enochic concepts profoundly influenced the eschatological beliefs of the early Christian community (Bauckham, 1998).

Divine Impacts

The impact of Enoch on Christianity has deep theological significance. Key Christian doctrines such as the second coming of Christ and the final judgment parallel themes in Enoch's writings, particularly on divine judgment and the vindication of the righteous. Enoch's depiction of a cosmic conflict between good and evil echoes the Christian belief in spiritual warfare and the eventual triumph of God's kingdom. Furthermore, Enoch's exploration of angels and demons expanded Christian perspectives on the spiritual realm, shaping discussions on the roles of these beings in God's grand design. The intricate tales of the Watchers and their fall introduced intricate concepts of sin, rebellion, and divine justice that resonated with Christian teachings on evil and the repercussions of going against God's will (De Jager, 2023b; Delp, 2018).

Continuing Legacy

Despite not being included in the canonical Bible, the Book of Enoch maintained a significant impact on Christian ideology over the ages. During the medieval era, it became intertwined with mystical and esoteric beliefs, captivating individuals drawn to profound spiritual revelations. The resurgence of curiosity in ancient manuscripts during the Renaissance propelled Enochic literature to the forefront of both scholarly inquiry and spiritual exploration, solidifying its influence on the cultural and intellectual landscape of the period (Ashcroft, 2022; De Jager, 2023c).

In today's world, the rediscovery of the Book of Enoch among the Dead Sea Scrolls has sparked a resurgence of interest and scholarly inquiry. These discoveries have confirmed the text's ancient origins and its importance in early Jewish and Christian contexts. Scholars today are delving into its theological, historical, and literary aspects, revealing new depths of meaning and influence.

The impact of the Book of Enoch goes beyond academic realms, as its rich symbolism and apocalyptic themes serve as inspiration for literature, films, and various media forms in popular culture. This enduring impact highlights the text's ability to captivate the human imagination and its relevance to ongoing spiritual and existential inquiries (De Jager, 2023a; De Jager, 2023b; De Jager 2023c).

Influence on Judaism

The Book of Enoch has deeply influenced Jewish mystical traditions, especially the Kabbalah, but has only briefly been mentioned in earlier chapters. Even though it is not part of the canonical Jewish scriptures, it has still provided profound spiritual insights and esoteric knowledge, shaping Jewish thought and mysticism. Therefore, it would be unwise to leave the information as is without further examining the influence it has had on more specific parts of Judaism.

The detailed cosmology, angelology, and apocalyptic themes of the Book of Enoch have been central to the development of Jewish mysticism over the centuries. From early Jewish apocalyptic thought to Kabbalistic teachings, the Book of Enoch offers timeless wisdom, continuing to inspire and illuminate the mystical path for those seeking to understand divine mysteries.

Enoch and Early Jewish Mysticism

In ancient Jewish mysticism, the Book of Enoch was highly respected for its detailed descriptions of the Heavens, angelic beings, and divine throne, offering a mystical view of the cosmos. Enoch's journey to Heaven and transformation into the angel Metatron is a central theme in Jewish mystical texts, symbolizing spiritual progression and divine insight. Metatron, depicted as a scribe bridging between God and humanity, signifies spiritual growth and wisdom. Enoch's narrative and angelic change highlight the human potential to achieve spiritual elevation and forge a direct connection with the divine.

Enoch was an important figure in ancient Jewish mysticism and was respected for sharing detailed insights about the Heavens. The Book of Enoch was highly valued as it explored the angelic realm and divine throne, offering a mystical perspective on the cosmos and celestial hierarchy. In its text, a significant event occurs when the main character transforms into the angelic figure called Metatron. This change represents a key point in Jewish mystical belief, indicating a move from earthly life to a higher spiritual realm. Metatron, shown as a writer and mediator connecting people with the divine, symbolizes spiritual knowledge and deep wisdom in Jewish mysticism (Schäfer, 2020; Jacobs & Blau, n.d.).

Metatron's role as a messenger connecting humans with God illustrates the opportunity for spiritual growth and the search for divine knowledge. Enoch, becoming Metatron, uncovers secret teachings on how to reach higher spiritual states and have a close bond with the spiritual realm. Enoch's journey to the Heavens highlights the noble nature of human existence, demonstrating the capacity to go beyond worldly boundaries and reach celestial realms. His story serves as a manual for seekers on a spiritual journey, offering wisdom on the significant influence of faith, perseverance, and a connection with the divine (Schäfer, 2020; Jacobs & Blau, n.d.).

Encompassed by mystique, Enoch's story involves intricately threading through celestial wonders and encounters with the divine that invites readers to contemplate the boundless enigmas of the universe. Through his interactions with celestial beings and metamorphosis into Metatron, profound avenues for philosophical reflection and spiritual examination emerge. Central to Enoch's narrative lies a profound teaching on spiritual growth and the pursuit of divine wisdom. By embodying the essence of Metatron, ancient wisdom-seekers found inspiration to seek profound truths, cultivate inner enlightenment, and forge meaningful connections with the universal spiritual essence (Schäfer, 2020; Jacobs & Blau, n.d.).

Enoch's journey is a powerful symbol of the enduring search for a direct connection with the divine. His evolution into Metatron reveals a pathway to deepening relationships with the divine, surpassing worldly bounds, and embracing spiritual awakening. The stories of Enoch and Metatron remain captivating within Jewish mysticism, inspiring spiritual seekers and mystics with their celestial encounters and divine wisdom. Their remarkable journey embodies the ageless pursuit of spiritual growth and divine unity.

The travels of Enoch symbolize the timeless quest to directly connect with the divine. His transformation into Metatron unveils a path to strengthening connections with the sacred, transcending earthly limitations, and embracing spiritual enlightenment. The tales of Enoch and Metatron hold a profound fascination in Jewish mysticism, fueling the spiritual endeavors of seekers and mystics through their celestial experiences and divine insights. Their extraordinary expedition epitomizes the eternal pursuit of spiritual development and unity with the divine.

The Book of Enoch and the Kabbalah

The mystical tradition of Kabbalah in Judaism has been greatly influenced by the themes and symbols found in the Book of Enoch. The elaborate descriptions of the universe and angelic hierarchy in the text closely mirror Kabbalistic beliefs about divine beings and the cosmos' structure. Kabbalah views the sefirot, the ten divine emanations that interact with the world, as a reflection of the orderly universe depicted in the Book of Enoch. In Kabbalistic philosophy, Enoch's journey and transformation into Metatron symbolizes the soul's quest through spiritual realms toward unity with the divine. This idea is fundamental in Kabbalistic rituals and meditations, as practitioners aim to progress through the sefirot and achieve deeper spiritual insight. The Book of Enoch provides a narrative foundation that enhances and complements Kabbalistic doctrines (Meiliken, 2010; Miller, n.d.).

The magical encounters shared in the Book of Enoch, like seeing the heavenly throne and the angel ranking, strongly connect with the Kabbalistic search for hidden wisdom and firsthand divine encounters. The focus on revealing divine insights lines up with the Kabbalistic practice of discovering the concealed teachings in the Torah and the mysteries of existence.

Influence on Later Jewish Mystical Texts

The ideas in the Book of Enoch have a lasting impact on later mystical Jewish writings like the Zohar, which is key to Kabbalah. The Zohar includes similar concepts and signs found in Enoch's texts, like vivid accounts of celestial realms and angelic-human connections. Stories of Rabbi Shimon bar Yochai's spiritual adventures in the Zohar mirror Enoch's visions, showing how these writings connect through time. Furthermore, the Book of Enoch's discussions about the end of the world and the eventual salvation of the good have had a significant impact on Jewish beliefs about the future. These ideas can also be seen in Kabbalah through the idea of fixing the world, where those who do good are important in helping to bring about the ultimate salvation. The Book of Enoch paints a picture of a renewed and cleansed world that aligns with this Kabbalistic notion, stressing how human deeds are linked to a higher purpose (Fishbane, 2023).

Contemporary Jewish Mysticism

In modern Jewish mystical teachings, the Book of Enoch remains a captivating source of inspiration and exploration. Its discussions on divine revelations, angelic structures, and universal fairness attract modern learners looking into Kabbalistic wisdom. The text's intricate symbols and deep spiritual reflections provide valuable insights for those curious about spiritual mysteries and cosmic understanding. Modern Kabbalists and researchers frequently revisit the Book of Enoch to unveil fresh meanings and link ancient mystical knowledge with present-day spiritual customs. Enoch's visions continue to fascinate many as they touch on humanity's timeless pursuit of wisdom, transcendence, and connection with the divine.

The Role of Angels and Divine Intermediaries

The detailed study of angels in the Book of Enoch has influenced Jewish mystical beliefs, with angels being viewed as links between God and humanity. The portrayal of the Watchers, their descent, and their interactions with people in the Book of Enoch helps explain the role of angels in the universe. In Kabbalah, angels are seen as messengers who do God's work and aid in spiritual growth, and consequently, the transformation of Enoch into Metatron highlights how humans can become angels through spiritual growth. This idea is reflected in Kabbalistic teachings, where seekers aim to surpass earthly limits for a direct connection with the divine. The Book of Enoch signifies the transformative power of the mystical journey (Robinson, 2005).

Integration Into Biblical Narratives

The ancient Book of Enoch offers powerful apocalyptic visions and intricate cosmological details that have deeply impacted the holy scriptures of significant faiths like Judaism and Christianity. This segment explores the seamless integration of diverse aspects from the Book of Enoch into the tapestry of these sacred stories, illuminating their religious and symbolic importance.

The incorporation of Enoch's profound concepts into the sacred scriptures of both Judaism and Christianity exemplifies the lasting impact of this age-old document. Its vivid apocalyptic illustrations, intricate explanation of the universe, and deep spiritual revelations have significantly shaped the religious storytelling in these prominent belief systems. Ranging from the prophetic writings of the Hebrew Scriptures to the end-time visions of the Christian New Testament, Enoch's substantial influence is unmistakable, enhancing the discussions on spirituality and theology.

When taking a deep plunge into how the Book of Enoch influences these recognized texts, we develop a richer understanding of the vibrant connection between apocalyptic writings and spiritual beliefs. By integrating Enochic motifs into the wider theological context, the text's importance is highlighted, enriching the intricate fabric of religious storytelling and symbolism.

Reflections in the Hebrew Bible

Though not in the Hebrew Bible, the Book of Enoch has had a great impact on important writings. It has shared ideas on God's judgments, angel ranks, and visions of the future by echoing Hebrew prophetic writings. For instance, in Daniel's book, with its end-time prophecies and heavenly beings, Enoch's descriptions feel quite alike.

Daniel's dreams of the Elderly Figure and the arrival of the "Son of Humanity" in the book of Daniel, Chapter 7, verses 9–14 (*NIV*, 2011), resemble Enoch's depiction of the celestial throne and the divine arbiter. This common theme implies that the writers of Daniel could have known about Enochic beliefs and integrated them into their own apocalyptic context. Moreover, the idea of an ultimate reckoning and the formation of God's reign, which are fundamental in both Enoch and Daniel, emphasize the mutual futuristic perspective in these writings (deSilva, 2012).

Mentions of sacred scriptures in the Old Testament, like the mention of the "Book of Life" in Daniel 12:1 and the "Book of Remembrance" in Malachi 3:16, mirror the Enochic concept of heavenly archives. Enoch speaks of celestial tablets that note down human actions and divine pronouncements, stressing the ideas of responsibility and judgment in the eyes of God. This theme of celestial recording mirrors a prevalent apocalyptic focus on divine fairness and the final destiny of mankind (Delp, 2018).

Influence on the New Testament

The New Testament makes frequent mention of the Book of Enoch, suggesting its impactful role in shaping the beliefs of early Christians. A notable reference is found in the Epistle of Jude, where Enoch's prophecies regarding the Lord's arrival, accompanied by countless saints to administer judgment, are acknowledged in Jude 1:14-15 (*NIV*, 2011). This reference highlights the ancient Christian perspective on the prophetic value and theological importance of the Book of Enoch (Davila, 2005).

The influence of the Book of Enoch can be seen in various New Testament writings, particularly in the apocalyptic and end-time themes found in the Gospels and Revelation. Jesus' frequent reference to himself as the "Son of Man," a significant figure in Enoch's visions, implies a direct connection between Enochic traditions and the portrayal of Jesus in the New Testament. This

Son of Man is presented as a divine judge who will oversee the final judgment, a role that closely resembles Enoch's description of the end-time figure. Revelation, with its vivid apocalyptic symbols and detailed depictions of heavenly realms, reflects the visions depicted in the Book of Enoch. The representation of the heavenly throne, the celestial beings, and the cosmic battle between good and evil in Revelation heavily borrows from the symbolic language and concepts of the Book of Enoch. This connection underscores the link between Jewish apocalyptic literature and Christian beliefs about the end times, highlighting their shared theological background (Bauckham, 1998).

Integration Into Early Christian Writings

As early Christian scholars and theologians like Tertullian and Origen interacted with the Book of Enoch, Tertullian especially supported the genuineness of Enoch. He was advocating for its validity by citing Jude's reference and its harmony with Christian beliefs about the end of days. He saw Enoch as a channel for divine knowledge, shedding light on angels, the universe, and the apocalypse (Nickelsburg & VanderKam, 2001).

While exercising prudence, Origen acknowledged the significance of Enoch's visions in elucidating the dynamics between the divine and the demonic. His mentions of Enoch in conversations about angelology and demonology underscore the impact of the text on the initial stages of Christian theological evolution. The elaborate depictions of the Watchers and their descent laid the groundwork for comprehending the source of malevolence and the universal conflict between virtue and wickedness (Nickelsburg & VanderKam, 2001).

Additionally, the broader influence of Jewish apocalyptic traditions on early Christian thought, including the use of the Book of Enoch, is discussed in studies of Jewish lore and its impact on various theological developments (Reeves, 1992).

Symbolic and Theological Parallels

The connections between the Book of Enoch and traditional texts reveal its deep influence on religious thoughts. Ideas like God's judgment, universal fairness, and the eventual salvation of the good echo through Jewish and Christian beliefs. These concepts are key in apocalyptic writings and overarching stories about sin, rescue, and the world's eventual renewal (Davila, 2005).

The detailed cosmological framework found in the book of Enoch beautifully complements the theological ideas present in traditional texts. By depicting angels as messengers between God and people, showcasing their execution of divine plans, and their involvement in future events, Enochic literature mirrors themes seen in different religions. This commonality in imagery underscores the connections between these texts and the long-lasting impact of Enochic beliefs (Reeves, 1992).

Global Religious Perspectives

The Book of Enoch has had a significant influence on Jewish and Christian traditions. It not only explores connections and disparities with non-Abrahamic faiths but also investigates how its themes resonate across different world religions, through symbols and narratives.

Enoch's ideas find broad appeal as they touch on humanity's search for meaning in the divine, the universe, and ethical principles. From the cyclical time in Hinduism to the cosmic battles of Zoroastrianism, from the beliefs in the ancient Egyptian afterlife to shamanic experiences, Enoch's insights draw similarities in various spiritual practices.

Global perspectives enhance our understanding of the universal importance of the Book of Enoch. Delving into these correlations gives us a glimpse into the shared beliefs of mankind's spiritual legacy, emphasizing a worldwide pursuit of purpose, fairness, and spiritual growth.

Parallels With Hinduism and Buddhism

In Hinduism, the idea of divine judgment and cosmic cycles shares similarities with the apocalyptic themes found in the Book of Enoch. Hindu scriptures such as the Bhagavad Gita and the Mahabharata describe how the universe goes through cycles of destruction and rebirth under the guidance of divine powers. This cyclical understanding of time, marked by repeated eras (yugas) culminating in a final judgment and restoration, mirrors Enoch's prophetic insights on divine judgment and the eventual creation of a just society (Delp, 2018).

Buddhism, especially in its Mahayana form, draws intriguing similarities with Enochian themes in its cosmology and eschatology. The concept of various Heavens and hells in Buddhism, where beings are reborn based on their actions, reflects the intricate heavenly realms and moral outcomes shown in Enoch. Additionally, the idea of bodhisattvas—enlightened beings who assist others—can be compared to Enoch's angelic entities, who serve as intermediaries and guides in the heavenly spheres (Ji & Wang, 2024),

Influences in Zoroastrianism

In the ancient faith of Zoroastrianism, there are similar ideas to those in the Book of Enoch. Both talk about a cosmic battle between good and evil, a final judgment, and the cleansing of the world. Zoroastrianism also speaks of a savior figure who will bring about the world's renewal, like the prophecies in Enoch (Encyclopaedia Iranica, 2012).

The detailed descriptions of the afterlife in Zoroastrian writings, such as the evaluation of souls and the consequences they face, echo Enoch's accounts of the ultimate judgment. The concept of a bridge (Chinvat Bridge) that departed souls traverse post-death, where their destiny is influenced by their actions in life, mirrors the ethical evaluations highlighted in Enoch's texts (Landes, 2016).

Comparisons With Ancient Egyptian Religion

Ancient Egypt's religious beliefs, filled with a diverse array of gods and intricate views on life after death, present captivating parallels to the Book of Enoch. While the Egyptian Book of the Dead comprises a series of incantations and ceremonies designed to steer the departed in the afterlife, it converges thematically with Enoch's accounts of celestial voyages and divine judgments. Both writings underscore the ethical scrutiny of spirits and the repercussions of their deeds in the afterworld (Mark, 2016).

The concept of Ma'at, a key concept in Egyptian beliefs representing truth, equilibrium, and universal order, aligns with the Enochian focus on fairness and keeping the cosmic balance intact. In Egyptian myths, the scenes of judgment, where a person's heart is compared to the feather of Ma'at, bear a resemblance to the final judgment accounts in Enoch that depict the separation of good and evil individuals (Mirza, 2016).

Shamanistic Traditions and Enochian Themes

Shamanic customs in different cultures often include venturing into the spiritual realm, conversing with gods, and discovering secret wisdom—themes fundamental to Enoch's story. For instance, in Siberian and Native American shamanism, the shaman's journey to higher realms or lower realms to acquire wisdom and advocate for their people mirrors Enoch's celestial voyages and his function as an intermediary (Alexander, 1977; Davila, 2005).

Shamanic traditions focus on the significance of spiritual visions and a shaman's skill to move between earthly and divine realms, much like Enoch, who held roles as a visionary and messenger. Both shamanic customs and Enoch stories stress the importance of ethical behavior and accountability for one's deeds, underlining a shared emphasis on moral values and spiritual responsibility (Blum, 2018).

Modern Spiritual Movements

In modern times, the ideas and symbols introduced in the Book of Enoch have resonated across different spiritual and esoteric paths. The New Age movement, particularly centered on spiritual growth, universal awareness, and human change, reflects themes akin to Enoch's teachings about heavenly wisdom and ascension. The New Age movement's focus on angelic support, spiritual progress, and the forthcoming transition to an elevated phase of awareness mirrors the transformative and enlightening parts of Enoch's experiences (Akin, 2021).

Similarly, theosophical lessons draw inspiration from Enoch's stories, blending facets of Eastern beliefs,

Western mystical practices, and ancient traditions. Enoch's elaborate tales of the universe, angels, and apocalyptic insights align with the theosophical pursuit of secret knowledge and comprehension of divine structures (Ashcroft, 2022).

As we rummage deeper through the modern reinterpretations and influences of Enochian literature in the coming chapter, we will uncover how these ancient narratives continue to shape contemporary thought and spirituality.

Chapter 7:
Enoch in the Modern Age

In the quiet corners of libraries and the bustling discourse of online forums, the ancient whispers of the Book of Enoch continue to weave their way into contemporary thought and culture. This text, steeped in mysticism and apocalyptic visions, stirs both debate and fascination. As we explore modern interpretations and cultural resonance of Enoch's prophecies, we are drawn into a vibrant scheme of theological and scholarly discussions that bridge the ancient with the modern.

The Book of Enoch sparks discussions beyond religious scholarship, resonating with contemporary audiences through themes of divine judgment, celestial hierarchies, and eschatological visions. Its exclusion from the biblical canon has only heightened its allure, casting it as a forbidden fruit ripe for rediscovery. Scholars debate its origins, influence on apocalyptic literature, and reasons for its omission from the canon, touching on fundamental questions about divine justice and the ethical use of knowledge.

Beyond academia, the Book of Enoch has inspired a range of artistic and media representations. The 2014 movie *Noah*, directed by Darren Aronofsky, draws heavily on Enochian themes, particularly the Watchers. Literature, visual arts, and music have also embraced Enoch's prophecies, using its vivid imagery and dramatic narratives to explore themes of redemption, divine justice, and human frailty. This creative expression highlights the text's enduring relevance and captivates modern audiences with its blend of myth, legend, and biblical lore.

In the digital age, online communities and social media platforms buzz with discussions about the Book of Enoch. Enthusiasts share interpretations while debating theological implications and exploring connections between Enoch's visions and contemporary events. This digital engagement reflects a broader trend of rediscovering ancient texts and seeking new meanings in their timeless messages.

The Book of Enoch continues to challenge and inspire contemporary theology, prompting reflection on the nature of sacred texts and the criteria by which they are judged. The questions it raises about divine justice, human destiny, and the cosmos are as relevant today as they were millennia ago. Theologians and spiritual seekers find in Enoch's prophecies profound insights and a catalyst for deep reflection.

As we journey through this chapter, we will explore the myriad ways in which the Book of Enoch has been interpreted, debated, and represented in modern times. We will plunge into theological discussions, examine its impact on contemporary thought, and trace its influence across various forms of art and media. The story of Enoch, with its blend of the mystical and the moral, continues to captivate and inspire, reminding us of the enduring power of ancient wisdom to illuminate the present and guide us into the future.

Theological Debates

As the ancient and enigmatic text that it is, the Book of Enoch has provoked a myriad of theological debates in the modern age. As scholars, theologians, and religious enthusiasts engage with its contents, the discussions surrounding its authenticity, historical accuracy, and theological implications continue to evolve. This section delves into the key modern theological issues and discussions about the Book of Enoch, setting the stage for a deeper exploration of its place in contemporary theology.

Authenticity and Canonical Status

One of the most contentious debates centers on the authenticity and canonical status of the Book of Enoch. Unlike the canonical books of the Bible, the Book of Enoch has a complex history of acceptance and rejection within various religious traditions. As has been previously mentioned, early Christian writers such as Tertullian and Origen referenced Enoch; its influence and potential canonical status during the early Christian period can be considered heavily advocated. However, its eventual exclusion from the Jewish and Christian canons has led to ongoing debates about its legitimacy and divine inspiration.

Modern scholars analyze the Book of Enoch using historical-critical methods to explore its authorship and composition timeline. Traditionally believed to be penned by Enoch, Noah's great-grandfather, contemporary research generally places the text's origin between the 3rd century BCE and the 1st century CE. This timeline suggests the compilation spans several centuries, prompting debates on its prophetic legitimacy and the degree to which it embodies genuine divine inspiration versus later interpretive constructs.

Historical Accuracy and Context

The historical accuracy of the Book of Enoch is another focal point of modern theological debates. Scholars scrutinize its descriptions of pre-flood events, angelic hierarchies, and cosmological visions as they compare them to archaeological findings and other ancient texts. While some argue that the Book of Enoch provides valuable insights into the religious and cultural milieu of ancient Judaism, others contend that its mythological elements undermine its historical reliability.

Enoch's vivid descriptions of the Watchers have sparked particular interest and controversy for this storyline, while rich in symbolic meaning, challenge modern readers to discern their historical basis. Some scholars propose that the Watchers' story reflects ancient Near Eastern myths reinterpreted within a Jewish apocalyptic framework, while others see it as a unique and original contribution to Jewish angelology.

Theological Ramifications

The theological implications of the Book of Enoch extend beyond questions of authenticity and historical accuracy. The text's apocalyptic themes, detailed angelology, and visions of divine judgment and redemption have profound implications for understanding the nature of God, the cosmos, and human destiny. Enoch's portrayal of a multi-tiered Heaven, populated by various angelic beings, offers a complex cosmology that challenges simplistic interpretations of the divine realm.

One of the key theological issues is the Book of Enoch's depiction of divine justice. Enoch's visions of the final judgment, where the righteous are rewarded and the wicked are punished, resonate with but also expand upon the eschatological themes found in canonical texts. This has led to debates about the nature of salvation, the role of divine mercy, and the ultimate fate of humanity. Enoch's detailed descriptions of the afterlife provide a rich source for theological reflection and have influenced both Jewish and Christian understandings of eschatology (Fitzmyer, 1977).

Modern Scholarly Views

Modern scholarly views on the Book of Enoch are diverse, reflecting a range of interpretive approaches and theological perspectives. Some scholars view the text as a valuable historical document that sheds light on the religious landscape of Second Temple Judaism. They argue that Enoch provides critical insights into the development of Jewish apocalypticism, angelology, and cosmology. For instance, the Book of Enoch is often studied to understand early Jewish mystical traditions and its influence on later religious texts, including the New Testament (Alexander, 1977; Editors of Encyclopaedia Britannica, 2020).

Others, however, approach the Book of Enoch with caution, questioning its historical accuracy and theological coherence. They point to its complex textual history, the presence of mythological elements, and its exclusion from the canonical scriptures as reasons to treat it as a secondary source. This cautious approach underscores the ongoing debates about the nature of sacred texts and the criteria for determining their authenticity and authority. Scholars like Davila (2005) highlight the issues of pseudepigraphy and the challenges in tracing the book's origins, while Bauckham (1998) emphasizes the theological implications and the book's reception history in both Jewish and Christian contexts.

Enoch In Contemporary Theology

In the ever-evolving landscape of contemporary theology, the Book of Enoch has emerged as a fascinating and contentious subject of study. The theological debates surrounding the Book of Enoch set the stage for a deeper exploration of its place in contemporary theology. As we delve into how modern theologians and scholars engage with Enoch's teachings, we will uncover the ways in which this ancient text continues to inspire, challenge, and provoke thought in the modern age.

The Book of Enoch's apocalyptic visions, angelic hierarchies, and themes of divine justice and mercy offer rich material for contemporary theological reflection. Whether viewed as a historical curiosity, a source of mystical insight, or a prophetic revelation, the Book of Enoch remains a vibrant and dynamic text that speaks to the enduring human quest for understanding the divine and the cosmos.

Theological Exploration and Doctrinal Debates

Contemporary theologians often turn to the Book of Enoch to explore themes that resonate with modern spiritual and ethical concerns. Enoch's vivid descriptions of celestial realms, angelic hierarchies, and divine judgment provide a framework for discussing the nature of the divine, the cosmos, and the moral order. Scholars like George W.E. Nickelsburg and James C. VanderKam (2001; 2004) have contributed significantly to the academic study of Enoch, examining its influence on Jewish apocalypticism and early Christian thought.

One of the key areas where Enoch's writings are influential is in the discussion of angelology and demonology. The detailed accounts of the Watchers, the fallen angels, and their interactions with humanity offer a unique perspective on the nature of good and evil, divine justice, and the consequences of sin. Modern theologians use these narratives to explore the complexities of free will, the origins of evil, and the role of supernatural beings in the moral and spiritual development of humanity (Nickelsburg & VanderKam, 2001; Nickelsburg & VanderKam, 2004).

Influence on Modern Eschatology

Enoch's apocalyptic visions have had a deep influence on modern eschatological ideas. The depiction of the ultimate judgment in the text, where the good receive their due rewards and the wicked face punishment, resonates with concepts present in Jewish and Christian beliefs about the end times. As a result, theologians have been prompted to revisit established doctrines concerning the end of days, the resurrection of the deceased, and the formation of a fresh, divine framework (Nickelsburg & VanderKam, 2001).

In Christian theology, the Book of Enoch's influence is particularly evident in discussions about the Second Coming of Christ and the final judgment. The text's descriptions of cosmic upheavals, angelic interventions, and the ultimate triumph of good over evil provide a rich source of imagery and symbolism for interpreting New Testament prophecies. Theologians like Richard Bauckham (1998) have explored how Enoch's apocalyptic visions shape contemporary Christian eschatological expectations and the theology of hope and renewal.

Ethical and Moral Implications

The ethical and moral teachings embedded in Enoch's writings are another focal point for contemporary theologians and have thus been discussed in previous chapters. The text's emphasis on divine justice, the consequences of sin, and the rewards for righteousness offer valuable insights into the nature of moral accountability and the pursuit of virtue. Modern theologians often use Enoch's moral lessons to address contemporary ethical issues, such as social justice, environmental stewardship, and human rights (Bagley, n.d.). The text's warnings about the consequences of moral decay and the importance of upholding divine laws resonate with current discussions about ethical leadership, societal responsibility, and the role of religion in promoting moral values. These teachings inspire a call to action, urging believers to live in accordance with divine principles and strive for a just and compassionate society.

Integration Into Liturgical Practices

In addition to its theological implications, the Book of Enoch has found a place in contemporary liturgical practices and spiritual rituals. Some religious communities incorporate readings from Enoch into their worship services, using its apocalyptic visions and moral teachings to inspire reflection and devotion. This integration reflects a growing appreciation for the text's spiritual depth and relevance to modern religious life.

Scholarly Perspectives on Authenticity

The authenticity and historical accuracy of the Book of Enoch are subjects of significant scholarly debate. Modern scholars utilize historical-critical methods to investigate the text's origins, its compilation over centuries, and its context within ancient Jewish literature. Some scholars, such as Nickelsburg and VanderKam (2001), argue that Enoch is a pseudepigraphical work reflecting later interpretive traditions. Others emphasize its historical significance, noting its influence on Jewish apocalypticism, angelology, and early Christian thought (Smith, 2023; Townsend, 2020).

Scholars like Michael A. Knibb (2009) and John J. Collins (1998) have contributed to the critical study of Enoch, examining its textual history, theological themes, and influence on early religious traditions. Their work highlights the complexity of the text and its multifaceted nature, inviting further exploration and debate about its role in the history of religious literature.

Contemporary Relevance and Ongoing Debates

The ongoing discussions among theologians concerning the Book of Enoch highlight its lasting significance and the intrigue it still evokes. When theologians and scholars delve into its text, they unveil fresh layers of interpretation and establish links between Enoch's age-old revelations and modern spiritual queries. This vibrant interaction between history and the current era emphasizes the enduring charm of the text and its ability to address the human experience throughout history.

In contemporary theology, Enoch is seen as a connection linking the teachings of old with the questions of today, providing perspectives that not only question and motivate but also stir contemplation. Whether regarded as a piece of history, a repository of esoteric wisdom, or a future-focused disclosure, the Book of Enoch holds a critical position in theological discourse, influencing conversations on the divine, the universe, and ethical principles.

Moving into the next section, we will explore the ways the lessons of Enoch have become part of today's theological discussions, shaping current views on scripture, spiritual matters, and the concept of divine messages. This exploration of Enoch's intricate and mysterious realm keeps shedding light on the profound insights into human comprehension and the ongoing pursuit of spiritual wisdom.

Enoch and Popular Culture

In the world of heavy metal, the dark, apocalyptic themes of Enoch find new life, while filmmakers reimagine ancient myths, drawing from its deep well of stories. The Book of Enoch serves as a bridge between the ancient and the contemporary, the sacred and the secular, inviting us to ponder the divine mysteries, the complexities of moral choice, and the ultimate fate of humanity.

The Cultural Impact of Enoch

With the cultural impact of the Book of Enoch being profound, it stretches across centuries and various forms of media, from literature and visual arts to film and popular culture. Enochian themes deeply influence modern artistic and literary expressions with their defining apocalyptic visions, angelic conflicts, and divine judgment—yet they continue to inspire and captivate. The cultural impact of the Book of Enoch is a testament to its timeless appeal and profound narrative power.

The exploration of Enoch's influence in popular culture not only highlights its historical significance but also its relevance to contemporary artistic and intellectual pursuits. As we delve further into the cultural impact of Enoch, we uncover new layers of meaning and interpretation, revealing the enduring power of this ancient text to illuminate the mysteries of the divine and the human condition.

Enoch in Modern Literature

The Book of Enoch has served as a rich source of inspiration for modern literature, providing themes and motifs that resonate with contemporary readers. The text's intricate narratives of celestial journeys and cosmic battles offer a compelling framework for novelists and poets exploring existential and metaphysical questions.

One notable example is H.P. Lovecraft (1928), who drew upon Enochian themes in his works, particularly the notion of forbidden knowledge and cosmic horror. Lovecraft's mythos, filled with ancient deities and otherworldly entities, echo the apocalyptic and supernatural elements found in Enoch. Similarly, contemporary fantasy authors often weave Enochian lore into their world-building, crafting narratives that explore the boundaries between the divine and the mortal, the known and the unknown.

Literature has long drawn from the rich well of the Book of Enoch's narratives. The text's dramatic tales of the Watchers, the Nephilim, and Enoch's celestial journeys offer a treasure trove of themes and motifs for novelists and poets alike. Writers across genres have tapped into Enochian lore to craft stories that resonate with both ancient mystery and contemporary relevance.

Modern literary works have also been directly inspired by or adapted from the Book of Enoch. Authors such as Neil Gaiman (1989–1996) and Philip Pullman (1995–2000) have incorporated Enochian themes into their novels, blending myth, religion, and fantasy to create rich, multi-layered narratives. Gaiman's "Sandman" series (1989–1996), for example, includes references to Enochian lore, exploring themes of destiny, morality, and the supernatural.

Philip Pullman's "His Dark Materials"-trilogy (1995–2000) similarly draws upon Enochian themes, particularly in its depiction of angelic beings and cosmic conflict. These modern adaptations highlight the text's versatility and ability to inspire new interpretations and stories that speak to contemporary issues and concerns.

Cinematic Interpretations

The film industry has also embraced the dramatic potential of the Book of Enoch. Darren Aronofsky's film *Noah* (2014) is a prominent example, integrating elements from Enoch, particularly the portrayal of the Watchers. These fallen angels, reimagined as giant stone creatures, play a crucial role in the narrative, helping Noah build the ark and defend against enemies. Aronofsky's creative liberties with Enochian lore sparked considerable debate and brought the ancient text into mainstream cinematic consciousness.

Other films and TV series have similarly drawn inspiration from Enochian themes, using apocalyptic visions and angelic conflicts as aids while exploring themes of morality, divine justice, and human frailty. This ongoing engagement with Enochian narratives in film highlights their timeless appeal and capacity to resonate with contemporary audiences.

Visual Arts and Symbolism

Visual artists have long been captivated by the dramatic and mystical themes of the Book of Enoch. Over the centuries, painters, illustrators, and sculptors have depicted scenes from the text, capturing its celestial visions and apocalyptic warnings. These artistic representations highlight the tension between divine order and chaos, good and evil, and the mortal and the immortal. In medieval and Renaissance art, depictions of angels and demons often drew upon the detailed descriptions found in Enoch. Artists used these themes to explore complex theological and moral questions, creating works that were both visually stunning and intellectually provocative. In contemporary art, the influence of Enoch continues, with digital artists and illustrators using modern techniques to reinterpret the text's timeless themes for a new audience.

The interactive medium of video games has also embraced Enochian mythology. Games that delve into apocalyptic themes, angelic conflicts, and quests for forbidden knowledge often draw upon the narratives found in the Book of Enoch. Titles like *Darksiders* (2010) and *Bayonetta* (2009) incorporate elements of Enochian lore, using the text's rich array of characters and themes to enhance their storytelling and gameplay mechanics. In these games, players might encounter the Watchers, engage in battles reminiscent of the cosmic struggles described in Enoch, or embark on quests to uncover hidden truths. The immersive nature of video games allows players to experience the dramatic and often harrowing world of Enochian prophecy firsthand, making the ancient text relevant in a new and dynamic context.

Enoch in Music and Performing Arts

The influence of the Book of Enoch extends significantly into music and the performing arts, particularly within genres that delve into dark, mystical, and apocalyptic themes. Metal bands frequently reference Enochian lore in their lyrics and imagery, drawing on themes of divine rebellion and cosmic warfare. The dramatic intensity and narrative depth of Enoch's texts lend themselves well to the powerful and visceral expressions found in metal music. For instance, bands like Metallica and Iron Maiden have incorporated elements of Enochian lore, especially the tales of fallen angels and apocalyptic battles, into their music to create rich, evocative experiences for their audiences.

For Metallica, while they do not directly reference the Book of Enoch in their songs, their work often explores themes of rebellion, destruction, and cosmic struggle, which are consistent with the Enochian narrative. Songs like *The Four Horsemen* (1983) and *Ride the Lightning* (1984) reflect apocalyptic themes and the battle between good and evil, resonating with the dramatic tone of the Book of Enoch.

Iron Maiden, however, has more explicit connections to Enochian themes in their lyrics. The song *The Fallen*

Angel (2000) from the album *Brave New World* references the concept of a fallen angel rising again and preparing for Armageddon, directly aligning with the themes of divine rebellion and cosmic warfare found in the Book of Enoch. Additionally, their track *2 Minutes to Midnight* (1984) from the album *Powerslave* deals with impending Armageddon, echoing the apocalyptic visions described in Enoch.

Moreover, musicians in the metal and gothic genres, in general, often reference the Book of Enoch in their works. The text's dark, apocalyptic tone and its exploration of divine rebellion resonate deeply with the aesthetic and philosophical underpinnings of these genres. Visual artists also draw inspiration from Enoch's vivid descriptions of heavenly realms and cosmic battles, resulting in paintings, illustrations, and digital art projects that reinterpret the ancient themes for modern audiences.

In the realm of performing arts, theatrical performances and dance productions have also embraced Enochian themes. These adaptations often focus on the dramatic and moral conflicts within Enoch, exploring themes of sin, redemption, and divine justice. Avant-garde theater and modern dance companies, for example, use the vivid imagery and complex characters of Enoch to create visually and emotionally compelling performances that engage contemporary audiences on multiple levels.

Overall, the Book of Enoch continues to inspire a wide range of artistic expressions, demonstrating its enduring influence and capacity to engage and resonate with creators and audiences in various artistic domains.

Analysis of Key Media Influences, Popular Media, and Enoch in Academic and Public Discourse

The profound cultural impact of the Book of Enoch is evident in its widespread influence on a variety of media forms. Through an exploration of how Enochian themes have been reimagined to suit contemporary settings in literature, film, and art, we gain insight into the lasting importance of Enoch's visions, which continue to captivate and provoke thought.

Within literature, the exploration of forbidden knowledge, divine judgment, and cosmic conflicts echoes contemporary existential and philosophical inquiries. The realm of film embraces storytelling opportunities through Enochian narratives, enabling filmmakers to delve into deep moral and spiritual dilemmas. Similarly, in the realm of visual arts, the vibrant imagery of the text serves as an artistic platform to delve into the conflicts between good and evil, as well as the dichotomy of order and chaos.

Popular forms of media frequently spark theological contemplation in viewers when they explore the Book of Enoch. Movies, literature, and video games influenced by Enochian concepts not only entertain but also initiate discussions on profound spiritual and moral inquiries. By delving into the portrayals of the Watchers, audiences are compelled to ponder themes like sin, redemption, and divine judgment, thus encouraging introspection on ethical and spiritual consequences while drawing resemblances to present-day matters of power, liberty, and accountability.

Besides serving as entertainment and art, the Book of Enoch holds significant sway over discussions in academic circles and public forums. Scholars and theologians actively delve into its content during discussions, debates, and scholarly works, emphasizing its profound historical relevance and influence on religious ideologies. With such scholarly focus, the Book of Enoch transitions from a specialized topic to a subject of more widespread cultural fascination.

The fascination with Enoch is clearly seen through the growing number of online forums, blogs, and social media conversations. These platforms serve as a space where enthusiasts and scholars come together to exchange views and understandings, nurturing a lively community dedicated to Enochian studies and fan culture. This online interaction showcases the timeless allure of the text and its knack for captivating a wide range of people on various online platforms.

The speculative allure of the Book of Enoch extends into popular media, inspiring numerous works of fiction and entertainment. Films like *Noah* (2014) and TV shows such as Kripke's *Supernatural* (2005–2020) incorporate elements from Enoch, particularly the narratives of the Watchers and Nephilim. These portrayals often blend traditional interpretations with creative liberties, resulting in engaging but sometimes controversial depictions. Darren Aronofsky's *Noah* presents the Watchers as fallen angels who assist Noah in building the ark, sparking debate about the use of apocryphal texts in mainstream entertainment. Similarly, TV shows and novels that draw on Enochian themes contribute to the text's mystique and provoke discussions about the boundaries between fiction and religious tradition.

Controversial Theories and Speculations

The Book of Enoch has always been a subject of fascination and controversy, inspiring a myriad of theories and speculations. In the modern age, this ancient text continues to stir debate among scholars, theologians, and conspiracy theorists alike. Therefore, it seems only fitting to dive deep into some of the more contentious and speculative ideas surrounding the Book of Enoch, examining the reasons behind their appeal and the implications they hold for our understanding of this enigmatic scripture.

With the wide range of interpretations it inspires, from ancient aliens and genetic manipulation to secret Masonic knowledge and modern-day prophecies, the Book of Enoch serves as a fertile ground for speculative thought and imaginative exploration. While many of these theories remain highly contentious and lack scholarly consensus, they reflect the text's profound impact on human curiosity and the quest for understanding the divine and the mysterious.

Whether viewed through the lens of scholarship, conspiracy, or creative adaptation, it is safe to say that the Book of Enoch remains a powerful and enigmatic source of inspiration.

Ancient Aliens and Enoch

One of the most popular and controversial theories associated with the Book of Enoch is the ancient astronaut hypothesis. Proponents of this theory suggest that the Watchers described in Enoch were, in fact, extraterrestrial beings who visited Earth in ancient times. This idea gained traction with the publication of Erich von Däniken's *Chariots of the Gods?* in 1968, which posited that many ancient texts, including the Book of Enoch, contain evidence of alien encounters (von Däniken, 1968).

Advocates of the ancient astronaut hypothesis emphasize the elaborate accounts of the Watchers' arrival on Earth and their engagements with humans as suggestive of highly advanced technological entities. They posit that the celestial characteristics ascribed to the Watchers might signify depictions of spacecraft and the teachings they shared with humanity, such as metallurgy and astronomy, could be viewed as technological progress instigated by visitors from beyond our planet. This concept is considered largely theoretical and frequently met with skepticism from conventional academics due to its absence of concrete evidence and dependence on pseudo-scientific explanations.

Nephilim and Genetic Manipulation

Another speculative theory revolves around the Nephilim, the offspring of the Watchers and human women. Some theorists propose that the Nephilim were the result of genetic manipulation by the Watchers. According to this view, the Watchers possessed advanced genetic knowledge, which they used to alter the human genome, creating beings with extraordinary abilities and size (Universe Unriddled, 2024).

This theory intersects with modern conspiracy narratives about secret government experiments and hidden histories. It suggests that the Nephilim's extraordinary traits were not merely mythological but were instead the product of deliberate genetic engineering. Critics of this theory argue that it stretches the interpretations of ancient texts beyond their intended meanings and lacks credible scientific support (Universe Unriddled, 2024).

The Book of Enoch and Freemasonry

The Book of Enoch has also found its way into the lore of Freemasonry, a fraternal organization with historical roots in the medieval stonemason guilds. Some Masonic traditions hold that the Book of Enoch contains secret knowledge passed down through the ages. This idea is partly based on the Masonic legend of Enoch, who is said to have discovered hidden wisdom and preserved it in two great pillars for future generations (*The Legend of Enoch*, n.d.).

Freemasons believe that these pillars contain knowledge of the divine, the cosmos, and moral truths, aligning with their own quest for enlightenment and moral improvement. This connection between Enoch and Freemasonry adds a layer of mystique and secrecy to the text, suggesting that it holds keys to ancient wisdom that have been guarded through the centuries (*The Legend of Enoch*, n.d.).

Enoch and the Apocryphal Texts

The absence of the Book of Enoch in the official Biblical canon has generated significant interest regarding its contents and intentions. There are various speculations proposing that the exclusion was a deliberate choice to suppress its contentious concepts and potential challenges to traditional teachings. Notably, the Book of Enoch contains elaborate narratives of apocalyptic revelations, portraying the actions of angels and demons, elements perceived as too unconventional or mysterious for inclusion in the Bible. Early religious scholars criticized certain views presented in Enoch's writings as heretical, especially those related to prophecies and intricate angelic structures, which diverged from mainstream Jewish and Christian doctrines (Meisfjord, 2020).

The idea frequently linked with this viewpoint is the concept that the Book of Enoch holds concealed insights concerning the cosmos, humanity's purpose, and the metaphysical struggle between good and evil. Advocates maintain that these concealed insights were possibly regarded as extremely risky or destabilizing for broad dissemination, resulting in the book being pushed to the sidelines. Additionally, the book's omission might have been affected by its imaginative features, like the Nephilim and the Watchers, which did not have support from other historical or archaeological references (Smith, 2023)

Additionally, the Book of Enoch gained popularity among the early Jewish and Christian groups yet encountered resistance because it lacked clear apostolic authorship and conflicted with established beliefs. As the biblical collection took shape, writings failing to align with strict theological standards or deemed overly imaginative were left out to ensure a cohesive and consistent body of sacred texts (Scott, 2024; Smith, 2023)

The omission of the Book of Enoch from the Bible emphasizes the intricate methods involved in establishing the canon, reflecting on the diverse theological and practical factors that determined the inclusion of certain texts.

Modern-Day Prophecies and Enoch

In contemporary religious contexts, certain groups and individuals assert that the Book of Enoch harbors prophecies that bear significance in the present era. They analyze the apocalyptic imagery within Enoch as foretellings of ongoing or impending occurrences, encompassing natural calamities, political turbulence, and worldwide disputes. Such analyses frequently link Enoch's visionary accounts with current global happenings, proposing that we are currently witnessing the prophesied era, according to Enoch.

Enoch's prophetic readings can evoke a feeling of immediacy and importance, yet many question their credibility due to the absence of thorough interpretative methods. Detractors believe that these analyses may fuel sensationalism and alarmism instead of fostering a reflective dialogue with the text.

As we look into the various interpretations and meanings attributed to the Book of Enoch in present-day religious settings, it becomes clear that the themes of apocalyptic visions and divine intervention are not exclusive to this ancient text. Similar stories and beliefs have arisen in diverse cultures and time periods, each presenting unique viewpoints on the end of the world, celestial conflicts, and humanity's role in the grand scheme of things. In the upcoming chapter, "Across Cultures and Time," we will examine these comparable stories and myths, contrasting the prophetic insights of Enoch with those from other cultural heritages. Through this comparative analysis, our goal is to discover the common threads and shared human anxieties that go beyond time and place, shedding light on how different societies have wrestled with the enigmas of the universe and the destiny of mankind.

Chapter 8:
Across Cultures and Time

In the swirling mists of antiquity, where myth and history intertwine, the Book of Enoch stands as a testament to the boundless reach of ancient human imagination. If you attempt to picture an ancient library, where every scroll and tablet is a portal to another worldview, that would be the contents of this chapter. The Book of Enoch, with its vivid tales of angels, divine judgments, and apocalyptic visions, invites us to consider its place within the broader context of global mythology and religious thought. It beckons us to explore the celestial realms of Mesopotamian deities, the heroic sagas of Greek mythology, the cosmic battles of Hindu scriptures, and the profound mysteries of Norse legends. Each tradition offers a unique lens through which we can view the Book of Enoch, revealing striking similarities and fascinating differences.

From ancient Mesopotamian narratives such as the Enuma Elish and the epic of Gilgamesh to Norse mythology's Prose Edda with its depictions of apocalyptic events, various mythologies across cultures delve into celestial conflicts and divine interactions. The Ancient Mesopotamian tales explore the intertwining of divine entities with humanity, prompting profound moral and existential inquiries. Greek mythology's Titanomachy and the tale of Prometheus echo Enoch's celestial struggles and the Watchers' transmission of forbidden wisdom. Hindu mythology's Matsya avatar draws parallels to Enoch's flood narratives, emphasizing themes of divine judgment and salvation. The Norse mythology, with its accounts of Ragnarök, the final battle of the world, reflects Enochian apocalyptic beliefs, revealing a universal mythic structure that transcends cultural confines. Egyptian mythology, rich in intricate afterlife beliefs as detailed in the Egyptian Book of the Dead, intersects with Enochian concepts of celestial realms and divine judgment.

The Book of Enoch is part of a global tradition of storytelling that seeks to explain the mysteries of existence. Its narratives echo themes found in diverse traditions, suggesting a shared human experience and a common quest for meaning. Connections between the Book of Enoch and other apocalyptic literature, such as the Book of Daniel and the Revelation of John, highlight its influence on the development of eschatological thought within the Abrahamic traditions. Global flood myths, appearing in cultures from Mesopotamia all the way to the Americas, illustrate the widespread nature of these themes. The parallels between the flood narrative in the Book of Enoch and similar stories in other cultures, like the Epic of Gilgamesh and the story of Manu in Hindu tradition, highlight universal concerns with divine retribution and the preservation of life.

This chapter conducts a detailed comparison to reveal the common themes and distinct characteristics of the Book of Enoch within the expansive realm of ancient mythology. By scrutinizing these parallels, we attain an understanding of enduring enigmas that have intrigued humanity for ages: exploring the essence of divinity, pondering the soul's journey, and contemplating the ultimate fate of the world. This scrutiny showcases the

Book of Enoch as not only a pivotal piece of apocalyptic literature but also a vital link uniting the spiritual and mythological legacies of diverse global civilizations.

Similar Myths in Different Cultures

In the vast and intricate web of ancient mythology, certain themes appear time and time again, echoing through different cultures and eras. The Book of Enoch finds parallels in the myths and legends of numerous civilizations. In weaving together these diverse narratives, we see how the Book of Enoch is part of a global tradition of storytelling that seeks to explain the mysteries of existence. The similarities and differences among these ancient texts reveal a shared human experience and a common quest for understanding the cosmos, the divine, and our place within it.

Mesopotamian Civilization

Ancient Mesopotamian texts like the Epic of Gilgamesh and the Enuma Elish share striking parallels with the themes in the Book of Enoch. These narratives delve into interactions between the divine and humans, celestial voyages, myths of creation, and the pursuit of timeless wisdom, reflecting the intricate tales woven within the Enochian text. By looking into these resemblances, a comprehension of the timeless themes threading through ancient mythologies emerges, highlighting the intricate blend of cultural and spiritual elements in early civilizations.

The common themes of divine-human interactions, celestial quests, apocalyptic imagery, and the pursuit of eternal knowledge link the Epic of Gilgamesh and the Enuma Elish with the Book of Enoch. These parallels highlight humanity's enduring intrigue with the divine, the quest for immortality, and the cosmic battle between order and chaos. The quests for eternal life by Gilgamesh and Enoch's heavenly journeys both accentuate the thirst for knowledge and the boundaries set by the divine. Depicting the world's creation through godly conflicts, the Enuma Elish mirrors the celestial strife in Enoch's visions. The various interactions among divine beings emphasize a universal fascination with the origins and structure of the universe, influenced by divine will and conflict (*The Enumah Elish*, n.d.; Kynes, 2023; Wright, 2019).

By exploring these parallels, we position the Book of Enoch within the broader framework of ancient myths, revealing the timeless nature of these themes and their lasting relevance in understanding the mysteries of existence.

The Epic of Gilgamesh

The Epic of Gilgamesh, an ancient Sumerian literary masterpiece, tells the story of Gilgamesh, who is the respected ruler of Uruk. This epic examines themes such as mortality, companionship, and the desire for immortality, akin to the celestial aspects in the Book of

Enoch. Gilgamesh's quest to find the immortal survivor of a great flood, Utnapishtim, parallels Enoch's heavenly travels in search of divine wisdom. Utnapishtim, similar to Noah in biblical stories, is forewarned about a flood and builds a huge ark to save his family and creatures, thus reflecting Enoch's tale. This connection emphasizes the exchanges between the divine and mortal, focusing on the transmission of crucial knowledge for human existence (*The Enumah Elish*, n.d.; Wright, 2019).

In both writings, the theme of connections between humans and divine beings is explored. The Book of Enoch tells the tale of the Watchers descending to Earth and interacting with humans by sharing forbidden knowledge, which, by extension, leads to their downfall. Similarly, in the Epic of Gilgamesh, gods influence human events and the fates of individuals, highlighting the intertwining of heavenly and earthly realms, a common theme in ancient mythologies (Kynes, 2023; Wright, 2019).

In both the Epic of Gilgamesh and the Book of Enoch, a significant idea is the concept of a massive flood as punishment from the divine. The flood story is used to purify the world of its corrupt residents, representing a reset of the moral balance orchestrated by a higher power. This shared theme indicates a wider belief that floods are tools of divine judgment and rebirth. Additionally, the Epic of Gilgamesh explores the pursuit of eternal life and the eventual acknowledgment of mortality, while Enoch's tale delves into seeking celestial wisdom and embracing one's place in a spiritual hierarchy. Both characters experience profound changes through their encounters with divine beings, showcasing the transformative influence of divine insight and the eternal human pursuit of knowledge (*The Enumah Elish*, n.d.; Wright, 2019).

Enuma Elish

The Enuma Elish, the Babylonian creation myth, provides another rich comparison to the Book of Enoch. The text describes the creation of the world through a series of divine battles; it primarily focuses on the conflict between the god Marduk and the primordial chaos represented by Tiamat. The themes of divine conflict and creation in the Enuma Elish mirror the celestial battles and the establishment of order in the Book of Enoch.

In the Enuma Elish, when Marduk defeated Tiamat and then shaped the world from her remains, it was seen as a triumph of order prevailing over chaos. This story resembles the clashes between the angels who rebelled and those who remained faithful in the visions of Enoch. The struggles between the divine entities in these plots emphasize the eternal battle between order and chaos, a prevalent theme in ancient myths. The creation story in the Enuma Elish depicts complex relationships among the gods, each having specific roles and powers. Similarly, the Book of Enoch elaborates on the duties and impacts of different angels on the human world. The organized hierarchy of the divine beings in these texts portrays a universe where the divine realm is meticulously structured and significantly intertwined with the destiny of mankind (Klamm, n.d.; Christian Ministries International, n.d.).

The Enuma Elish also touches upon the ideas of punishment and reward from divine beings, where the gods give out fairness based on faithfulness or defiance. Similarly, in the Book of Enoch, the Watchers experience harsh outcomes for going against divine rules, focusing on the idea of fair judgment by divine forces. These concepts highlight a common belief in a moral system that is upheld by higher entities. Additionally, both texts stress the significance of divine wisdom and its passing down to humans. In the Enuma Elish, Marduk organizing the world reflects the sharing of divine knowledge, and in contrast, in the Book of Enoch, when the Watchers share forbidden wisdom, it brings both enlightenment and disorder, showcasing the double-sided aspect of divine insight (*The Enumah Elish*, n.d.; Klamm, n.d.; Wright, 2019).

Greek Mythology

Studying Greek myths like the Titanomachy and the story of Prometheus shows many similarities in themes with the tales in the Book of Enoch. Both Greek myths and Enoch explore themes of rebellion against the divine, sharing forbidden knowledge, and dealing with the outcomes of these actions. This illustrates how ancient societies pondered comparable existential and spiritual inquiries.

The Titanomachy, an epic battle between the Olympian gods and the Titans, reflects the cosmic battles detailed in Enoch. It highlights the quest for divine power and the creation of universal harmony. Likewise, the tale of Prometheus, who resisted Zeus to give fire and wisdom to mankind, mirrors the account of the Watchers in Enoch. Both Prometheus and the Watchers challenge the divine rule, share hidden knowledge with people, and endure harsh consequences (Kapach, 2023; Panovski, 2023; Wagner, 2019).

These Greek myths provide valuable insights into the universal themes of divine rebellion and forbidden knowledge found in the Book of Enoch. By comparing these stories, we gain a deeper appreciation for the shared human concerns and the enduring relevance of these themes across different cultures and times.

The Titanomachy

The Titanomachy, also known as the Battle of the Titans, is a fundamental tale in Greek mythology. It recounts the grand conflict between the Titans, led by Cronus, and the Olympian gods, led by Zeus. This story symbolizes a shift from an older system to a new divine rule. It draws parallels to a story in the Book of Enoch, where divine beings, called the Watchers, disobey God and face consequences. The Titanomachy commences with Cronus, who, anxious about a prophecy predicting his downfall by one of his offspring, eats each newborn. Yet, his wife, Rhea, rescues the youngest, Zeus, who matures and challenges Cronus and the Titans. Following an intense battle, Zeus and the Olympian deities triumph, sending the Titans to Tartarus. This tale reflects on themes of insurrection and divine justice, akin to those seen in the Book of Enoch (English Plus, 2024; *Titanomachy*, 2020; Panovski, 2023).

The parallel between the Book of Enoch and the tale of the Watchers is striking, for both the Titans in Greek mythology and the Watchers are powerful beings who rebel against a higher divine authority and suffer dire consequences for their transgressions. The battle between the Titans and the Olympians can be seen as a cosmic struggle between chaos and order, much like the conflict between the Watchers and the forces of divine retribution. In both narratives, the triumph of the newer divine order (the Olympians and the angels loyal to God) over the older, rebellious entities (the Titans and the Watchers) symbolizes the restoration of cosmic balance and divine justice. In addition, both myths focus on family disagreements and betrayal. Cronus eating his children to avoid being overthrown is similar to the Watchers going against their original goal, leading to their punishment (English Plus, 2024; *Titanomachy*, 2020; Panovski, 2023).

Both of these stories demonstrate how excessive pride can lead to serious consequences, putting emphasis on the looming prospect of divine punishment for those who overstep their boundaries.

Prometheus

The story of Prometheus, the Titan who defied Zeus to bring fire to humanity, bears striking thematic resemblances to the Watchers' imparting of forbidden knowledge to humans in the Book of Enoch. Prometheus's actions and the resulting punishment underscore the tension between divine authority and the quest for knowledge, a theme central to both myths.

Prometheus, named for his ability to think ahead as his name means "forethought," is shown as a strong supporter of humankind. He defies Zeus by taking fire from the gods and sharing it with humans, symbolizing the growth and strengthening of humanity. As a consequence of his rebellion, Prometheus faces never-ending suffering, imprisoned on a rock where his liver is eaten daily by an eagle, only to regenerate every night (Atsma, 2017; Cartwright, 2013).

This story shows obvious similarities with the tale of the Watchers in the Book of Enoch, as they also face severe consequences for challenging God's authority. Sharing forbidden knowledge with humanity, whether it's Prometheus or the Watchers, highlights how enlightenment can have both positive and dangerous outcomes when one rebels against divine rule. The retribution faced by Prometheus and the Watchers accentuates the overarching theme of divine justice and the consequences of hubris. The eternal torment of Prometheus and the confinement of the Watchers deep within the Earth stand as potent reminders of the constraints set by the divine order and the fallout of crossing those boundaries (Cartwright, 2013; Universe Unriddled, 2024).

Additionally, both stories highlight how knowledge can bring about great change. In Greek myths, fire symbolizes more than just heat and light—it also signifies the birth of civilization and intellectual growth. Similarly, the wisdom shared by the Watchers results in important progress for humanity, although it comes with a price of moral decay and divine disapproval. These tales show us that knowledge can be a double-edged sword, offering power while also posing a risk of leading to ruin.

Comparative Analysis

The Clash of the Titans and the Tale of Prometheus provide valuable comparative frameworks for exploring the themes of rebellion, retribution, and the pursuit of wisdom in the Book of Enoch. These Greek myths and Enochian accounts examine the intricate dynamics between divine entities and humanity, shedding light on the complexities of order versus chaos, authority versus rebellion, and the pursuit of knowledge versus the allure of corruption.

In both the Titanomachy and the Book of Enoch, those divine beings who challenge the established order suffer grave repercussions, emphasizing the inevitable hand of divine justice. These myths mirror a widespread cultural fascination with the demarcations between divine and mortal domains and the repercussions of transgressing those bounds.

The tale of Prometheus highlights the transformative force of forbidden knowledge, echoing the narrative of the Watchers found in the Book of Enoch. These myths vividly portray the two-sided nature of enlightenment, offering cautionary insights into the pitfalls of unchecked ambition.

Hindu Scriptures

The ancient Hindu scriptures, particularly the Bhagavata Purana and the Mahabharata, present narratives rich in divine intervention, cosmic order, and moral dilemmas, themes that closely resonate with those found in the Book of Enoch. By examining these texts, we can draw compelling parallels between the apocalyptic and interventionist themes of Enoch and the stories of divine avatars and epic battles in Hindu mythology.

The stories found in the Bhagavata Purana and the Mahabharata give a deep understanding of divine involvement, ethical challenges, and apocalyptic views, which also appear in the Book of Enoch. Exploring these

Hindu texts allows us to acknowledge the common mythological elements that go beyond cultures and mirror widespread worries regarding the divine, ethics, and the universe's harmony (*Bhagavata Purana*, n.d.; *Read Mahabharata in English*, n.d.).

In Hindu mythology, the avatars of Vishnu, particularly the Matsya avatar, provide compelling parallels to the flood narratives found in the Book of Enoch. Matsya, the great fish who saves humanity and sacred texts from a cosmic deluge, mirrors the preservation themes in Enoch's apocalyptic visions. Within this plot, the focus is on how divine beings intervene in human matters to protect knowledge and life. The tale of Matsya appears in numerous old writings, such as the *Bhagavata Purana* and the *Matsya Purana*. These ancient texts recount how Matsya forewarns Manu, the first man, about a looming catastrophic flood, guiding him to construct a vessel for his rescue, along with various wise individuals and every type of vegetation and creature. This act of safeguarding knowledge and life closely mirrors the flood story in the Book of Enoch, underscoring the essential role of divine assistance in safeguarding existence (*Matsya Avatar Story*, n.d.; Mythic Whispers, 2023; Iqbal, 2023).

The Bhagavata Purana

The Bhagavata Purana, one of the major Puranic texts of Hinduism, is renowned for its elaborate narratives about the god Vishnu, who descends to Earth in various avatars, or so-called incarnations, to restore cosmic order and protects the moral law, dharma (*Bhagavata Purana*, n.d.; *Read Mahabharata in English*, n.d.). These stories of divine intervention are closely similar to the apocalyptic themes in the Book of Enoch, where celestial beings descend to Earth, although often with more catastrophic consequences. In the Bhagavata Purana, Vishnu incarnates in numerous forms, including the fish (Matsya), the turtle (Kurma), the boar (Varaha), and the lion-man (Narasimha), each time to save the world from impending doom or to vanquish evil. The Matsya Avatar, for instance, involves Vishnu saving the sacred Vedas from a great flood, a narrative that echoes the flood myth and divine intervention found in many ancient cultures, including the story of Noah's Ark in the Judeo-Christian tradition and the global flood myths linked to Enoch (*Matsya Avatar Story*, n.d.; Mythic Whispers, 2023).

The apocalyptic and interventionist themes in the Book of Enoch, particularly the descent of the Watchers and their impact on humanity, bear a thematic resemblance to Vishnu's avatars. While the Watchers' descent leads to moral corruption and divine retribution, Vishnu's avatars are aimed at restoring balance and righteousness. Both narratives, however, highlight the profound impact of divine beings interacting with the mortal realm, leading to significant cosmic and moral consequences (*Matsya Avatar Story*, n.d.; Mythic Whispers, 2023).

The Bhagavata Purana's focus on dharma and the preservation of cosmic order (*Bhagavata Purana*, n.d.; *Read Mahabharata in English*, n.d.) parallels the ethical and moral dimensions found in the Book of Enoch. Enoch's visions often involve divine judgment and the eventual restoration of order, reflecting a similar concern for maintaining the balance between good and evil. These texts highlight the universal theme of divine intervention as a means to rectify moral and cosmic imbalances, a concept central to many religious traditions.

Mahabharata

The Mahabharata, one of the greatest epic narratives in Hindu literature, encompasses a wide array of themes, including divine intervention, moral dilemmas, and epic battles (*Read Mahabharata in English*, n.d.; *Bhagavata Purana*, n.d.), which resonate strongly with the narratives in the Book of Enoch. The ancient tale penned by the wise Vyasa illustrates the intricate dynamics between deities and mortals, much like the exchanges between the Watchers and mankind as documented in the Book of Enoch.

One of the central stories of the Mahabharata is the Kurukshetra War, a cataclysmic battle between the Pandavas and the Kauravas, which involves numerous divine interventions. The Bhagavad Gita, a part of the Mahabharata, features a profound discourse between Prince Arjuna and the god Krishna, who serves as his charioteer. Krishna, an incarnation of Vishnu, reveals divine wisdom and guidance to Arjuna, addressing deep ethical and philosophical dilemmas (*Matsya Avatar Story*, n.d.; Mythic Whispers, 2023).

The themes of divine guidance and moral struggle in the Mahabharata can be compared to the Book of Enoch's emphasis on divine revelations and ethical teachings. Enoch receives visions and guidance from God, which he then imparts to humanity, similar to how Krishna imparts divine knowledge to Arjuna. Both texts explore the complexities of moral choices and the consequences of actions, emphasizing the role of divine wisdom in navigating these dilemmas (*Bhagavata Purana*, n.d.; *Read Mahabharata in English*, n.d.).

Spectacular battles and divine actions in the Mahabharata closely resemble the cosmic clashes and divine actions in the Book of Enoch. The descent of the Watchers and the resulting disorder they cause are similar to the clashes between gods and demons in the Mahabharata, as they compete for dominance, greatly affecting the human world (*Matsya Avatar Story*, n.d.; Mythic Whispers, 2023).

The Mahabharata's exploration of dharma and adharma, meaning unrighteousness (*Read Mahabharata in English*, n.d.; *Bhagavata Purana*, n.d.), parallels the moral oppositions present in the Book of Enoch. Both texts depict a world where the struggle between good and evil plays out on a cosmic scale, with divine beings influencing the outcomes. This emphasis on moral and ethical struggles underscores the universal concerns of ancient cultures regarding the nature of justice and the role of divine intervention.

Comparative Analysis

When we look at the Bhagavata Purana and the Mahabharata alongside the Book of Enoch, we see that despite coming from different cultures and religions, these old texts have similar ideas about gods getting involved in human affairs, people facing tough moral choices and predicting disastrous future events. These stories show how humans are intrigued by the divine's role in our world.

In the Bhagavata Purana, Vishnu's avatars act as divine interventions to bring back balance to the universe. This concept ties in with the apocalyptic prophecies found in Enoch, where celestial beings come down to impact human affairs. Likewise, the Mahabharata's portrayal of divine direction and grand battles reflects the cosmic conflicts and ethical lessons seen in Enoch.

The similarities between mythological themes across various cultures show how people all over the world have explored similar deep questions through their stories. By comparing the narratives in these texts, we can gain a deeper understanding of what makes the Book of Enoch distinctive within the context of ancient literature as a whole.

Norse Mythology

Norse mythology, encapsulated in the Prose Edda, presents a fascinating blend of tales about how the world began, epic battles, and important life lessons that echo similar themes in the Book of Enoch. Written by Snorri Sturluson, an Icelandic scholar in the 13th century, the Prose Edda is a key source that sheds light on the myths of the Norse gods. Within these stories, readers uncover the origins of the world, the intriguing dynamics between deities and giants, and the cyclical cycle of destruction and renewal during Ragnarok, mirroring the dramatic divine clashes and end-times prophecies of the Book of Enoch.

Norse mythology, with its rich cosmology and apocalyptic prophecies, provides another fascinating parallel. The Prose Edda's tales of Ragnarök (Summerville, 2022), the end-of-the-world battle, share striking similarities with Enochian apocalypticism. The themes of cosmic renewal and the struggle between good and evil are prevalent in both traditions, highlighting a shared mythic structure that transcends cultural boundaries.

The Norse myth of Yggdrasil, the world tree that connects the Heavens, Earth, and underworld (*Yggdrasil*, n.d.), parallels the cosmological visions in the Book of Enoch. Both texts depict a universe intricately connected by divine realms and governed by the actions of celestial beings.

The Prose Edda and the Book of Enoch offer rich, overlapping themes of creation, divine interaction, and apocalyptic visions. Through the lens of Norse mythology, we can appreciate the broader context in which the Book of Enoch exists, recognizing the shared motifs that pervade ancient mythological and religious literature. These narratives not only reflect the concerns and values of their respective cultures but also contribute to a universal mythological heritage that continues to captivate and inspire.

Creation and Cosmic Order

The Prose Edda begins with the story of the world's creation, where the primordial void, Ginnungagap, gives birth to the first beings: Ymir, the giant, and Audhumla, the cow. From Ymir's body, the gods Odin, Vili, and Vé create the world (Summerville, 2022; *Yggdrasil*, n.d.). This creation myth sets the stage for a universe governed by a delicate balance of order and chaos, a theme that resonates with the cosmological framework in the Book of Enoch.

In the Book of Enoch, the cosmos is meticulously structured, with heavenly realms inhabited by angels and earthly domains populated by humans. Enoch's visions often depict a universe where divine beings influence earthly affairs, reflecting a cosmic order similar to that in Norse mythology. Both texts underscore the importance of maintaining balance within the universe, with divine beings playing crucial roles in preserving or disrupting this order.

The Prose Edda is replete with stories of gods and giants interacting, often resulting in conflict and strife. The gods, such as Odin, Thor, and Loki, engage with giants in battles that shape the fate of the world (Summerville, 2022; *Yggdrasil*, n.d.). These interactions mirror the narratives in the Book of Enoch, where the Watchers, a group of fallen angels, descend to Earth, interact with humans, and ultimately cause chaos.

One striking parallel is the story of the Watchers teaching forbidden knowledge to humans, leading to moral corruption and divine retribution. This narrative echoes the myth of Prometheus in Greek mythology, who defies Zeus to bring fire to humanity, and the actions of Loki in Norse mythology. Loki, often depicted as a trickster and a disruptor of order (Summerville, 2022; *Yggdrasil*, n.d.), parallels the Watchers in his role as a bringer of chaos. Both Loki and the Watchers challenge the divine order, resulting in significant consequences for both divine and human realms.

Apocalyptic Visions: Ragnarok and the End of Days

Ragnarok, the Norse apocalypse, is a central theme in the Prose Edda, depicting a cataclysmic battle between gods and giants that leads to the world's destruction and subsequent rebirth. This narrative shares several thematic elements with the apocalyptic visions in the Book of Enoch, where cosmic battles between good and evil forces culminate in divine judgment and the establishment of a new world order.

In the Prose Edda, Ragnarok involves a series of foreboding events, such as the death of Balder, the binding and eventual escape of Loki, and the arrival of the giant Surt with his flaming sword. These events lead to a final, devastating battle, resulting in the deaths of many gods, including Odin and Thor, and the submersion of the world in water. However, from this destruction emerges a new, purified world, symbolizing renewal and hope (Arqadic, 2024; Editors of Encyclopaedia Britannica, 2023; *Ragnarök*, 2023).

The Book of Enoch similarly envisions a final judgment in which the wicked are punished, and the righteous are rewarded. Enoch's apocalyptic visions include the binding of evil spirits, the cleansing of the Earth, and the establishment of a new, harmonious world under divine rule. Both texts emphasize the cyclical nature of creation, destruction, and rebirth, reflecting ancient beliefs in the inevitability of cosmic renewal.

Comparative Analysis

The Prose Edda and the Book of Enoch share important teachings through their stories about gods and catastrophic events. In Norse myths, tales of deities and giants frequently emphasize bravery, faithfulness, and the certainty of destiny. The behaviors of the divine beings, especially during Ragnarok, highlight the significance of valor and selflessness as they bravely face their future with dignity.

The Book of Enoch highlights ideas of fairness and doing the right thing. It tells a story about the Watchers who fell from grace and faced punishment for disobeying divine rules. Enoch's visions stress the significance of being good and following divine laws, echoing the moral values found in Norse mythology.

When comparing the Prose Edda to the Book of Enoch, several thematic parallels emerge, despite the cultural and temporal differences between these texts. In both stories, gods connect with humans, causing important impacts on the universe and morality. Both texts portray apocalyptic scenarios with epic clashes between good and evil, resulting in the world's end and rebirth.

These parallels highlight the universal nature of certain mythological themes and the shared human fascination with the divine, the moral order, and the fate of the world. By examining the Prose Edda alongside the Book of Enoch, we gain a deeper understanding of how different cultures have addressed similar existential questions through their mythological narratives.

Egyptian Mythology

The ancient Egyptian "Book of the Dead" is a compilation of spells and rituals intended to guide the deceased through the afterlife. This funerary text, often written on papyrus and placed in tombs, includes various spells designed to protect and assist the deceased on their journey through the afterlife, ensuring they safely navigate the challenges they might encounter. The spells serve multiple purposes, such as defending against evil spirits, enabling the deceased to overcome obstacles, and ensuring they are judged favorably by the gods (*Book of the Dead*, n.d.; *Egyptian Book of the Dead*, n.d.).

The Book of the Dead is particularly renowned for its detailed portrayal of the journey through the underworld and the judgment of souls, themes that parallel the Book of Enoch. Both texts emphasize the role of divine judgment and the journey through heavenly realms, reflecting similar concerns about morality and the afterlife in their respective cultures. This comparison highlights the shared motifs across ancient mythologies and religious texts, demonstrating a universal human endeavor to understand and navigate the mysteries of existence (Jarus, 2022; *Egyptian Book of the Dead*, n.d.).

The narrative of Osiris, the god of the afterlife who is resurrected and judges the dead (Macquire, 2021), parallels the eschatological themes in the Book of Enoch. Both traditions emphasize the cyclical nature of life and death, the importance of moral conduct, and the promise of divine judgment.

The Journey Through the Afterlife

The Book of the Dead is an ancient Egyptian funerary text consisting of spells, charms, and incantations designed to help the deceased navigate the afterlife and reach the Field of Reeds, an eternal paradise. The text dates back to the New Kingdom (circa 1550–1070 BCE) but draws on earlier traditions from the Pyramid Texts and Coffin Texts. It was intended to protect and empower the soul (ba) and the spirit (ka) during their perilous journey (Mark, 2016; *Book of the Dead*, n.d.).

Similarly, the Book of Enoch, particularly in the sections known as the Astronomical Book and the Book of the Heavenly Luminaries, describes Enoch's journeys through different realms of the cosmos, guided by angelic beings. Enoch's ascensions provide a vision of the heavenly order and the places of judgment reserved for the righteous and the wicked. These visionary journeys emphasize the moral and cosmological order upheld by divine beings, echoing the protective and guiding functions of the Book of the Dead (Nickelsburg, n.d.; Universe Unriddled, 2022).

Central to both texts is the concept of divine judgment. In the Book of the Dead, the deceased undergoes the Weighing of the Heart ceremony before the god Osiris and a tribunal of 42 judges. The heart of the deceased is weighed against the feather of Ma'at, the goddess of truth and justice. A heart heavy with sin is devoured by Ammit, the soul-eating monster, condemning the individual to oblivion. Conversely, a heart that balances with Ma'at allows the soul to enter the eternal Field of Reeds (*The Underworld and the Afterlife in Ancient Egypt*, 2023; Mark, 2016).

The Book of Enoch similarly focuses on divine judgment, where angels, including the Watchers, are judged for their transgressions, and humanity is judged for its righteousness or wickedness. Both the Book of the Dead and the Book of Enoch highlight interactions between divine beings and mortals. In the Book of the Dead, various deities assist the deceased in navigating the afterlife, including Anubis, who oversees the embalming process and guides souls to the afterlife, and Thoth, who records the outcomes of the Weighing of the Heart. These deities play essential roles in ensuring that the deceased receives the proper rites and passes through the trials of the afterlife (*Book of the Dead*, n.d.; Mark, 2016). Similarly, the Watchers in the Book of Enoch descend to Earth and corrupt humanity with forbidden knowledge, resulting in divine punishment. The Nephilim, offspring of the fallen angels, exemplify the consequences of divine interference with human affairs. This is a theme that resonates with the protective and guiding roles of the gods in the Book of the Dead.

The Book of the Dead and the Book of Enoch also share apocalyptic and cosmological themes. The Book of the Dead includes spells that address the creation and destruction of the world, emphasizing the cyclical nature of existence and the ongoing struggle between order and chaos. For example, Spell 17 recounts the creation of the world by the god Atum and describes the threats posed by chaotic forces that must be overcome to maintain cosmic order (*Book of the Dead*, n.d.; Mark, 2016).

The Book of Enoch also contains apocalyptic visions that depict the ultimate triumph of good over evil. Enoch's prophecies foretell the coming of a new age, where the righteous are rewarded, and the wicked face eternal punishment. The text's detailed accounts of battles between angels and demons emphasize the constant effort to maintain divine justice and order in the universe.

Comparative Analysis

When we look at the Book of the Dead alongside the Book of Enoch, we can notice some similar themes. These texts focus on the passage through mystical worlds, led by heavenly figures, and stress the significant part played by divine judgment in deciding the destiny of spirits. They also shed light on the connections between divine and human domains, the necessity of upholding ethical and universal harmony, and the apocalyptic prophecies envisioning the final victory of righteousness over wickedness.

Still, these texts have unique features influenced by their cultural backgrounds. The Book of the Dead is deeply connected to Egyptian beliefs in the afterlife and the significance of funeral practices, showcasing a culture with a strong focus on death and the rituals associated with the afterlife. On the other hand, the Book of Enoch presents a Jewish perspective centered on apocalyptic themes, highlighting concepts like divine judgment, celestial conflicts, and the eventual salvation of the righteous. This aligns with prevalent ideas in Jewish teachings about the end times.

Connections With Other Apocalyptic Literature

The Book of Enoch is a captivating and mysterious piece that has fascinated scholars, theologians, and everyday readers for many years. Its vivid visions of the end times, intricate views of the universe, and moral teachings make it stand out among other ancient texts. Enoch's visions are not unique occurrences; they share common themes with various apocalyptic texts, especially those from the Jewish tradition, like the Book of Daniel. In this part, we will examine the similarities between Enoch's visions and other apocalyptic writings, revealing how these links enrich our knowledge of ancient beliefs about the end of the world.

The stories of great floods found in different cultures around the world, from Mesopotamia to the Americas, show how these themes are widespread. Comparing the flood story in the Book of Enoch to similar tales in other cultures, like the Epic of Gilgamesh and the tale of Manu in Hindu beliefs, highlights how humans across the globe share a common interest in divine punishment and the survival of life.

The Book of Enoch stands as a significant work within the genre of apocalyptic literature, offering profound insights into divine judgment, cosmology, and hopeful views of the end times. Its connections with other apocalyptic texts, such as the Book of Daniel, highlight common themes and motifs found in ancient Jewish and Christian beliefs. Exploring these similarities gives us a better understanding of the shared interests and dreams that influenced these visionary writings. The Book of Enoch still holds significance in the wider scope of apocalyptic literature, offering timeless thoughts on the eternal battle between good and evil, the mysteries of the cosmos, and the eventual triumph of the righteous.

The Book of Daniel

The Book of Enoch shares many themes with other apocalyptic literature such as the Book of Daniel and the Revelation of John. These texts include divine revelations, cosmic battles, and prophetic visions of the end times. The influence of Enoch is evident in these later works, highlighting its foundational role in shaping apocalyptic literature.

The Book of Daniel, written during the Maccabean revolt (circa 167–164 BCE), offers visions revealing divine secrets about the end times, the fate of the righteous and the wicked, and the triumph of God's kingdom. Both Enoch and Daniel emerged during periods of significant upheaval, reflecting the existential anxieties and hopes of their communities. Notably, both texts use visionary journeys to convey divine knowledge (Nickelsburg & VanderKam, 2004).

In the Book of Enoch, Enoch is taken up by angels to witness the workings of the heavens, the places of judgment, and the fate of souls, detailed in the Astronomical Book and the Book of the Heavenly Luminaries. Similarly, Daniel's visions reveal the future of earthly kingdoms and the ultimate establishment of God's dominion. For example, Daniel 7 describes a vision of four great beasts representing successive empires, culminating in divine judgment and the establishment of an everlasting kingdom (Collins, 1998; *NIV*, 2011, Daniel 7:9-14) (Nickelsburg & VanderKam, 2004).

Both Enoch and Daniel use rich apocalyptic imagery and symbolism. Enoch's visions include scenes of cosmic upheaval, such as stars falling and mountains melting (Draper, 1882, Enoch 1:6-9). Similarly, Daniel's visions are laden with symbolic imagery, like the ram and the goat in Daniel 8, representing the Medo-Persian and Greek empires, respectively. Such symbolism conveys complex historical and theological truths and underscores the inevitability of divine justice (Collins, 1998).

Central to both texts is the theme of divine judgment and redemption. In Enoch, the Watchers—fallen angels who taught forbidden knowledge—are severely judged, and the earth is purified through a deluge. This emphasizes the moral order upheld by divine beings and the vindication of the righteous (Draper, 1882, Enoch 10:12-16). Similarly, Daniel emphasizes divine judgment and redemption, with scenes like the Ancient of Days judging the beasts (Collins, 1998; *NIV*, 2011, Daniel 7:9-10; Nickelsburg & VanderKam, 2004).

Both texts depict cosmic battles between good and evil. In Enoch, archangels like Michael and Gabriel lead the fight against the Watchers, symbolizing the triumph of divine order over chaos. Daniel describes angelic warfare involving Michael, reflecting the earthly struggles of the Jewish people and assuring divine intervention (Collins, 1998; *NIV*, 2011, Daniel 10-12; Nickelsburg & VanderKam, 2004).

Comparative Analysis With Other Apocalyptic Literature

The Book of Enoch and the Book of Daniel are not alone in their apocalyptic themes. Similar motifs can be found in other ancient texts, such as the Book of Revelation in the New Testament and the Sibylline Oracles, a collection of prophetic writings attributed to the Sibyls. These texts, like Enoch and Daniel, are characterized by visionary journeys, symbolic imagery, and themes of divine judgment and redemption.

The Book of Revelation

The Book of Revelation, penned by John of Patmos, mirrors themes found in Enoch and Daniel. John describes cosmic chaos, battles involving angels, and God's triumph. The visuals of falling stars (*NIV*, 2011, Revelation 6:13) and Satan being confined in a deep pit (*NIV*, 2011, Revelation 20:1-3) reflect Enoch's celestial turmoil and punishment of defiant angels. Similar to the messages of Enoch and Daniel, Revelation conveys hope and assurance to the faithful (Swindoll, n.d.).

The Sibylline Oracles

The ancient Sibylline Oracles talk about the end of times and predictions about the future. These writings, created over many years, make predictions about God's judgment, massive disasters, and the beginning of a peaceful era. The Oracles focus on good behavior and punishment from the gods, similar to the teachings in Enoch. By using symbols and visions, these texts are linked to the wider tradition of apocalyptic literature (Editors of Encyclopaedia Britannica, 2021).

Enoch and Global Flood Myths

The theme of a great flood as divine judgment and a means of renewal is a powerful and pervasive motif found in many ancient cultures. We have already touched base on this concept in previous chapters; however, in regard to other cultures, it deserves a wee mention. The Book of Enoch presents a compelling narrative of a flood sent by God to purge the Earth of the wickedness introduced by the fallen Watchers and their offspring, the Nephilim. This tale of cataclysm and salvation echoes through various flood myths across the world, notably in the Mesopotamian Epic of Gilgamesh and the Hindu story of the Matsya Avatar in the Bhagavata Purana, both of which have been previously mentioned. However, for the sake of the analysis, they have both been included in this section for by examining these stories a bit more in-depth, we can draw fascinating parallels that illuminate the shared human experience of contemplating divine justice and cosmic renewal, and therefore, it deserves a place in this chapter.

The Gilgamesh Epic

The Epic of Gilgamesh, an ancient Sumerian text, is one of the earliest known literary works, and it contains a flood narrative that shares striking similarities with the flood story in the Book of Enoch. In the epic, the hero Gilgamesh embarks on a quest for eternal life and encounters Utnapishtim, a character who, like Noah in the Bible and figures in Enoch, survives a great flood sent by the gods to destroy humanity. Utnapishtim tells Gilgamesh about the divine warning he received, the boat he built to save his family and animals, and the eventual resting of the vessel on a mountain after the waters receded (*The Enumah Elish*, n.d.; Kynes, 2023; Wright, 2019).

Both the Epic of Gilgamesh and the Book of Enoch portray the flood as an act of divine judgment. In Enoch, the flood is decreed by God to cleanse the Earth of the corruption brought about by the Watchers and their progeny (Draper, 1882, Enoch 10:1-11). Similarly, in the Epic of Gilgamesh, the gods decide to send a flood to wipe out humanity due to its transgressions, although the exact reasons vary slightly between different versions of the epic.

The motif of a select few being forewarned and saved is central to both narratives. Utnapishtim, like Noah, receives instructions from the gods to build a vessel and preserve life. This aspect underscores the theme of divine mercy intertwined with judgment, reflecting the idea that while divine justice is inevitable, so is the possibility of salvation for the righteous.

After the floodwaters recede in both narratives, there is a sense of renewal and a fresh start for humanity. In Enoch, the flood marks the end of the era of the Watchers' dominion and the beginning of a new, purified world. Utnapishtim's tale similarly concludes with a new beginning, as the flood's survivors go on to repopulate the Earth. This theme of renewal emphasizes the cyclical nature of destruction and rebirth, a concept deeply embedded in many ancient mythologies.

Hindu Mythology: The Matsya Avatar

In Hindu mythology, the story of the Matsya Avatar of Vishnu presents another fascinating parallel to Enoch's flood narrative. In this tale, Lord Vishnu takes the form of a fish (Matsya) to save Manu, the progenitor of humans, from an impending deluge. Matsya warns Manu about the flood, instructs him to build a boat, and guides the vessel during the flood, ensuring the preservation of seeds, plants, and animals to regenerate life (*Matsya Avatar story*, 2023; Mythic Whispers, 2023).

In the story of Matsya, similar to the Enochian flood tale, there's a divine warning involved. Vishnu takes on the form of Matsya and visits Manu to alert him about the impending flood. He provides Manu with thorough guidance on how to get ready and what to safeguard. This special divine help emphasizes the gods' care for sustaining life and harmony, even as they deliver verdicts.

In both stories, the emphasis on preserving life—seeds, plants, animals, and humans—accentuates a broader theme of continuity and regeneration. The flood serves not just as a punishment but as a means to cleanse and renew the world, ensuring that life can begin anew in a purified state.

The ethical implications of divine intervention are significant in both narratives. In the Book of Enoch, the flood is a response to the moral corruption brought by the Watchers, whose teachings of forbidden knowledge

244

lead humanity astray (Draper, 1882, Enoch 7:1-6). The flood is thus a means to restore moral order. In the Hindu myth, Manu's righteousness is highlighted as the reason for his salvation, and his role as the progenitor of a new human race underscores the importance of dharma (righteousness) in maintaining cosmic balance.

Both stories convey the message that divine beings are deeply invested in the moral state of the world and that divine judgment serves to correct deviations from this moral order. This emphasis on ethical conduct aligns with broader themes in religious and mythological narratives, where divine favor is often linked to moral rectitude.

Comparative Analysis

These mentioned flood myths, while originating from diverse cultures, share core elements that reflect common human concerns about divine justice, moral order, and the continuity of life. The Book of Enoch's flood story, the Epic of Gilgamesh, and the Matsya Avatar narrative all involve:

1. **Divine judgment**, for each story portrays the flood as an act of divine judgment against moral and ethical corruption.

2. **Forewarning and preparation**, as the protagonists receive divine warnings and

instructions, emphasizing the possibility of salvation through obedience and righteousness.

3. **Preservation and renewal**, considering that the preservation of life and subsequent renewal of the world are central themes, highlighting a cycle of destruction and rebirth.

By comparing these stories, we can see how various cultures have used the idea of a flood to delve into topics like fairness from the gods, good behavior, and starting anew in the universe. The similarities in these tales hint at a common human background and a joint effort to understand gods, nature, and the moral rules that guide people.

As we finish comparing ancient flood legends and their common themes, we see that these stories, coming from various cultures, have key elements that show universal human worries. Tales about divine judgment, prophetic signals, readiness, and the need for rebirth highlight how humans strive to make sense of life's rules and the morals set by higher powers. Moving forward to the final chapter, "What Lies Ahead?", we will explore future academic research trends on this subject, focusing on how interdisciplinary approaches and technological advancements can further unravel the complexities of these ancient texts, offering deeper insights into their historical, cultural, and theological contexts. This forward-looking analysis will highlight emerging methodologies and the potential for new discoveries that can enhance our understanding of humanity's perennial quest to decipher the divine and the moral fabric of the universe.

Chapter 9:
What Lies Ahead?

As we stand at the crossing point of antiquated intelligence and modern request, the Book of Enoch calls us into a wealthy and sweeping field of exploration. With its visions and esoteric knowledge, significant dreams, and obscure information, it has captured the creative energy of researchers, scholars, and otherworldly searchers for centuries. The future of engagement with the Book of Enoch promises to be as dynamic and multifaceted as its past, advertising modern avenues for scholarly inquiry, interdisciplinary dialogue, and spiritual exploration.

In the corridors of academia, where the hushed conversations of scholars echo through time, with the discussions bridging the gap between the ancient past and the emerging future. At the heart of these conversations is The Book of Enoch, a glimmer of enigmatic allure that invites scholars to unearth its secrets and to consider its implications for our understanding of biblical history and beyond. As we peer into the horizon, we see a landscape where new research trends and scholarly interests are beginning to take shape, each thread contributing to a tapestry of knowledge that is both intricate and expansive.

In the academic research field, the Book of Enoch serves as a rich resource for fresh studies. Scholars are realizing more and more the importance of reassessing conventional biblical writings using Enochian texts as a guide to delve into early Christian beliefs and how they affected Judaic and Christian end-time perspectives. This revival of interest goes beyond just scholarly pursuits; it stems from a strong desire to uncover the roots of religious concepts and learn how ancient manuscripts can influence modern spiritual beliefs.

Think about the new directions in academic research, where experts are exploring the Book of Enoch beyond its historical value. They view it as a dynamic piece that still motivates and poses questions for present-day readers. This evolving scholarly curiosity spans various areas like theology, literature, and cultural studies. The blending of these different subjects brings the potential for innovative perspectives on the text, giving rise to interpretations that balance academic excellence with spiritual depth.

Today, technology is greatly influencing the changing field of studying old texts. The use of digital tools and methods in the humanities is leading to exciting opportunities for exploring Enochian texts. Picture this: digital versions of the Book of Enoch with notes and connections to other texts, creating a detailed and interactive resource for scholars. These technological progressions go beyond just making things easier; they mark a significant change in how we connect with ancient knowledge, making it accessible to more people and encouraging cooperation among researchers worldwide.

Solving the mysteries of the Book of Enoch is now a team effort involving a mix of different fields like archaeology, anthropology, and cognitive science. This collaboration of the interdisciplinary approaches is giving researchers a more complete view of the text, showing how knowledge from various areas can work together to shed light on ancient writings and even impact modern discussions.

The Book of Enoch holds importance not only in scholarly circles but also in spiritual realms. It serves as a wellspring of inspiration and direction for those on a quest for a profound connection with the divine. Through its visions and teachings, the book strikes a chord with individuals exploring deeper spiritual insights. Touching on themes like divine judgment, cosmic harmony, and the eternal conflict between good and evil, the Book of Enoch presents a distinctive outlook on spiritual matters. These timeless themes remain just as pertinent in modern times, offering a treasure trove of wisdom for present-day spiritual enthusiasts.

Additionally, the Book of Enoch is crucial for conversations between people of different faiths, connecting various religious beliefs. Its discussions on fairness, angels, and the end of times are relevant to many religions, creating a shared understanding and unity among faith groups. Looking ahead, the *Book of Enoch* can help spark important discussions among diverse religious groups, encouraging respect and teamwork.

Could you imagine a future where the Book of Enoch is not just a subject of scholarly inquiry but a touchstone for spiritual growth and interfaith harmony? In such a future, the text serves as a guidepost, illuminating the path toward a deeper understanding of the divine and our place in the cosmos. The engagement with Enoch's visions becomes a journey of discovery, one that transcends disciplinary boundaries and religious differences, fostering a sense of global interconnectedness.

As we venture into the unknown, the Book of Enoch remains a steadfast companion, its ancient wisdom guiding us toward new horizons of knowledge and spiritual insight. On this journey, we are not merely passive recipients of ancient wisdom; we are active participants in a dynamic process of discovery and interpretation. The future of Enochian studies is one of vibrant intellectual and spiritual engagement, a future where the ancient and the modern converge in a harmonious dance of inquiry and revelation.

Academic Research Trends

As we go further into studying the mysterious Book of Enoch, exciting new trends and methods in academic research are changing how we view this ancient text. Scholars from different fields are using creative ways to reveal the mysteries in Enoch's writings, offering new insights and discovering hidden meanings. In the upcoming discussion, we will examine these growing research interests and the innovative methods shaping the study of the Book of Enoch in new and fascinating ways.

Theological and Doctrinal Studies

The Book of Enoch has long been a subject of interest in theological and doctrinal studies, and this trend continues to grow. Modern theologians are re-examining Enoch's teachings and their implications for contemporary religious thought. This includes exploring the book's influence on early Christian doctrines, particularly in the context of angelology and eschatology. Scholars are also investigating how Enoch's visions and prophecies align with or diverge from canonical biblical texts. This comparative approach not only deepens our understanding of the Book of Enoch but also highlights its unique contributions to Judeo-Christian theology (VanderKam, 1996; Nickelsburg, n.d.).

Comparative Religious Studies

Comparative religious studies is an emerging field that examines the Book of Enoch alongside other religious texts and traditions. This approach highlights the similarities and differences between Enoch's visions and the mythologies of other ancient cultures, such as the Mesopotamian, Egyptian, and Greek traditions. By situating the Book of Enoch within this broader religious context, researchers can better understand its place in the history of human spirituality.

Comparative religious studies is a growing field that examines the Book of Enoch in relation to other religious writings and beliefs. Researchers explore how Enoch's visions compare to stories from ancient cultures such as Mesopotamia, Egypt, and Greece. By comparing the Book of Enoch to these texts, scholars can see how beliefs and ideas were shared or altered across different societies, helping to place Enoch within the broader context of human history and spirituality (Nickelsburg & VanderKam, 2004; Collins, 1998).

Enoch's visions are not isolated stories but part of a larger web of beliefs and traditions. By examining similarities and differences in other cultures' stories, we gain a clearer picture of the human experience through time. Understanding the Book of Enoch within the context of other religious texts is like fitting a puzzle piece into the whole picture, revealing how different pieces create a comprehensive view of human spirituality.

Comparing Enoch's visions to other mythologies uncovers common themes and ideas that may be universal across cultures. This approach shows how certain beliefs or stories resonate with humans regardless of time or place. Studying the Book of Enoch alongside other texts highlights shared themes or motifs, providing insights into what was significant to ancient people (Collins, 1998; *Book of the Dead*, n.d.).

Looking at Enoch's visions in the context of other traditions brings history to life, illustrating how people in the past viewed the world, their gods, and their place in the universe. Comparative religious studies also reveal how spiritual beliefs evolved over time. By examining how Enoch's visions compare to other texts, we can trace the development of ideas across different cultures. When we integrate Enoch's visions with other mythologies, we construct a diverse and intricate blend of beliefs spanning centuries and civilizations, appreciating the diversity of human spiritual expression. Researchers use a cross-cultural approach to understand the Book of Enoch, adding depth and complexity to its place in the religious landscape.

Cultural and Literary Analysis

Another burgeoning area of interest is the cultural and literary analysis of the Book of Enoch. Researchers are examining the text through the lens of literary theory, exploring its narrative structures, themes, and stylistic elements. This approach reveals the Book of Enoch as a complex literary work, rich in symbolism and allegory (Culler, 2011; deSilva, 2012, Wells, 2011).

Cultural analysis, meanwhile, focuses on the impact of Enochian themes on various cultural traditions and practices. By studying how different communities have interpreted and adapted Enoch's teachings, scholars can trace the text's influence across time and space, providing insights into its enduring relevance (Ludlow, 2021; Universe Unriddled, 2024).

Social and Political Contexts

Contemporary academic research is now more focused on exploring the social and political backgrounds that influenced the creation and reception of the Book of Enoch. This involves analyzing how the text played a part in the social and political setting of Second Temple Judaism, as well as how it was received and interpreted during times of religious and political turmoil. By delving into these backgrounds, scholars can gain a deeper understanding of the Book of Enoch beyond its religious and literary aspects, seeing it as a document shaped by and responding to the real-world social and political issues of its era. This approach can unveil fresh insights and significance, enhancing our grasp of Enoch's teachings and their enduring influence on future generations (Bisbee, 2022; Perkins, 2011).

Emerging Scholarly Interests

The Book of Enoch is gaining new popularity among scholars, sparking exploration into new areas. This research is not only enhancing our understanding of the book's history and theology but also highlighting its impact on early Christian beliefs and its special role in Second Temple Jewish writings. This part delves into these emerging scholarly interests, offering a fascinating look at where Enochian studies are headed.

Influence on Early Christian Thought

One of the most intriguing areas of emerging scholarly interest is the influence of the Book of Enoch on early Christian thought. Researchers are increasingly examining how the themes of judgment and divine intervention in Enoch shaped the development of Christian eschatological beliefs. This line of inquiry reveals how foundational the Book of Enoch was to early Christians, offering insights into the theological and doctrinal underpinnings of nascent Christianity.

For instance, the Book of Enoch's detailed descriptions of the judgment of the wicked and the reward of the righteous resonate strongly with early Christian eschatology, as seen in texts such as the Book of Revelation. Scholars argue that Enoch's visions of a final judgment where the righteous are vindicated, and the wicked are punished provided a blueprint for early Christian teachings about the end times. This connection underscores the Book of Enoch's role in shaping the apocalyptic imagination of early Christianity, influencing its narratives about divine justice and cosmic order (Townsend, 2020; VanderKam, 1996).

The impact of Enoch on early Christian thought is also evident in the way New Testament writers referenced Enochian themes. The epistle of Jude, for example, directly quotes the Book of Enoch, demonstrating the text's authoritative status among some early Christian communities. This direct citation highlights the deep integration of Enochian literature into the theological framework of early Christianity, prompting scholars to re-evaluate the boundaries of the Christian canon and the fluidity of scriptural traditions during this formative period (Hermann, 2023).

Comparative Studies With Other Apocryphal Texts

Another field gaining attention involves comparing the Book of Enoch to other ancient texts that did not make it into the Bible. By placing Enoch alongside other writings from the same era, scholars hope to uncover what sets it apart and how it connects to the beliefs of that time. This method not only sheds light on Enoch's special characteristics but also helps in grasping the deeper meanings behind its messages and symbols.

Researchers are particularly interested in how the Book of Enoch engages with themes common in other apocryphal texts, such as angelology, cosmology, and eschatology. For instance, texts like the Book of Jubilees and the Testaments of the Twelve Patriarchs share overlapping themes with Enoch, such as the role of angels in divine governance and the unfolding of eschatological events. By comparing these texts, scholars can trace the development of these themes across different works, revealing the dynamic interplay of ideas within Second Temple Judaism (Kolenkow, 1986; Kugler, 2001).

This comparative approach is also shedding light on the Book of Enoch's unique narrative strategies and theological innovations. For example, the detailed cosmological descriptions in Enoch, which include elaborate depictions of the Heavens and the underworld, stand out even among other apocalyptic writings. These vivid portrayals not only reflect Enoch's unique visionary experiences but also underscore its role in shaping Jewish and Christian conceptions of the cosmos (Jonge, 1990).

Interdisciplinary research goes beyond just studying various apocryphal texts. Scholars gain deeper insight into the Book of Enoch by examining it alongside writings from the Second Temple era. This exploration helps uncover the special nature of Enoch's visions and how they relate to other apocalyptic texts. One way researchers could explore the Book of Enoch is by comparing it to the Book of Jubilees, which is another apocryphal text that also talks about themes like angelic wrongdoing and punishment from divine powers. These comparisons help us see how the Book of Enoch influenced and mirrored the religious and end-time beliefs of its time. We will explore the field of interdisciplinary studies more in-depth later in this chapter.

Technological Advances and Enoch Studies

The dawn of the digital age has revolutionized many fields of study, and the realm of ancient texts is no exception. As the complex and enigmatic piece of literature that it is, the Book of Enoch has particularly benefited from these technological advancements.

Digital humanities, a field that combines traditional humanities scholarship with computational methods, is transforming how scholars engage with texts like Enoch. By leveraging tools such as text mining, semantic analysis, and digital editions, researchers are uncovering new insights and connections that were previously obscured.

The use of digital humanities in examining the Book of Enoch is changing how experts look at this ancient text. By utilizing methods like text analysis, semantic evaluations, and high-tech imagery, scholars are discovering fresh perspectives and links that shift our comprehension of Enoch's position in the realm of apocalyptic writings. With technology evolving, the upcoming times for Enoch research seem to hold more energy and creativity, providing intriguing chances to delve into this mysterious and significant text.

The implementation of digital humanities brings a fresh perspective to researching the Book of Enoch. Through digital tools and technologies, scholars can now delve deeper into the text with accuracy and thoroughness. For example, converting ancient manuscripts into digital formats enhances access to and safeguards these priceless materials. Additionally, digital tools aid in intricate textual examination by uncovering patterns and deviations in various manuscript versions, shedding light on the text's journey through time.

Sophisticated imaging tools, like multispectral imaging, help reveal hidden or harmed parts of text, providing fresh insights and understandings. These advancements in technology are creating fresh opportunities for study, enabling researchers to delve into the Book of Enoch with exceptional thoroughness and precision.

Digital Humanities and the Book of Enoch

Digital humanities projects have opened up unprecedented opportunities for exploring the Book of Enoch. One of the most significant contributions of this field is the development of digital editions of ancient manuscripts. These editions are not mere transcriptions but are enriched with features that facilitate deeper textual analysis and comparison (Viola, 2022).

For example, digital platforms allow scholars to annotate texts collaboratively, adding layers of scholarly commentary that can be updated and expanded over time. This dynamic approach to annotation contrasts sharply with the static nature of print editions, enabling a more interactive and evolving scholarly discourse (Battershill, 2023). Moreover, digital editions often incorporate high-resolution images of the original manuscripts, allowing researchers to examine the physical characteristics of the text, such as marginalia, ink color, and parchment quality. These details can provide valuable context for interpreting the text and understanding its historical transmission.

One of the most important trends in Enochian studies is the application of digital humanities. This field leverages advanced digital tools and techniques to analyze and interpret ancient texts. Digitization of manuscripts, for instance, has made the Book of Enoch more accessible to scholars worldwide, fostering collaborative research and enabling more precise textual analysis.

Digital humanities also involve the use of software for linguistic analysis, which can uncover patterns and structures within the text that might not be apparent through traditional methods. These tools allow researchers to perform detailed comparisons between the Book of Enoch and other ancient texts, identifying linguistic similarities and differences that shed light on the text's origins and influences (Viola, 2022).

Text Mining and Semantic Analysis

Text mining and semantic analysis are powerful tools that digital humanities scholars use to explore the linguistic and thematic depths of the Book of Enoch. Text mining involves the computational extraction of information from large volumes of text, identifying patterns and trends that would be difficult to discern manually. For instance, text mining can track the frequency and distribution of specific themes or motifs within the Book of Enoch, revealing how certain ideas evolve throughout the text or compare to other contemporaneous works (Feldman & Sanger, 2007).

Semantic analysis goes a step further by examining the relationships between words and concepts within the text, uncovering deeper meanings and connections. An example of semantic analysis in action is exploring Enoch's apocalyptic themes in relation to other ancient apocalyptic literature. By comparing the semantic fields of Enoch with those of texts like the Book of Daniel, scholars can identify common motifs and unique features, shedding light on the distinctiveness and influence of Enoch's visions (Feldman et al., 1997; Song & Chambers, 2014).

Textual Criticism and Paleography

Emerging trends in textual criticism and paleography are also revolutionizing the study of the Book of Enoch. Textual criticism involves the meticulous examination of different manuscript versions to reconstruct the most accurate text possible. This approach is particularly valuable for the Book of Enoch, which exists in various versions and languages, including Ge'ez, Aramaic, and Greek. Paleography, the study of ancient handwriting, complements textual criticism by helping scholars date and authenticate manuscripts. By analyzing the writing styles and materials used in different copies of the Book of Enoch, researchers can trace the text's transmission history and better understand its evolution over time (Comfort, 2005; Finegan, 1974).

Comparative Studies and Digital Editions

Digital tools in the humanities help researchers carry out detailed comparisons. By digitizing various manuscripts of the Book of Enoch, scholars can easily compare different versions of the text. This feature proves especially useful for complex texts such as Enoch, which are available in various languages and editions.

Especially analyzing the text online allows researchers to follow how it evolved, seeing how different scribes and translators understood and changed it over the years. This method can unveil details about how the Book of Enoch spread through history, showcasing the different ways it was received in various societies and time periods.

For example, by comparing the Ethiopic version of Enoch with fragments found among the Dead Sea Scrolls, researchers can identify significant differences and similarities that inform our understanding of how the text was used and understood in different Jewish communities. These comparative studies can also illuminate the broader cultural and religious contexts in which Enoch was read and revered.

Interactive Digital Tools

Interactive digital tools are another aspect of modern Enoch studies. Platforms that support the creation and sharing of digital annotations allow scholars to build a collective knowledge base around the Book of Enoch. These tools enable researchers to link passages of the text with relevant scholarly articles, historical documents, and other primary sources, creating a rich, interconnected web of information. Such interactivity enhances the collaborative nature of scholarship, breaking down the barriers of geographical and institutional isolation. Scholars from around the world can contribute to and benefit from a shared digital repository of knowledge, fostering a more inclusive and comprehensive understanding of the Book of Enoch (Sharma, 2023; Smeda et al., 2014).

Advanced Imaging Techniques

Advancements in imaging technology have also had a significant impact on the study of ancient texts. Techniques such as multispectral imaging allow scholars to recover faded or damaged portions of manuscripts, revealing text that has not been seen for centuries. These technologies can uncover hidden annotations, corrections, or even entire sections of text that were previously unreadable. For the Book of Enoch, such technologies have been invaluable in reconstructing the text and providing a clearer picture of its original form. High-resolution imaging can also aid in the identification of scribal hands, helping to determine the provenance and date of different manuscript copies (Chabries et al., 2015; University of Michigan News, 2009).

Interdisciplinary Approaches

The Book of Enoch, with its complex visions, ethical dilemmas, and divine interventions, has transcended traditional theological studies. Scholars from various disciplines, including psychology, philosophy, and anthropology, are exploring this ancient text to expand our understanding and highlight its broader scholarly relevance.

Traditionally rooted in biblical scholarship and theology, the study of the Book of Enoch is now embracing interdisciplinary research. Integrating insights from archaeology, anthropology, and literary studies provides a more holistic understanding of the text. This approach contextualizes Enoch's writings within the broader tapestry of ancient cultures and civilizations, revealing previously overlooked connections. For example, archaeological findings corroborate historical and cultural references in the Book of Enoch, enriching interpretations of its visions and prophecies (Bacchi, 2023; Szonyi, 2015).

Emerging scholarly interests increasingly embrace interdisciplinary research. Methods from literary studies, anthropology, and digital humanities offer new perspectives on the Book of Enoch. Literary analysis examines the text as a complex narrative, exploring its structure, symbolism, and rhetorical strategies to uncover deeper meanings and highlight its artistry alongside its doctrinal content (Szonyi, 2015). Anthropological perspectives study the social and cultural contexts of the Book of Enoch's production and reception, providing insights into the lived experiences and worldviews of the communities that embraced Enochian literature (Bacchi, 2023).

These interdisciplinary approaches reveal the multifaceted nature of the Book of Enoch and its significance across various fields of study. By engaging with the text through multiple lenses, scholars uncover new dimensions of Enoch's visions and their implications for both ancient and modern readers. These perspectives enrich our understanding and underscore the enduring relevance of the Book of Enoch in contemporary scholarship.

Psychological Dimensions of Visionary Experiences

The Book of Enoch captures attention with its rich descriptions of visionary encounters. These profound visions, brimming with vivid details and deep insights, provide a rich area for psychological exploration. Experts in psychology are especially keen on delving into the mental and emotional mechanisms that drive these encounters.

Psychologists are exploring how the intense visions described in the Book of Enoch might reflect altered states of consciousness. The vivid descriptions of celestial realms and divine beings suggest experiences that could be akin to what modern psychology recognizes as mystical or transcendental states. These states are often characterized by a sense of unity, timelessness, and profound insight, aligning closely with Enoch's encounters (Wittmann & Hurd, 2018).

Altered states of consciousness, such as those induced by meditation, hypnosis, or even certain psychological conditions, offer a broader lens through which to view and understand these experiences. Researchers are now considering how these altered states might provide a framework for interpreting the visionary experiences documented in ancient texts like the Book of Enoch (Smith, 2015; Ward, 1989).

Additionally, the Book of Enoch offers a special view of how getting messages from the Heavens affects a person's mind. In the book, we see Enoch often struggling with the heavy burden of the insights he gets and the duties that come with them. You can look at this using the idea of cognitive dissonance theory, which suggests that people feel mental strain when they have conflicting thoughts or face new facts that go against what they already believe.

Philosophical Engagement With Ethics and Justice

Philosophers have always found the Book of Enoch fascinating because it raises important ethical and moral issues. The text explores topics like how God's justice works, the choices people make freely, and what happens as a result of moral and ethical decisions. These ideas connect with long-standing philosophical discussions about fairness and the moral duties that people have.

One of the central ethical dilemmas in the Book of Enoch involves the transgression of the Watchers, the fallen angels who defy divine commandments by mingling with humans and teaching them forbidden knowledge. This act of defiance and its catastrophic consequences provide a rich framework for exploring issues of free will and moral accountability. Philosophers examine whether the Watchers' actions can be understood as a manifestation of free will and, if so, what this implies about the nature of their guilt and punishment (Blum, 2018).

Moreover, the idea of fairness in how God judges people in the Book of Enoch brings up some deep philosophical issues. The book describes a universe where God's punishments and rewards match how individuals behave morally. It's like following a strict moral code and doing what's right. Yet, it also sparks conversations about whether God's judgments are fair and reasonable, particularly when we consider the harsh punishments mentioned.

Anthropological Insights Into Cultural and Ritualistic Contexts

Anthropologists approach the Book of Enoch from a cultural and ritualistic perspective, aiming to situate the text within the broader spectrum of ancient Near Eastern religious practices. This approach involves examining the cultural and historical context in which the Book of Enoch was composed and used, shedding light on its significance within ancient societies. One area of interest is the ritualistic aspects described in the text. The Book of Enoch includes detailed accounts of celestial journeys and encounters with divine beings, which can be interpreted as reflecting ritualistic practices. These descriptions provide insights into how ancient communities might have engaged in rituals intended to facilitate communication with the divine or to gain spiritual insights (Ramshaw, n.d.).

Anthropologists also explore the socio-political context of the Book of Enoch. The text's emphasis on divine judgment and the downfall of corrupt rulers can be seen as a reflection of the socio-political tensions of the time. This perspective helps to understand the Book of Enoch not only as a religious text but also as a commentary on the social and political dynamics of the ancient Near East.

Future Directions

The future of Enochian studies is set to be both vibrant and multifaceted, with emerging trends and new methodologies continuously reshaping our understanding of the Book of Enoch. Scholars are increasingly utilizing interdisciplinary approaches, blending insights from anthropology, theology, and literary studies to uncover more of the text's hidden depths. These approaches provide new insights into the text's cultural, ritualistic, and socio-political contexts, enriching our appreciation of its significance in ancient societies (Barker, 2005; Reed, 2017).

Technological innovations, such as artificial intelligence (AI) and machine learning, are poised to revolutionize the study of ancient texts like the Book of Enoch. AI algorithms can analyze textual variations and generate new hypotheses about the relationships between Enoch and other apocalyptic literature, offering more sophisticated analyses than ever before. These tools can help predict how different versions of the text might have evolved, providing a clearer picture of its historical development (Ramshaw, n.d.).

Moreover, digital humanities are enabling more interactive and immersive ways to engage with the Book of Enoch. Virtual reality (VR) and augmented reality (AR) technologies can create immersive experiences that allow both scholars and the public to explore the themes and settings of the text in new and engaging ways. Imagine a VR experience that takes users on a journey through Enoch's celestial visions, offering a vivid, first-person perspective on the text's apocalyptic imagery (Reed, 2017).

The integration of these technologies with traditional scholarly methods is not only enhancing our understanding of Enoch but also expanding the horizons of biblical and apocryphal scholarship. This interdisciplinary approach is ensuring that the study of the Book of Enoch remains a dynamic and evolving field, rich with potential for discovery and understanding. Scholars are continually exploring new areas of interest, promising even more groundbreaking discoveries in the future.

The Book of Enoch stands as a testament to the enduring power of ancient texts to inspire and challenge us. Its complex narratives, profound theological insights, and rich cultural contexts make it a fascinating subject of study across various disciplines. As research trends continue to evolve, the Book of Enoch will undoubtedly remain a pivotal focus of academic inquiry, offering new insights into the religious and intellectual heritage of humanity. By embracing new methodologies and interdisciplinary approaches, scholars are ensuring that this ancient text continues to provide valuable guidance and inspiration as we navigate the complexities of the modern world (Barker, 2005; Reed, 2017).

Future Directions in Interdisciplinary Studies

The future of Enoch studies lies in continued interdisciplinary collaboration. By integrating insights from psychology, philosophy, and anthropology, scholars can develop a more nuanced understanding of the *Book of Enoch* and its enduring significance. These interdisciplinary approaches not only enrich the study of Enoch but also demonstrate the text's relevance across diverse fields of inquiry. As technology advances, new methodologies will further enhance interdisciplinary research. Digital humanities tools, such as text-mining and semantic analysis, will continue to facilitate comparative studies and uncover new connections between Enoch and other ancient texts. This dynamic interplay between disciplines promises to yield fresh insights and foster a deeper appreciation of the *Book of Enoch* within the broader landscape of human knowledge (Barker, 2005; Reed, 2017).

Spiritual and Religious Relevance

The Book of Enoch continues to captivate contemporary readers and spiritual seekers, providing a profound and enigmatic window into ancient wisdom and esoteric knowledge. As modern spirituality evolves, the Book of Enoch's themes of divine intervention, cosmic justice, and the interplay between the celestial and terrestrial realms are finding new expressions and interpretations. This section explores the potential developments in how the Book of Enoch might influence contemporary spiritual practices, highlighting its growing relevance and the ways it is being integrated into modern religious thought and practice.

The Book of Enoch remains a dynamic and influential text, deeply woven into the fabric of contemporary spirituality. Its rich themes of divine intervention, cosmic justice, and spiritual transformation resonate across various spiritual traditions and practices, offering timeless wisdom for modern seekers. As interest in the Book of Enoch grows, its relevance will continue to expand, inspiring new interpretations and applications in the ever-evolving landscape of spirituality.

Revival of Mystical Traditions

One of the most significant developments in contemporary spirituality is the revival of interest in mystical traditions. The Book of Enoch offers a rich tapestry of mystical visions and celestial journeys that resonate with modern seekers looking for deeper spiritual experiences. The text's detailed descriptions of Enoch's ascents to the heavenly realms and his encounters with angelic beings provide a framework for understanding mystical experiences within a biblical context (Reed, 2017).

Modern mystics and spiritual practitioners are drawing on the Book of Enoch to explore concepts such as the hierarchy of angels, the nature of divine knowledge, and the process of spiritual ascension. This revival is not limited to scholarly circles but is permeating popular spirituality, where books, workshops, and online courses delve into the mystical teachings of Enoch, offering practical guidance for spiritual development (Barker, 2005; Ramshaw, n.d.).

Integration Into Esoteric Practices

Esoteric traditions, including Kabbalah, Theosophy, and modern-day mysticism, are increasingly incorporating the Book of Enoch into their teachings. The text's intricate cosmology and revelations about the divine order resonate with esoteric principles, making it a valuable resource for those seeking to understand the hidden aspects of reality. In Kabbalistic studies, the Book of Enoch is used to explore the nature of the Sephirot and angelic hierarchies, offering insights into the structure of spiritual worlds and pathways of divine emanation. Theosophical societies also draw on Enochian themes to discuss the evolution of consciousness and the role of spiritual beings in guiding human development (Barker, 2005).

Influence on New Age Movements

The New Age movement, with its eclectic blend of spiritual beliefs and practices, has embraced the Book of Enoch for its emphasis on celestial guidance, spiritual transformation, and apocalyptic visions. These elements align with New Age themes of awakening, enlightenment, and global transformation. Practitioners are drawing inspiration from the Book of Enoch for meditative practices, spiritual rituals, and healing modalities (Barker, 2005; Reed, 2017).

One notable example is Enochian magic, a system of ceremonial magic based on angelic communications received by John Dee and Edward Kelley in the 16th century. Although distinct from the Book of Enoch, Enochian magic incorporates themes of angelic hierarchies and divine messages, bridging ancient texts and modern spiritual practices (Barker, 2005).

In New Age spirituality, the Book of Enoch is seen as a valuable resource that provides insights into the structure of the spiritual universe and offers practical guidance for personal and collective spiritual growth. The text's rich descriptions of Enoch's ascents to the heavenly realms and encounters with divine beings serve as a framework for understanding mystical experiences within a broader spiritual context (Ramshaw, n.d).

As New Age practitioners continue to explore the teachings of the Book of Enoch, they are finding new

273

ways to integrate its wisdom into their spiritual practices, thus enriching the modern spiritual landscape with ancient insights.

Ethical and Moral Reflections

The Book of Enoch continues to influence contemporary religious thought, particularly through its emphasis on divine judgment and moral conduct. The text's portrayal of the consequences faced by the Watchers for their transgressions, contrasted with the rewards granted to the righteous, offers a profound commentary on the importance of ethical behavior and the pursuit of justice. This ancient narrative provides a robust framework for modern discussions on the nature of sin, repentance, and redemption (Barker, 2005; Reed, 2017).

Religious communities are engaging with the Book of Enoch to delve into themes of accountability, forgiveness, and moral responsibility. The vivid depictions of the fate of the wicked versus the salvation of the just serve as powerful tools for exploring these timeless themes. The text's insights into ethical behavior and divine justice resonate deeply within these communities, fostering a renewed interest in the moral teachings found within its verses (Ramshaw, n.d.).

By examining the Book of Enoch, scholars and practitioners alike are finding valuable lessons on the consequences of moral failings and the rewards of virtuous living. This engagement highlights the text's enduring relevance and its ability to provide guidance on ethical conduct in both personal and communal contexts (Barker, 2005).

Potential for Future Developments

Looking ahead, the Book of Enoch is likely to continue influencing contemporary spirituality in several key areas:

1. **Digital engagement:** As technology advances, digital platforms will play a crucial role in disseminating the teachings of the Book of Enoch. Online study groups, digital editions, and interactive tools will make the text more accessible to a global audience, fostering a deeper engagement with its themes.

2. **Ecological spirituality:** The Book of Enoch's apocalyptic visions and emphasis on cosmic order have significant implications for ecological spirituality. The text's warnings about divine judgment and the importance of maintaining harmony with the natural world resonate with contemporary concerns about environmental stewardship and sustainability.

3. **Personal spiritual growth:** The text's emphasis on spiritual ascension and the pursuit of divine knowledge will continue to inspire individuals seeking personal growth and transformation. Spiritual retreats, guided meditations, and workshops based on

Enochian themes will offer practical pathways for seekers to connect with the divine.

4. **Academic research:** Ongoing scholarly research will continue to uncover new dimensions of the Book of Enoch, shedding light on its historical, cultural, and theological significance. Interdisciplinary studies will further enrich our understanding of the text, bridging the gap between academic scholarship and spiritual practice.

The Role of Enoch in Interfaith Dialogue

The Book of Enoch serves as a distinctive and valuable platform for interfaith dialogue, fostering mutual understanding among diverse religious traditions. By exploring themes such as angels, cosmology, and prophecy, the text offers rich material for theological discussions that resonate with believers across different faiths. Enoch's teachings on divine justice, cosmic order, and the interplay between good and evil provide common ground for meaningful conversations, highlighting both shared spiritual heritage and unique contributions of each tradition (Ramshaw, n.d.; Reed 2017).

In interfaith forums, scholars and religious leaders use the Book of Enoch to examine commonalities and differences among Judaism, Christianity, Islam, and other religions. This dialogue promotes respect and collaboration, demonstrating the text's role as a catalyst for deeper understanding and cooperation among faith communities. The historical and theological contexts of the Book of Enoch also offer a framework for understanding the development of religious thought, enriching academic and spiritual exchanges (Barker, 2005).

As global interconnectedness increases, the Book of Enoch continues to emerge as a significant text in interfaith initiatives. Its universal themes resonate widely, providing a foundation for discussions about the nature of the divine, the role of angels, and eschatological beliefs. By integrating the Book of Enoch into these dialogues, religious communities can foster greater understanding, respect, and collaboration, contributing to a more harmonious and enlightened world.

Angelology: A Shared Curiosity

One of the most compelling aspects of the Book of Enoch is its detailed exploration of angelology, which has captivated religious scholars and practitioners across various faith traditions. In Judaism, angels are considered messengers of God, integral to the divine plan. Christianity shares this perspective but often emphasizes the protective and intercessory roles of angels. The Book of Enoch offers intricate descriptions of angelic hierarchies, their duties, and their interactions with humanity, providing a rich basis for interfaith dialogue (Reed, 2017).

This detailed angelology invites comparisons and discussions about the roles of angels in different religious texts. For instance, Ethiopian Christianity, which regards the Book of Enoch as canonical, offers unique insights into angelic beings, enriching the dialogue with distinctive perspectives. These conversations help illuminate the similarities and differences in how angels are perceived and understood across various traditions, fostering a deeper appreciation for the diverse ways in which the divine is conceptualized (Ramshaw, n.d.).

The Book of Enoch thus serves as a common ground for interfaith dialogue, enabling scholars and practitioners to explore shared themes and distinct beliefs. This engagement not only enhances theological understanding but also promotes mutual respect and cooperation among different religious communities. As these dialogues continue, they contribute to a more nuanced and comprehensive understanding of angelology within the broader context of religious studies.

Cosmology: Understanding the Universe

The cosmological themes in the Book of Enoch, including its descriptions of the structure of the Heavens, the movement of celestial bodies, and the nature of the universe, mirror the cosmological inquiries present in many religious traditions. In Judaism, Christianity, and Islam, cosmology intertwines with theology to explain the nature of creation and the order of the universe. Enoch's vivid cosmology provides a rich platform for interfaith discussions, allowing scholars and religious leaders to explore how different religions perceive the universe's creation and divine order (Barker, 2005; Reed, 2017).

These discussions can lead to a deeper appreciation of each tradition's cosmological views and theological implications. By comparing Enoch's cosmology with those found in other sacred texts, scholars and religious leaders can identify similarities and differences that shape each faith's understanding of the divine cosmos. This comparative approach not only enhances our understanding of the Book of Enoch but also fosters mutual respect and deeper insight into the theological frameworks of various religious traditions (Ramshaw, n.d.).

Prophecy: Visions of Divine Justice

Prophetic literature, a cornerstone of many religious traditions, offers profound insights into divine will, justice, and the future. The Book of Enoch is rich with apocalyptic visions and prophecies describing the end times, the judgment of the wicked, and the rewards for the righteous. These themes resonate with the prophetic traditions in Judaism, Christianity, and Islam, where concepts of divine justice and eschatology play significant roles (Arsena, 2023; Taylor, n.d).

The Book of Enoch intertwines visions and celestial phenomena to present a complex tapestry of apocalyptic foretelling. It vividly depicts the fate of the world, showcasing the destiny of both the righteous and the wicked. Enoch's visions of the future, particularly those recorded in the Parables, offer a glimpse of end times, where divine judgment is meted out, rewarding the just and punishing the unrighteous (Arsena, 2023).

In interfaith dialogue, the prophetic themes of the Book of Enoch can enhance mutual understanding of how different faiths envision the end times and divine judgment. Discussions can explore how Enoch's portrayal of universal judgment aligns with or diverges from eschatological views in other religious texts. This comparative analysis fosters broader conversations about the nature of divine justice, the role of humanity, and the hope for redemption and renewal (Reed, 2017; Taylor, n.d.).

By examining these prophetic themes, scholars and religious leaders can appreciate the commonalities and differences in eschatological beliefs across various traditions. This not only enriches theological understanding but also promotes respect and cooperation among different faith communities, contributing to a more harmonious interfaith dialogue (Arsena, 2023; Reed, 2017).

Historical and Theological Contexts

The Book of Enoch is a helpful resource for grasping the history and beliefs of the people in the ancient Near East. During a time when Jewish apocalyptic writings were thriving, it influenced the early Christian ideas and the shaping of religious beliefs. For when we look at the Book of Enoch in its historical setting, discussions between different faiths can reveal how they have common origins but evolved in separate ways. This historical view can help us better understand how these faiths are connected and emphasize the distinct influences each tradition has on the broader religious scene.

Case Studies in Interfaith Dialogue

Several interfaith initiatives have successfully used the Book of Enoch as a focal point for dialogue. Academic conferences and workshops have brought together scholars from Jewish, Christian, and Ethiopian Orthodox backgrounds to discuss Enoch's teachings. These dialogues often focus on common themes such as the nature of divine beings, the structure of the universe, and the ethical implications of prophetic visions. For example, the interfaith symposium held at the University of Chicago brought scholars from various religious backgrounds to explore the Book of Enoch's influence on early Christian thought and its relevance to contemporary theological debates (Arsena, 2023; Taylor, n.d.).

The symposium highlighted the text's role in shaping concepts of divine justice and human responsibility, offering diverse perspectives that enriched participants' understanding. By examining the Book of Enoch, scholars, and religious leaders were able to delve into its impact on theological concepts across different traditions, fostering a deeper appreciation for its historical and spiritual significance (Barker, 2005; Reed, 2017).

These initiatives demonstrate the Book of Enoch's potential as a unifying text for interfaith dialogue, providing a common ground for exploring complex theological themes. The discussions generated by these events not only enhance academic scholarship but also promote mutual respect and cooperation among different faith communities, contributing to a more harmonious interfaith landscape.

Implications for Divine Justice and Redemption

Enoch's depiction of a judgment that applies to everyone has a deep impact on conversations between different faiths regarding fairness from gods and the act of being saved. The detailed storytelling of what happens to the bad people and the good people echoes themes found in various religions, sparking conversations about what justice really means and if there's a chance for forgiveness.

In these conversations, people can discuss things like: What do various religions think about divine fairness? What standards are used for making decisions, and how do they show the moral and ethical lessons of each belief system? How do ideas about being saved and pardoning others show up when talking about divine decisions? These talks help everyone grasp the similar principles and unique doctrines that form how each faith looks at fairness and being saved.

Enoch's vivid depiction of universal judgment provides a powerful foundation for interfaith dialogues on divine justice and redemption. His narratives, detailing the fate of both the wicked and the righteous, resonate deeply across various religious traditions, prompting meaningful conversations about justice and the possibility of forgiveness. These discussions often explore key questions about divine fairness, the criteria for judgment, and how these standards reflect the moral and ethical teachings of different faiths. Additionally, they examine how ideas of salvation and forgiveness are integrated into concepts of divine judgment, highlighting both shared values and unique doctrines.

Engaging with Enoch's teachings allows participants to gain a richer understanding of the principles underlying their beliefs. The Book of Enoch acts as a bridge, fostering mutual respect and understanding among diverse faith communities. By examining these themes, scholars and religious leaders can plunge into the profound implications of divine justice and redemption, enhancing their comprehension of these fundamental theological concepts. As the exploration of Enoch's visions continues, it provides enduring insights and inspiration, connecting ancient wisdom with contemporary spiritual inquiry.

Conclusion

The ancient text known as the Book of Enoch presents a myriad of vivid visions, prophecies, and otherworldly travels, providing deep wisdom on beliefs about divine fairness, human ethics, and the harmony of the universe. Our journey into this book has revealed various key ideas and revelations, all shedding light on the mysterious nature of this profound manuscript.

Revealing intricate insights into the universe's structure, the celestial voyages of Enoch shed light on the roles played by angelic entities and the divine blueprint for humankind. These divine revelations highlight the interconnectedness between the heavenly and earthly domains while accentuating how celestial harmony influences human affairs. Through the elaborate depictions of Enoch, we gain a distinctive insight into the ancients' perception of a cosmos meticulously arranged. This cosmic panorama serves not only as a plot canvas but as a crucial element in grasping the core themes of justice, morality, and humanity's role in the grand design of the divine. The heavenly journey of Enoch and his interactions with divine entities emphasize the deep connection between the mortal and sacred worlds, indicating a significant blending of earthly and spiritual dimensions, where human actions resonate throughout the universe.

Central to the Book of Enoch are the prophecies that outline the triumph of righteousness and the fall of the wicked. The Apocalypse of Weeks and the Animal Apocalypse provide symbolic narratives that depict historical epochs and eschatological visions, stressing the cyclical nature of sin, judgment, and redemption. These prophecies offer a framework for understanding history and the future, presenting a divine timetable where each phase of human existence is marked by specific moral and spiritual challenges. The cyclical nature of these prophecies suggests that history is not linear but rather a series of recurring patterns, each culminating in divine judgment and renewal. This perspective encourages readers to view their own lives within this grand cosmic cycle and, in doing so, recognize the ongoing struggle between good and evil and the ever-present possibility of redemption.

The book intricately threads moral obligations throughout its storytelling, encouraging readers to seek goodness and follow sacred rules, as well as grasp the outcomes of rebellion. The tales of the Watchers and their decline demonstrate the risks associated with forbidden wisdom and the resulting ethical decay. These stories act as impactful symbols of the wrongful use of authority and information, which, in a way, emphasizes the moral quandaries that emerge when divine limits are trespassed. The Watchers, celestial entities who descend to Earth and share prohibited knowledge with humans, represent the dangers of pride and the disastrous results of challenging divine structure. Their loss of favor and the resultant disorder highlights the significance of modesty, compliance, and ethical self-control.

The prophecies of Enoch also portray a final judgment where divine justice prevails, separating the righteous from the wicked and establishing a new, harmonious world. These themes resonate deeply with eschatological beliefs in various religious traditions, reinforcing the hope for ultimate redemption and cosmic renewal. The idea of a final reckoning is a strong symbol of the ethical responsibility that forms the basis of human life. It focuses on the fact that every deed, regardless of its scale, carries universal importance and that a supreme power will ensure fairness in the end. This belief in the afterlife provides an instructive fable as well as a hopeful assurance: a cautionary tale for those who deviate from the ethical way and a reassurance of salvation and everlasting tranquility for the faithful ones.

The messages that can be found and interpreted within the Book of Enoch hold relevance in present-day discussions surrounding spirituality and morality, as well as philosophy. In the current era, discussions around divine fairness, moral responsibility, and the relationship between wisdom and morals remain as crucial as ever. Notably, the story of the Watchers mirrors contemporary anxieties regarding the moral consequences of progress in science and technology. Similar to how the Watchers shared forbidden knowledge, which resulted in disorder and moral decay, modern scientific and technological advancements present moral quandaries that call for thoughtful reflection and moderation. The significant focus on redemption and ethical behavior promotes a contemplative and accountable approach to personal and communal actions, urging individuals to ponder the wider effects of their conduct on the society they inhabit.

Ongoing research and dialogue about the Book of Enoch are crucial for several reasons. Further study can uncover deeper historical and theological contexts, enhancing our understanding of, for example, early Jewish and Christian thought. The Book of Enoch offers a unique glimpse into the religious and cultural milieu of the Second Temple period, a time of significant theological development and transformation. By examining the text within its historical context, scholars can gain insights into the religious beliefs, practices, and concerns of ancient communities. This understanding can, in turn, inform our interpretations of other ancient texts and enhance our appreciation of the complex interplay between religion, culture, and history.

Utilizing methods from anthropology, literary studies, and digital humanities can offer new perspectives on the text, perhaps revealing its multifaceted nature and enduring significance. Anthropological approaches can shed light on the cultural and social dynamics that shaped the creation and transmission of the Book of Enoch, while literary studies can explore the text's narrative structure, symbolism, and thematic elements. Not to mention the uncovering of artistic and rhetorical techniques used to convey its messages. On the other hand, digital humanities can facilitate the analysis and dissemination of the text, thus making it more accessible to scholars as well as the public. These interdisciplinary approaches can thereby enrich our understanding of the Book of Enoch and highlight its relevance to contemporary issues.

Exploring parallels between the Book of Enoch and other cultural myths and religious texts can provide a broader understanding of universal themes and human concerns. Many of the themes in the Book of Enoch, such as the struggle between good and evil, the quest for knowledge, and the hope for redemption, are echoed in myths and religious narratives from diverse cultures around the world. By comparing these narratives, scholars can identify common motifs and themes that reflect fundamental human concerns and aspirations. This comparative approach can foster a deeper appreciation of the shared spiritual heritage of humanity and promote cross-cultural dialogue and understanding.

Reaching the end of our expedition across the pages of the Book of Enoch, we are encouraged to recollect the enduring sagacity enshrined within its storyline. This text prompts us to ponder over our ethical duties, the repercussions of our deeds, and the perpetual veracities governing the universe. It beckons intellectuals, truth-seekers, and readers of all kinds to plunge into its enigmas, to query, to absorb, and to evolve. Let the revelations from the Book of Enoch motivate you to chart new scholarly or spiritual routes, partake in meaningful conversations, and aspire toward a life harmonized with celestial precepts of fairness, virtue, and concord. In the continual pursuit of enlightenment, the Book of Enoch shines as a guiding light, traversing us through the intricacies of being and pushing us toward a tomorrow where celestial insight and human endeavor merge to sculpt a fair and enlightened society.

The ethical and moral lessons embedded in the Book of Enoch are particularly relevant in today's complex and often morally ambiguous world. In a time when technological advancements and scientific discoveries are rapidly transforming our world, the Book of Enoch puts strong emphasis on ethical restraint and moral responsibility as it offers a timely reminder of the potential consequences of unchecked ambition and hubris. It calls on individuals and societies to carefully consider the ethical implications of their actions and to strive for a balance between innovation and moral integrity.

As we reflect on the insights and themes explored in the Book of Enoch, we are reminded of the importance of ongoing research and dialogue. The diverse array of visions, predictions, and ethical teachings within the text provides a plethora of substance for academic inquiry and introspection. By persisting in the examination of the Book of Enoch, we can enhance our comprehension of antiquated religious ideologies and their relevance to present-day challenges. Additionally, we can cultivate a deeper admiration for the intricate interaction between religion, customs, and chronicles, acknowledging how ancient writings persist in influencing our perception of the universe and our position within it.

Summary

Introduction to the Book of Enoch

- Bridges the celestial and terrestrial, unveiling divine secrets through visions and prophecies.

- Written by Enoch, the seventh patriarch, beloved by God and taken to Heaven without experiencing death.

- Provides insights into divine mechanics, angelic hierarchies, and their influence on cosmic events.

- Challenges traditional religious doctrines and pushes the boundaries of spiritual understanding.

- Explores the origins, symbolism, and impact of the Book of Enoch on religious thought.

Significance and Historical Context

- Revered and reviled, its canonicity is disputed, yet its influence is undeniable.

- Shaped theological thought during the Second Temple period.

- Emerged from the Jewish apocalyptic tradition, reflecting concerns with divine judgment and cosmic justice.

- Influenced by and influenced multiple faiths, including Judaism and Christianity.

Journey and Historical Preservation

- Initially composed between the 3rd century BCE and 1st century CE.

- Early segments like the "Book of the Watchers" date back to the 3rd century BCE.

- Transmitted through various cultures, including Jewish, Greek, and Ethiopian communities.

- Preserved by the Ethiopian Orthodox Church, integrated into their canon.

- Rediscovered through the Dead Sea Scrolls, reaffirming its historical significance.

Themes and Narratives

- Detailed descriptions of Heaven, angelic hierarchies, and apocalyptic visions.

- Central themes of divine justice, moral responsibility, and the fate of humanity.

- Tales of the Watchers illustrates the dangers of forbidden knowledge and the consequences of rebellion.

- Prophecies of final judgment emphasize the separation of the righteous and wicked, ultimate redemption, and cosmic renewal.

Influence on Religious Thought

- Profound impact on Jewish eschatological thought and early Christian theology.

- Referenced in the New Testament, specifically the Epistle of Jude.

- Influenced early Christian apocryphal writings and theological discussions.

- Provided a theological framework for understanding divine justice and human morality.

Relevance to Contemporary Issues

- Mirrors modern anxieties about scientific and technological advancements.

- Emphasizes ethical restraint and moral responsibility in the face of progress.

- Promotes a reflective and responsible approach to personal and communal actions.

- Encourages ongoing research and dialogue to uncover deeper historical and theological contexts.

Scholarly Approaches and Methodologies

- Utilizes anthropology, literary studies, and digital humanities to offer new perspectives.

- Anthropological approaches reveal cultural and social dynamics shaping the text.

- Literary studies explore narrative structure, symbolism, and thematic elements.

- Digital humanities facilitate analysis and dissemination, making the text accessible to scholars and the public.

Comparative Analysis With Other Texts

- Identifies common motifs and themes reflecting fundamental human concerns.

- Fosters a deeper appreciation of the shared spiritual heritage of humanity.

- Promotes cross-cultural dialogue and understanding through comparative studies.

Enduring Wisdom and Future Exploration

- Invites readers to reflect on ethical duties, consequences of actions, and eternal truths.

- Encourages intellectuals and truth-seekers to delve into its mysteries.

- Inspires new scholarly or spiritual paths, meaningful conversations, and a life aligned with divine principles.

- Serves as a guiding light, urging toward a future where divine wisdom and human action coalesce for a just and enlightened world.

Ethical and Moral Lessons

- Relevant in today's complex and morally ambiguous world.

- Calls for careful consideration of ethical implications of actions.

- Strives for a balance between innovation and moral integrity.

- Reflects the importance of ongoing research and dialogue in understanding ancient religious ideologies and their relevance to present-day challenges.

Legacy and Ongoing Impact

- Continues to influence religious and philosophical discussions.

- Highlights the intricate interaction between religion, culture, and history.

- Recognized as a vital component of ancient apocalyptic traditions.

- Encourages a deeper understanding of the interplay between ancient texts and modern spiritual inquiries.

In conclusion, the Book of Enoch invites us to embark on a journey of exploration and discovery with its timeless wisdom and enduring messages. Let the insights from the Book of Enoch inspire you to explore new academic or spiritual paths, deepen your understanding of ancient religious thought, and strive for a life aligned with divine principles of justice, righteousness, and harmony. In the ever-evolving quest for understanding, the Book of Enoch stands as a guiding light, paving our way through the complexities of existence and urging us toward a future where divine wisdom and human action coalesce to create a just and enlightened world.

Glossary

- **Angelology:** The study of angels, exploring their nature, roles, and influence within various religious traditions.

- **Apocalyptic Literature:** A genre of religious writing that reveals a divine vision of the end times, the collapse of earthly kingdoms, and the ultimate salvation of the faithful. This literature is characterized by symbolic, often cryptic language that interprets present and future events as divine acts.

- **Apocalyptic Lore:** Narratives or teachings concerning the end of the world or dramatic changes to the cosmic order, often filled with symbolic imagery.

- **Apocalyptic Prophecy:** Refers to revelations that foretell significant and often cataclysmic events that are believed to lead up to the ultimate fate of the world. These prophecies are typically rooted in divine revelation and are integral to various religious narratives concerning the end times.

- **Canonicity:** Refers to the acceptance of a text as a part of the official scriptures by a religious community. This term is crucial in discussions about whether specific writings, like the Book of

Enoch, are recognized as authoritative religious texts.

- **Celestial:** This term is associated with the sky or Heaven, commonly used to refer to aspects or entities that are above our worldly experience and often linked to the divine or sublime.

- **Cosmic Events:** Phenomena that occur on a scale beyond the earthly, encompassing events in the universe that can have spiritual or symbolic significance.

- **Cosmological Speculations:** Thoughts or theories about the universe's structure, origins, and the fundamental nature of its components. These often blend scientific and philosophical perspectives with spiritual or religious beliefs.

- **Crossroads of Civilizations:** Describes a pivotal point where diverse cultural, historical, and geographical influences converge, leading to significant cultural exchange and the shaping of social and religious identities.

- **Cultural Synthesis:** The process through which elements from different cultures merge to create new cultural expressions. This synthesis can occur through the blending of languages, traditions, religions, or philosophical ideas, often resulting in a rich and varied cultural landscape.

- **Diaspora:** The dispersion of any people from their original homeland. In religious and historical contexts, this term often describes communities that maintain a strong sense of cultural identity while adapting to new environments and influences.

- **Divine Judgment:** The assessment or decree believed to come from a divine source, determining the moral value of actions and the fate of souls.

- **Divine Revelation:** This term encapsulates the communication from the divine to humans, revealing sacred truths and divine will through supernatural means such as visions or profound spiritual experiences.

- **Divine Secrets:** These are profound mysteries believed to be known only to the divine or through divine revelation, encompassing esoteric knowledge about the universe and spiritual realities.

- **Eschatological:** This concerns the part of theology that studies the ultimate destiny of the world and humanity. It often includes discussions about the end times, divine judgment, and the afterlife.

- **Eschatological Role of Angels:** Angels play vital roles in the eschatological visions of the Book of Enoch. They act as enforcers of divine judgment, carrying out God's decrees to ensure the delivery of divine justice.

- **Ethical Implications of Eschatological Themes:** The eschatological themes present in the Book of Enoch serve as ethical guides emphasizing the consequences of moral choices. Through vivid descriptions of divine judgment and the apocalypse, the text cautions readers to lead a righteous life.

- **Fallen Angels:** Celestial beings whose rebellion against divine order brings forth profound theological and ethical implications. Their story enriches the apocalyptic storyline of the Book of Enoch, serving as an allegory for understanding the interplay between divine justice and cosmic disorder.

- **Ge'ez:** An ancient language of Ethiopia that remains important in religious contexts, especially within the Ethiopian Orthodox Church. It is used in liturgical services and was the language into which the Book of Enoch was translated and preserved. **Hellenistic Period:** A historical era that began with the conquests of Alexander the Great and saw the widespread dissemination of Greek culture across the Mediterranean and into Asia. This period is characterized by the blending of Greek traditions with local cultures, significantly impacting art, architecture, language, and religion.

- **Heretical:** Describes beliefs or opinions that deviate from accepted norms or doctrines, especially in a religious context, often leading to controversy or conflict.

- **Hierarchies of Angels:** An ordered system where angels are ranked according to their status or roles within the celestial realm, reflecting their duties and powers.

- **Hope of Redemption:** Enoch's Book conveys a powerful message of hope and redemption interwoven with themes of judgment and retribution. It envisions the triumph of righteousness, the establishment of a new Heaven and Earth, and the fulfillment of divine pledges to restore harmony.

- **Human-Divine Interaction:** Explores the interactions and influences between humans and divine entities, emphasizing the reciprocal impact and the dynamic relationship that shapes theological narratives and human experiences.

- **Material:** Concerning physical substances or the tangible aspects of the world, as opposed to spiritual or ethereal dimensions.

- **Moral Complexity:** This refers to the intricate and often conflicting ethical dilemmas that challenge straightforward moral decision-making, highlighting the depth and ambiguity in ethical situations.

- **Mystical:** Pertaining to hidden or esoteric practices that seek direct communion with the divine or ultimate reality, transcending ordinary understanding.

- **Nephilim:** The offspring of the forbidden union between the Watchers and human women, powerful beings who were neither fully angelic nor entirely human. The Nephilim brought chaos and corruption to the world, challenging the established order and facing divine consequences.

- **Pharisees and Sadducees:** These terms refer to two prominent Jewish religious groups during the Second Temple period. The Pharisees were known for their strict observance of traditional and written law, while the Sadducees were more conservative, holding primarily to the Torah and rejecting later innovations.

- **Prophecies:** Insights or predictions about future events, often regarded as communicated through a divine or supernatural source, guiding or warning humanity.

- **Prophetic Visions:** Refers to revelations about future events or deeper spiritual truths, often given to prophets or seers by divine entities, which serve to guide, warn, or inform communities about divine will and the nature of reality.

- **Revelation:** The act of disclosing something not previously known, often seen in religious contexts as the divine unveiling of truth and knowledge.

- **Scriptural Status:** The classification of a religious text determines if it is officially accepted within a religious tradition as scripture. This status affects how the text is used and viewed within the community.

- **Seer:** An individual perceived as having the ability to see or perceive events beyond the scope of ordinary perception, often through divine or supernatural means.

- **Sinners:** In religious contexts, individuals who have acted contrary to divine law. The term is often used in religious texts to describe those who will face divine judgment.

- **Symbolism:** The use of symbols to represent deeper meanings or concepts, often allowing for complex ideas to be communicated with simplicity and depth.

- **Terrestrial:** This refers to elements related to the Earth or grounded in our everyday physical world, contrasting with what is considered celestial or otherworldly.

- **Theodicy:** A field of study within theology and philosophy that attempts to reconcile the existence of evil and suffering in the world with the notion of a benevolent and omnipotent divine being. It addresses the moral and philosophical questions concerning why a good deity would permit evil.

- **Theological Crises:** Periods marked by profound questioning or reassessment of religious beliefs within a community. These crises often stem from philosophical dilemmas, doctrinal disagreements, or external cultural pressures, challenging established religious orthodoxy.

- **Timeless Questions:** These are enduring philosophical and theological inquiries that humans have contemplated across centuries, dealing with the meaning of life, the nature of the universe, and the moral fabric of society.

- **Visions:** Experiences of seeing events or symbols not with the physical eyes but through spiritual or mystical perception, often involving revelations or deep insights.

- **Watchers:** A term specifically used to describe a group of angels in the Book of Enoch who were tasked with observing humanity but fell from grace due to their actions, illustrating themes of vigilance, temptation, and the consequences of divine disobedience.

References

Akin, J. (2021). *The mysterious Book of Enoch.* Catholic Answers. https://www.catholic.com/magazine/print-edition/the-mysterious-book-of-enoch

Alexander, P. S. (1977). The historical setting of the Hebrew Book of Enoch. *Journal of Jewish Studies, 28*(2), 156–180. https://doi.org/10.18647/826/jjs-1977

Anca, B. (2024). *Who are the Watchers in the Book of Enoch?* Bible Wings. https://biblewings.com/who-are-the-watchers-in-the-book-of-enoch/

Aronofsky, D. (Director). (2014). *Noah* [Film]. Paramount Pictures.

Arcadiq. (2024). *Ragnarök: The Norse apocalypse & end of the world in Norse mythology.* https://arcadiq.com/ragnarok-the-norse-apocalypse-in-norse-mytholog/

Arsena, P. (2023, July 6). *The Book of Enoch: Divine justice in the apocalyptic end times.* https://pamelaarsena.com/the-book-of-enoch-divine-justice-in-the-apocalyptic-end-times/

Ashcroft, R. (2022). *What is Renaissance philosophy's connection to mysticism?* TheCollector.

https://www.thecollector.com/what-is-renaissance-philosophy-mysticism/

Atsma, A., J. (2017). *Prometheus*. Theoi Project. https://www.theoi.com/Titan/TitanPrometheu s.html

The underworld and the afterlife in ancient Egypt. (2023, June 1). Australian Museum. https://australian.museum/learn/cultures/inter national-collection/ancient-egyptian/the-underworld-and-the-afterlife-in-ancient-egypt/

Bacchi, R. (2023). *Cultural anthropology and ancient texts.* Journal of Religious Studies.

Bagley, R. (n.d.). The Book of Enoch and its Importance to anyone interested in biblical history. Northeastern Seminary. https://blog.nes.edu/the_book_of_enoch_and _its_importance_to_anyone_interested_in_bibli cal_history

English Plus. (2024, January 25). *Clash of the Titans and Gods: Unraveling the epic Titanomachy.* English plus Podcast. https://englishpluspodcast.com/clash-

of-the-titans-and-gods-unraveling-the-epic-
titanomachy/

Barker, M. (2005). *The lost prophet: the book of Enoch and its influence on Christianity*. Sheffield Phoenix Press.

Battershill, C. (2023). The stories we tell: Project narratives, project endings, and the affective value of collaboration. *Digital Humanities Quarterly*, *017*(1). https://www.digitalhumanities.org/dhq/vol/17 /1/000665/000665.html

Bauckham, R. (1998). *The fate of the dead: Studies on the Jewish and Christian apocalypses*. Society of Biblical Literature.

Bhagavata Purana. (n.d.). Sanskrit Shiksha. https://sanskritshiksha.org/bhagavata-purana/

Bisbee, J. (2022, April 27). *Book note - Two gods in heaven: Jewish concepts of God in antiquity*. Ancient Jew Review. https://www.ancientjewreview.com/read/2022 /4/27/book-note-two-gods-in-heaven-jewish-concepts-of-god-in-antiquity

Black, M. (n.d.). *The strange visions of Enoch*. Biblical Archeological Society.

https://library.biblicalarchaeology.org/article/the-strange-visions-of-enoch/

Blum, J. (2018, June 21). *The Book of Enoch (2): The sin of the Watchers.* Biblical Hebrew and Holy Land Studies Blog. https://blog.israelbiblicalstudies.com/jewish-studies/the-book-of-enoch-2-the-sin-of-the-watchers/

Boccaccini, G. (1998). *Beyond the essene hypothesis: the parting of the ways between Qumran and Enochic Judaism.* W.B. Eerdmans.

Boccaccini, G. (2002). *Roots of Rabbinic Judaism: An intellectual history, from Ezekiel to Daniel.* W.B. Eerdmans.

Book of the Dead. (n.d.). The Fitzwilliam Museum. https://fitzmuseum.cam.ac.uk/explore-our-collection/highlights/E921904

Brand, M. (2016) *The Benei Elohim, the Watchers, and the origins of evil.* The Torah.com. https://www.thetorah.com/article/the-benei-elohim-the-watchers-and-the-origins-of-evil

Cain, S., Rylaarsdam, J. C., Flusser, D., Fredericksen, L., Bruce, F. F., Davis, H. G., Faherty, R. L., Grant, R. M., Sarna, N. M., Stendahl, K., & Sander, E. T. (2024, February 9). *The Book of Enoch.* Encyclopaedia Britannica.

https://www.britannica.com/topic/biblical-literature/The-Book-of-Enoch

Cartwright, M. (2013, April 20). *Prometheus.* World History Encyclopedia. https://www.worldhistory.org/Prometheus/

Chabries, D. M., Booras, S. W., & Bearman, G. H. (2015, January 2). Imaging the past: recent applications of multispectral imaging technology to deciphering manuscripts. *Antiquity*, *77*(296), 359–372. https://doi.org/10.1017/s0003598x00092346

Childs, K. (2019). *Enoch—the first librarians.* Swedenborg Foundation. https://swedenborg.com/enoch-the-first-librarians/

The Enumah Elish, Epic of Gilgamesh, and the Book of Genesis. (n.d.). https://www.christianministriesintl.org/the-enumah-elish-epic-of-gilgamesh-and-the-book-of-genesis/

Cohen, G. D., Greenberg, M., Feldman, L. H., Gaster, T. H., Silberman, L. H., Hertzberg, A., Novak, D., Pines, S., Vajda, G., Baron, S. W., Dimitrovsky, H. Z., Richard, J., & Schiff, D. (2024, July 3). *Hellenistic Judaism (4th century bce–2nd century ce).* Encyclopedia Britannica. https://www.britannica.com/topic/Judaism/H

ellenistic-Judaism-4th-century-bce-2nd-century-ce

Collins, J.J. (1998). *The apocalyptic imagination: An introduction to Jewish apocalyptic literature*. Eerdmans.

Comfort, P. W. (2005). *Encountering the manuscripts an introduction to New Testament paleography & criticism*. Nashville, Tenn. Broadman & Holman.

Culler, J. (2011). 6. Narrative. *Oxford University Press EBooks*, 83–94. https://doi.org/10.1093/actrade/97801996913 40.003.0006

Davidson, P. (2014, August 20). *The Book of Enoch as the background to 1 Peter, 2 Peter, and Jude*. Is That In The Bible? https://isthatinthebible.wordpress.com/2014/0 8/20/the-book-of-enoch-as-the-background-to-1-peter-2-peter-and-jude/

Davila, J. R. (2005). *The provenance of the Pseudepigrapha*. Brill.

Davies, P. R. (2024, May 9). *Dead sea scrolls*. Encyclopaedia Britannica. https://www.britannica.com/topic/Dead-Sea-Scrolls

De Jager, E. (2023a, December 25). *8 facts about the Book of Enoch and its content*. The Collector.

https://www.thecollector.com/book-of-enoch-facts/

De Jager, E. (2023b). *Archangels of the Apocrypha: Here's what you need to know.* TheCollector. https://www.thecollector.com/archangels-apocrypha/

De Jager, E. (2023c, November 28). *The fallen angels of Enoch: Vicious villains or virtuous victims?* TheCollector. https://www.thecollector.com/fallen-angels-enoch/

Denova, R. (2021, September 16). Enoch. *World History Encyclopedia.* https://www.worldhistory.org/Enoch/

Delp, R. (2018). *The impact of the Book of Enoch on Christianity and other religions.* https://www.christforafrica.org/images/delp_books/CS_The_Impact_of_the_Book_of_Enoch_on_Christianity.pdf

deSilva, D. A. (2012, January 24). The Book of Enoch: The order of God's cosmos and the consequences of violations. *Oxford University Press EBooks,* 101–140.

https://doi.org/10.1093/acprof:oso/97801953
29001.003.0005

De Young, S. (2020, July 31). *The book of the Watchers*. The
Whole Counsel Blog.
https://blogs.ancientfaith.com/wholecounsel/2
020/07/31/the-book-of-the-watchers/

Dorman, P. F., & Baines, J. R. (2024, June 24). *Ancient
Egyptian religion*. Encyclopaedia Britannica.
https://www.britannica.com/topic/ancient-
Egyptian-religion

Draper, W. F. (1882) *The Book of Enoch* (Schodde, G. H,
Trans.) Holy Books.
https://www.holybooks.com/wp-
content/uploads/The-book-of-Enoch.pdf

Editors of Encyclopaedia Britannica. (2020, June 18).
First Book of Enoch. *Encyclopaedia Britannica*.
https://www.britannica.com/topic/First-Book-
of-Enoch

Editors of Encyclopaedia Britannica. (2021, June 6).
Sibylline Oracles. *Encyclopaedia Britannica*.

https://www.britannica.com/topic/Sibylline-Oracles

Editors of Encyclopaedia Britannica. (2023, Aug 14). Ragnarök. *Encyclopaedia Britannica.* https://www.britannica.com/event/Ragnarok

Editors of Encyclopaedia Britannica. (2024a, March 6). George the Syncellus. *Encyclopaedia Britannica.* https://www.britannica.com/biography/George-the-Syncellus

Editors of Encyclopaedia Britannica. (2024b, April 23). James Bruce. *Encyclopaedia Britannica.* https://www.britannica.com/biography/James-Bruce

Editors of Encyclopaedia Britannica. (2024c, March 28). Levant. *Encyclopaedia Britannica.* https://www.britannica.com/place/Levant

Edzard, D. O., Frye, R. N., & von Soden, W. (2024, May 6). History of Mesopotamia. In *Encyclopedia Britannica.*

https://www.britannica.com/place/Mesopota
mia-historical-region-Asia

Encyclopaedia Iranica. (2011). *ENOCH, BOOKS OF.*
https://iranicaonline.org/articles/enoch-books-
of

Encyclopaedia Iranica. (2012). *ESCHATOLOGY i. In
Zoroastrianism and Zoroastrian Influence.*
https://iranicaonline.org/articles/eschatology-i

Feldman, R., Klösgen, W., & Ziberstein, A. (1997).
Document explorer: Discovering knowledge in
document collections. In Z. W. Raś & A.
Skowron (Eds.), *Proceedings of the Foundations of
Intelligent Systems: 10th International Symposium,
ISMIS'97 Charlotte, North Carolina, USA October
15–18, 1997* (pp. 137–146). Springer.

Feldman, R., & Sanger, J. (2007). Introduction to text
mining. In *The text mining handbook: Advanced
approaches to analyzing unstructured data* (pp. 1–10).
Cambridge University Press.

Finegan, J. (1974). Encountering New Testament
manuscripts; a working introduction to textual
criticism. *Internet Archive*. Grand Rapids, Mich.,
Eerdmans.

https://archive.org/details/encounteringnewt0
000fine

Fishbane, E. (2023, July 17). *Tikkun Olam: Repairing the world, healing God in Kabbalistic thought.* The Jewish Theological Seminary. https://www.jtsa.edu/torah/healing-god-in-kabbalistic-thought/

Fitzmyer, J. A. (1977, May 1). Implications of the new Enoch literature from Qumran. *Theological Studies Journal,* *38*(2). https://theologicalstudies.net/articles/implicati ons-of-the-new-enoch-literature-from-qumran/

Gaiman, N. (1989-1996). *The Sandman* (Vols. 1-10). DC Comics.

Geller, F. B. (2019). *Astronomical knowledge in the Slavonic apocalypse of Enoch: Traces of ancient scientific models.* mprl-series. https://www.mprl-series.mpg.de/proceedings/11/9/index.html

Geller, M. J. (2022). Fiction of a Jewish hellenistic Magical-Medical Paideai. *Journal of the American Oriental Society,* *142*(2). https://discovery.ucl.ac.uk/id/eprint/10152181 /1/Geller_JAOS%20142.2_Geller.pdf

Glickman, A. (2018, July 30). *What is the Book of Enoch? Who was Enoch? Originally published July 27-28, 2018.* BethShalom.

https://bethshalompgh.org/what-is-the-book-of-enoch-who-was-enoch-originally-published-july-27-28-2018/

Goodricke-Clarke, N. (2005). *Western Esotericism: A brief history of secret knowledge.* Taylor And Francis.

Gregory, B. (2017). *9 fascinating facts about the Archangels Michael, Gabriel, and Raphael.* EpicPew. https://epicpew.com/9-fascinating-facts-archangels/

Hermann, R. (2023, May 4). *The Book of Enoch and its influence on Christian thought.* The Outlaw Bible Student. https://outlawbiblestudent.org/the-book-of-enoch-and-its-influence-on-christian-thought/

Himmelfarb, M. (2010). *The apocalypse: A brief history.* Wiley-Blackwell.

Iron Maiden. (1984). *2 minutes to midnight.* On *Powerslave* [Album]. EMI.

Iron Maiden. (2000). *The fallen angel.* On *Brave New World* [Album]. EMI.

Isaac, E. (1983). New light upon the Book of Enoch from newly-Found Ethiopic Mss. *Journal of the*

American Oriental Society, *103*(2), 399–399. https://doi.org/10.2307/601461

Is the Book of Enoch inspired writing? Should the Book of Enoch be in the Bible? (n.d.). CompellingTruth. https://www.compellingtruth.org/book-of-Enoch.html

Iqbal, A. (2023, April 7). *Deluge of legends: The great flood and Noah's Ark in diverse mythologies.* Medium. https://22sebty22.medium.com/deluge-of-legends-the-great-flood-and-noahs-ark-in-diverse-mythologies-ecfa4a8b2015

Jacobs, J., & Blau, L. (n.d.). *MEṬAṬRON.* JewishEncyclopedia.com. https://www.jewishencyclopedia.com/articles/10736-metatron

Jarus, O. (2022, August 22). *Book of the Dead: The ancient Egyptian guide to the afterlife.* Livescience.com. https://www.livescience.com/ancient-egypt-book-of-the-dead

Jesus Without Baggage. (2018, August 6). *Judgment and punishment in the Book of Enoch.* https://jesuswithoutbaggage.wordpress.com/2018/08/06/judgment-and-punishment-in-the-book-of-enoch/

Ji, H., & Wang, J. (2024). Research on Buddhist cosmology from the perspective of religious comparison. *Religions*, *15*(6), 694. https://doi.org/10.3390/rel15060694

Jonge, M. de. (1990). Jewish Eschatology, early Christian Christology and the testaments of the twelve patriarchs, 180–90. Novum Testamentum Supplements 63. Leiden: Brill.

Kapach, A. (2023, March 10). *Greek titans*. Mythopedia. https://mythopedia.com/topics/greek-titans

Klamm, K. (n.d.). *The Enuma Elish and the Bible*. Bible Odyssey. https://www.bibleodyssey.org/articles/the-enuma-elish-and-the-bible/

Knibb, M. A. (2009). *Essays on the Book of Enoch and other early Jewish texts and traditions*. Brill.

Kolenkow, A. B. (1986). "Testaments: The literary genre 'Testament'." In *Early Judaism and its modern interpreters*, edited by Robert A. Kraft and George W. E. Nickelsburg, 259–67. The Bible and Its

Modern Interpreters. Atlanta, GA: Scholars Press.

Kripke, E. (Creator). (2005–2020). *Supernatural* [TV series]. Warner Bros. Television.

Kugler, R. A. (2001). *The testaments of the twelve patriarchs. Guides to Apocrypha and Pseudepigrapha*. Sheffield: Sheffield Academic Press.

Kynes, W. (2023). A suitable match: Eve, Enkidu, and the boundaries of humanity in the Eden narrative and the epic of Gilgamesh. *Harvard Theological Review, 116*(4), 491–513.

Landes, R. (2016, May 3). *Eschatology*. Encyclopaedia Britannica. https://www.britannica.com/topic/eschatology

Lloyd, E. (2017, October 27). *Mystery of the Watchers and Book Of Enoch – Fallen angels and their secret knowledge*. Ancient Pages. https://www.ancientpages.com/2017/10/27/mystery-of-the-watchers-and-book-of-enoch-fallen-angels-and-their-secret-knowledge/

Long, P. J. (2016a, June 3). *Enoch pleads with the watchers – 1 Enoch 12-16*. Reading Acts.

https://readingacts.com/2016/06/03/enoch-pleads-with-the-watchers-1-enoch-12-16/

Long, P. J. (2016b, July 6). *Enoch's journey through the heavens - 2 Enoch 1-22*. Reading Acts. Reading Acts. https://readingacts.com/2016/07/06/enochs-journey-through-the-heavens-2-enoch-1-22/

Long, P. J. (2016c). *The animal apocalypse, part 1 – 1 Enoch 85-90*. Reading Acts. https://readingacts.com/2016/06/22/the-animal-apocalypse-part-1-1-enoch-85-90/

Long, P. J. (2016d, M, May 31). *The fallen angels – 1 Enoch 6-8*. Reading Acts. https://readingacts.com/2016/05/31/the-fallen-angels-1-enoch-6-8/

Lovecraft, H. P. (1928). In *The call of Cthulhu*. (2009, August 20). Hplovecraft.com. https://www.hplovecraft.com/writings/texts/fiction/cc.aspx

Ludlow, J. W. (2021). *Enoch in the Old Testament and beyond*. In Belnap, D., L. & Schade, A., P. (2021). From Creation to Sinai (pp. 73-114). Religious Studies Center. https://rsc.byu.edu/creation-sinai/enoch-old-testament-beyond

Macquire, K. (2021, April 13). *Osiris: Egyptian God of the underworld and judge of the dead*. World History.

https://www.worldhistory.org/video/2449/osi
ris-egyptian-god-of-the-underworld-and-judge-
of/

Mark, J. (2016, March 24). *Egyptian Book of the Dead.*
World History Encyclopedia.
https://www.worldhistory.org/Egyptian_Book
_of_the_Dead/

McDonald, J. (2023). *Spiritual meaning: Lunar eclipse history
and symbolism.* Richard Alois.
https://www.richardalois.com/symbolism/luna
r-eclipse-symbolism

Mirza, U. (2016, November 28). Ancient Egyptian Book
of the Dead: Prayers, incantations, and other
texts from the Book of the Dead. In *Internet
Archive.* Wellfleet Press.
https://archive.org/details/the-ancient-
egyptian-book-of-the-dead-prayers-
incantations-and-other-texts-from-the-book-of-
the-dead

Meiliken, J. (2010, December 7). *Metatron in the beginning
and in the end of days.* Kabbalah Secrets.
https://kabbalahsecrets.com/metatron-in-the-
beginning-and-in-the-end-of-days/

Meisfjord, T. (2020, January 24). *The real reason The Book
of Enoch isn't in the Bible.* Grunge.

https://www.grunge.com/184258/the-real-reason-the-book-of-enoch-isnt-in-the-bible/

Metallica. (1983). *The four horsemen*. On *Kill 'Em All* [Album]. Megaforce Records.

Metallica. (1984). *Ride the lightning*. On *Ride the Lightning* [Album]. Megaforce Records.

Miller, M. (n.d.). *Worlds and emanations*. Kabbalah Online. https://www.chabad.org/kabbalah/article_cdo/aid/380376/jewish/Worlds-and-Emanations.htm

Mythic Whispers. (2023, June 7). *Matsya Avatar: The divine fish incarnation of Lord Vishnu*. Medium. https://medium.com/@kalpanamourya135/matsya-avatar-the-divine-fish-incarnation-of-lord-vishnu-dbc9cd6b168c

New International Version. (2011). Bible Gateway. https://www.biblegateway.com/versions/New-International-Version-NIV-Bible/#vinfo

Nickelsburg, G. W. E., & VanderKam, J. C. (2001). *1 Enoch: a commentary on the Book of 1 Enoch*. Minneapolis: Fortress Press.

https://archive.org/details/1enochcommentary
0002nick/page/n5/mode/2up

Nickelsburg, G.W.E. and Vanderkam, J.C. (2004) *1 Enoch: A new translation*. Minneapolis: Fortress Press.

Nickelsburg, G. W. E. (n.d.). *Dead sea scrolls spotlight: The Book of Enoch*. Biblical Archaeology Society. https://library.biblicalarchaeology.org/sidebar/dead-sea-scrolls-spotlight-the-book-of-enoch/

Yggdrasil. (n.d.). Norse Mythology. https://www.norsemythology.org/other/yggdrasil

Egyptian Book of the Dead: Unveiling the Ancient Egyptian funerary text secrets. (n.d.). Old World Gods. https://oldworldgods.com/egyptians/egyptian-book-of-the-dead/

Matsya Avatar story: Unveiling the ancient Hindu mythology and artistry. (n.d.). Old World Gods. https://oldworldgods.com/indian/matsya-avatar-story/

Oropeza, B. J. (2024, January 8). *The apocalypse of weeks In 1 Enoch: A neglected prophecy.* https://www.patheos.com/blogs/inchrist/2024

/01/the-apocalypse-of-weeks-in-1-enoch-a-neglected-prophecy/

Panovski, A. (2023, December 8). *Titanomachy: Greek mythology's fiercest battle.* TheCollector. https://www.thecollector.com/titanomachy-greek-mythology-battle/

Payton, J. (2024, January 10). *Decoding the symbolism in the Book of Enoch.* https://jeremypaytonbooks.com/2024/01/10/decoding-symbolism-book-enoch/

Perkins, N. (2011). *The Book of Enoch and Second Temple Judaism.* Electronic Theses and Dissertations. https://dc.etsu.edu/cgi/viewcontent.cgi?article=2588&context=etd

PlatinumGames. (2009). *Bayonetta* [Video game]. Sega.

Pullman, P. (1995-2000). *His dark materials* (Vols. 1-3). Scholastic.

Ramshaw, J. (n.d.). *The importance of the Book of Enoch.* Gateways of His Light.

https://www.gatewaysofhislight.com/bookofen och/enochisauthoritative/

Read Mahabharata in English. (n.d.). Mahakavya. https://www.mahakavya.com/mahabharata-english/

Reed, A. Y. (2017, July 28). Categorization, collection, and the construction of continuity: 1 Enoch and 3 Enoch in and beyond "Apocalypticism" and "Mysticism"1. *Method & Theory in the Study of Religion, 29*(3), 268–311. https://doi.org/10.1163/15700682-12341391

Reeves, J. C. (1992). *Jewish lore in Manichaean cosmogony: Studies in the Book of Giants traditions.* Hebrew University of Jerusalem.

Reich, A. (2022, December 12). *The Book of Enoch: What is the famous biblical Apocrypha? - explainer.* The Jerusalem Post. https://www.jpost.com/judaism/article-724679

Robinson, S. (2005). *The origins of Jewish apocalyptic literature: Prophecy, Babylon, and 1 Enoch.*

https://core.ac.uk/download/pdf/154466427.pdf

Rosenberg, D. (n.d.). *Introduction to Kabbalah*. Sefaria. https://www.sefaria.org/sheets/249697.12?lang=bi&with=all&lang2=en

Rudy, L. J. (2019). *What is Kabbalah? Definition and history*. Learn Religions. https://www.learnreligions.com/kabbalah-4771368

Sarata. (n.d.). *The Book of Enoch: Heavenly Luminaries*. https://sarata.com/bible/book/enoch/heavenlyluminaries.html

Schäfer, P. (2020, March 3). From the human Enoch to the lesser God Metatron. *Princeton University Press EBooks*, 99–133. https://doi.org/10.23943/princeton/9780691181325.003.0013

Scott, H. (2024, February 13). *Why isn't the Book of Enoch in the Bible*. The Holy Script. https://www.theholyscript.com/why-isn-t-the-book-of-enoch-in-the-bible/

Shanks, H. (2007). *The dead sea scrolls— Discovery and meaning*. Biblical Archeologica Society. https://www.muslim-

library.com/dl/books/English_The_Dead_Sea
_Scrolls_Discovery_and_Meaning.pdf

Sharma, S. (2023). *Supporting student engagement with technology.* Edutopia. https://www.edutopia.org/article/using-technology-support-student-engagement/

Smeda, N., Dakich, E., & Sharda, N. (2014, December 3). The effectiveness of digital storytelling in the classrooms: a comprehensive study. *Smart Learning Environments,* *1*(1). https://doi.org/10.1186/s40561-014-0006-3

Smith, C. (2015). *Altered states of consciousness.* Psychology Today. https://www.psychologytoday.com/intl/blog/shift/201508/altered-states-consciousness

Smith, S., H. (2023) *What is the Book of Enoch and should it be in the Bible?* Christianity.com. https://www.christianity.com/wiki/bible/what-is-the-book-of-enoch-and-should-it-be-in-the-bible.html

Song, M., & Chambers, T. (2014, January 1). Text mining with the Stanford CoreNLP. *Measuring Scholarly*

Impact, 215–234. https://doi.org/10.1007/978-3-319-10377-8_10

Summerville, T. (2022, December 7). *The Prose Edda: Summary and facts*. Norse Mythologist. https://norsemythologist.com/prose-edda/

Swindoll, C. (n.d.). *Book of Revelation overview*. Insight for Living Ministries. https://insight.org/resources/bible/the-apocalypse/revelation

Szink, T. L. (2008) The vision of Enoch: Structure of a masterpiece. *Journal of Book of Mormon Studies, 17*(1). https://scholarsarchive.byu.edu/cgi/viewconte nt.cgi?article=1437&context=jbms

Szonyi, K. (2015). *Interdisciplinary approaches to Enochian studies*. Academic Press.

Taylor, R. A. (n.d.). *Introduction to Old Testament apocalyptic literature*. The Gospel Coalition. https://www.thegospelcoalition.org/essay/intr

oduction-to-old-testament-apocalyptic-literature/

Tiller, P. A. (2016). *The animal apocalypse (1 Enoch 85-90)*. https://www.marquette.edu/maqom/tiller.pdf

Titanomachy. (2020, April 28). Livius.org. https://www.livius.org/sources/content/epic-cycle/titanomachy/

Townsend, C. (2020, October 1). Revisiting Joseph Smith and the availability of the Book of Enoch. *Dialogue: A Journal of Mormon Thought, 53*(3), 41. https://doi.org/10.5406/dialjmormthou.53.3.0041

The legend of Enoch. (n.d.). Universal Co-Masonry. https://www.universalfreemasonry.org/en/history-freemasonry/legend-of-enoch

Universe Unriddled. (2024, April 6) *The Book of Enoch and the Watchers*. Universe Unriddled. https://universeunriddled.com/post/the-book-of-enoch-and-the-watchers/

University of Michigan News. (2009). *High-tech imaging reveals hidden past in ancient texts*. https://news.umich.edu/high-tech-imaging-reveals-hidden-past-in-ancient-texts/

VanderKam, J. C. (1996). "1 Enoch, Enochic motifs, and Enoch in early Christian literature." In J. C.

VanderKam & W. Adler (Eds.), *The Jewish apocalyptic heritage in early Christianity* (pp. 33-101). Minneapolis: Fortress Press.

Van Hatten, J. (2022, December 16). *IMPORTANCE OF ENOCH AND THE BOOK OF ENOCH.* Faithwriters. https://www.faithwriters.com/article-details.php?id=215175

Vigil Games. (2010). *Darksiders* [Video game]. THQ.

Ragnarök. (2023, November 5). Viking Heritage. https://www.vikingheritage.net/blogs/viking/ragnarok

Viola, L. (2022, September 29). The humanities in the digital. *Springer EBooks*, 1–35. https://doi.org/10.1007/978-3-031-16950-2_1

von Däniken, E. (1968). *Chariots of the Gods? Unsolved mysteries of the past* (M. Heron, Trans.). G.P. Putnam's Sons.

Wagner, B. B. (2019, October 13). *Battle of the Gods, when Titans took on Zeus.* ww.ancient-Origins.net.

https://www.ancient-origins.net/myths-legends-europe/titanomachy-0012714

Ward, C. A. (1989). *Altered states of consciousness and mental health: A cross-cultural perspective.* SAGE Publications.

Watson, R. (2024). *Who was Tertullian?* TheCollector. https://www.thecollector.com/who-was-tertullian/

Wayne, L. (2020). *Is the Book of Enoch Scripture since it was found among the Dead Sea Scrolls?* Christian Apologetics & Research Ministry. https://carm.org/bible-general/is-the-book-of-enoch-scripture-since-it-was-found-among-the-dead-sea-scrolls/

Wells, K. (2011, January 1). Analysis of narrative structure. *Oxford University Press EBooks*, 62–81. https://doi.org/10.1093/acprof:oso/97801953 85793.003.0005

What is the Book of Enoch and should it be in the Bible? (n.d.). GotQuestions.

https://www.gotquestions.org/book-of-Enoch.html

Wittmann, M., & Hurd, P. (2018). *Altered states of consciousness: Experiences out of time and self.* The MIT Press.

Wright, T. (2019, May 17). *The Epic of Gilgamesh & the Bible.* Epicarchaeology.org. https://epicarchaeology.org/2019/05/17/the-epic-of-gilgamesh-the-bible/

Image References

8moments. (2018, June 19). *Pyramid, Giza, Egypt image* [image]. Pixabay. https://pixabay.com/photos/pyramid-giza-egypt-royal-tomb-3478575/

Apsolut. (2014, August 13). Fountain, Zeus, Water [image]. Pixabay. https://pixabay.com/photos/fountain-zeus-water-statue-travel-416657/

AstroGraphix_Visuals. (2016, July 4). *Eclipse Sun Space* [image]. Pixabay. https://pixabay.com/illustrations/eclipse-sun-space-moon-planet-1492818/

Djedj. (2018, September 7). *Temple, Jupiter, Roman* [image]. Pixabay.

https://pixabay.com/photos/temple-jupiter-roman-antique-3657496/

Durduhann. (2019, December 1). *Moon, Door, Flower* [image]. Pixabay. https://pixabay.com/photos/moon-door-traditional-building-4663701/

Fernando, Simpson. (2022, Oktober 8). *Art Mythology Ufo* [image]. Pixabay. https://pixabay.com/illustrations/art-mythology-ufo-alien-pyramid-7503007/

KELLEPICS. (2022, January 7). *Fantastic, Moon, Water.* [image]. Pixabay. https://pixabay.com/photos/fantastic-moon-water-boat-tree-6915749/

JancickaL. (2020, May 11). *Astronomical clock, Prague, Old town square* [image]. Pixabay. https://pixabay.com/photos/astronomical-clock-prague-5154957/

Oladimeji Ajegbile. (2019, September 7). *Glasses on a Open Book* [image]. Pexels.

https://www.pexels.com/photo/glasogon-lasglasogon-oppen-bok-2908773/

Pixabay. (2018, Oktober 7). *Scroll, Map, Treasure* [image]. Pixabay. https://pixabay.com/photos/scroll-map-treasure-map-certificate-3728646/

Pixabay. (2013, March 31). *Tree of Life* [image]. Pexels. https://www.pexels.com/photo/ljus-gryning-natur-solnedgang-268533/

Pixundfertig. (2022, January 27). *Noah's ark, Sea, Seagull* [image]. Pexels. https://pixabay.com/photos/noahs-ark-sea-seagull-ship-ark-6968364/

PublicDomainPictures. (2012, February 27). *Livestock, Animals, Nature* [image]. Pixabay. https://pixabay.com/photos/livestock-animals-sheep-mammals-17482/

Ri_Ya. (2019, December 19). *Star of david, Emblem, Jewish* [image]. Pixabay. https://pixabay.com/photos/star-of-david-emblem-jewish-bible-4703731/

Robert_C. (2016, September 20). *Alphabet, Bible, Book image* [image]. Pexels.

https://pixabay.com/photos/alphabet-bible-book-old-book-1679750/

Samirsmier. (2022, September 9). *Qumran national park, Qumran, Archeology* [image]. Pixabay. https://pixabay.com/photos/qumran-national-park-qumran-7438379/

SamuelFJohanns. (2019, April 28). *Pen, Calligraphy, Fountain* [image]. Pixabay. https://pixabay.com/photos/pen-calligraphy-fountain-pen-font-4163403/

Sergeitokmakov. (2020, February 10). *Angel Fallen Model* [image]. Pixabay. https://pixabay.com/illustrations/angel-fallen-model-silhouette-4834921/

Sinousxl. (2021, January 16). *Milky way, Galaxy, Stars* [image]. Pixabay. https://pixabay.com/photos/milky-way-galaxy-stars-cosmos-5905903/

Sspiehs3. (2016, Oktober 28). *Cross, Sunset, Silhouette* [image]. Pixabay. https://pixabay.com/photos/cross-sunset-silhouette-god-1772560/

www.ingramcontent.com/pod-product-compliance
Lightning Source LLC
Chambersburg PA
CBHW070340090426
42733CB00009B/1235